Mac OS X Panther
for Unix Geeks

Other Macintosh resources from O'Reilly

Related titles

Learning Cocoa with Objective-C

Learning Unix for Mac OS X Panther

Applescript: The Definitive Guide

AppleWorks 6: The Missing Manual

Running Mac OS X Panther

Mac OS X Panther in a Nutshell

Mac OS X: The Missing Manual

Mac OS X Panther Pocket Guide

Mac OS X Unwired

Mac OS X Hacks

Mac OS X Hints

Macintosh Books Resource Center

mac.oreilly.com is a complete catalog of O'Reilly's books on the Apple Macintosh and related technologies, including sample chapters and code examples.

A popular watering hole for Macintosh developers and power users, the Mac DevCenter focuses on pure Mac OS X and its related technologies, including Cocoa, Java, AppleScript, and Apache, just to name a few. It's also keenly interested in all the spokes of the digital hub, with special attention paid to digital photography, digital video, MP3 music, and QuickTime.

Conferences

O'Reilly & Associates bring diverse innovators together to nurture the ideas that spark revolutionary industries. We specialize in documenting the latest tools and systems, translating the innovator's knowledge into useful skills for those in the trenches. Visit *conferences.oreilly.com* for our upcoming events.

Safari Bookshelf (*safari.oreilly.com*) is the premier online reference library for programmers and IT professionals. Conduct searches across more than 1,000 books. Subscribers can zero in on answers to time-critical questions in a matter of seconds. Read the books on your Bookshelf from cover to cover or simply flip to the page you need. Try it today with a free trial.

Mac OS X Panther
for Unix Geeks

Brian Jepson and Ernest E. Rothman

O'REILLY®

Beijing · Cambridge · Farnham · Köln · Paris · Sebastopol · Taipei · Tokyo

Mac OS X Panther for Unix Geeks
by Brian Jepson and Ernest E. Rothman

Published by O'Reilly Media, Inc., 1005 Gravenstein Highway North, Sebastopol, CA 95472.

O'Reilly Media, Inc. books may be purchased for educational, business, or sales promotional use. On-line editions are also available for most titles (*safari.oreilly.com*). For more information, contact our corporate/institutional sales department: (800) 998-9938 or *corporate@oreilly.com*.

Editor:	Chuck Toporek
Production Editor:	Philip Dangler
Cover Designer:	Emma Colby
Interior Designer:	David Futato

Printing History:

October 2002:	First Edition. Originally published under the title *Mac OS X for Unix Geeks*.
February 2004:	Second Edition.

 This book uses RepKover™, a durable and flexible lay-flat binding.

ISBN: 0-596-00607-1

Table of Contents

Part IV.   Serving and System Management

Part V.   Appendixes

Preface

Once upon a time, Unix came with only a few standard utilities and, if you were lucky, it included a C compiler. When setting up a new Unix system, you'd have to crawl the Net looking for important software: Perl, *gcc*, *bison*, *flex*, *less*, Emacs, and other utilities and languages. That was a lot of software to download through a 28.8 kbps modem. These days, Unix distributions come with much more, and it seems like more and more users are gaining access to a wide-open pipe.

Free Linux distributions pack most of the GNU tools onto a CD-ROM, and now commercial Unix systems are catching up. IRIX includes a big selection of GNU utilities, Solaris comes with a companion CD of free software, and just about every flavor of Unix (including Mac OS X) now includes Perl. Mac OS X comes with many tools, most of which are open source and complement the tools associated with Unix.

This book serves as a bridge for Unix developers and system administrators who've been lured to Mac OS X because of its Unix roots. When you first launch the Terminal application, you'll find yourself at home in a Unix shell, but like Apple's credo—"Think Different"—you'll soon find yourself doing things a little differently. Some of the standard Unix utilities you've grown accustomed to may not be there, */etc/passwd* and */etc/group* have been supplanted with something called NetInfo, and when it comes to developing applications, you'll find that things like library linking and compiling have a few new twists to them.

Despite all the beauty of Mac OS X's Aqua interface, you'll find that some things are different on the Unix side. But rest assured, they're easy to deal with if you know what to do. This book is your survival guide for taming the Unix side of Mac OS X.

Audience for This Book

This book is aimed at Unix developers, a category that includes programmers who switched to Linux from a non-Unix platform, web developers who spend most of their time in *~/public_html* over an *ssh* connection, and experienced Unix hackers. In catering to such a broad audience, we chose to include some material that advanced users might consider basic. However, this choice makes the book accessible to all Unix programmers who switch to Mac OS X as their operating system of choice, whether they have been using Unix for one year or ten. If you are coming to Mac OS X with no Unix background, we suggest that you start with *Learning Unix for Mac OS X Panther* (O'Reilly) to get up to speed with the very basics.

Organization of This Book

This book is divided into five parts. *Part I* helps you map your current Unix knowledge to the world of Mac OS X. *Part II* discusses compiling and linking applications, and *Part III* takes you into the world of Fink and covers packaging. *Part IV* discusses using Mac OS X as a server and provides some basic system management information. *Part V* provides useful reference information.

Here's a brief overview of what's in the book:

Part I, *Getting Around*
> This part of the book orients you to Mac OS X's unique way of expressing its Unix personality.

> Chapter 1, *Inside the Terminal*
>> This chapter provides you with an overview of the Terminal application, including a discussion of the differences between the Terminal and your standard Unix *xterm*.

> Chapter 2, *Startup*
>> This chapter describes the Mac OS X boot process, from when the Apple icon first appears on your display to when the system is up and running.

> Chapter 3, *Directory Services*
>> Use this chapter to get started with Mac OS X's powerful system for Directory Services, which replaces or complements the standard Unix flat files in the */etc* directory.

> Chapter 4, *Printing*
>> This chapter explains how to set up a printer under Mac OS X, and shows you around CUPS, the open source printing engine under Mac OS X's hood.

Chapter 5, *The X Window System*
> In this chapter, you'll learn how to install and work with the X Window System on Mac OS X.

Chapter 6, *Multimedia*
> This chapter discusses working with multimedia, including burning CDs, displaying video, and manipulating images.

Chapter 7, *Third-Party Tools and Applications*
> This chapter introduces some third-party applications that put a new spin on Unix features, such as virtual desktops, SSH frontends, and TeX applications.

Part II, *Building Applications*
> Although Apple's C compiler is based on the GNU Compiler Collection (GCC), there are important differences between compiling and linking on Mac OS X and on other platforms. This part of the book describes these differences.

Chapter 8, *Compiling Source Code*
> This chapter describes the peculiarities of the Apple C compiler, including using macros that are specific to Mac OS X, working with precompiled headers, and configuring a source tree for Mac OS X.

Chapter 9, *Libraries, Headers, and Frameworks*
> Here we'll discuss building libraries, linking, and miscellaneous porting issues you may encounter with Mac OS X.

Chapter 10, *Perl*
> This chapter describes the version of Perl that ships with Mac OS X, as well as optional modules that can make your Perl experience that much richer.

Part III, *Working with Packages*
> There are a good number of packaging options for software that you compile, as well as software you obtain from third parties. This part of the book covers software packaging on Mac OS X.

Chapter 11, *Fink*
> In this chapter, you'll learn all about Fink, a package management system and porting effort that brings many open source applications to Mac OS X.

Chapter 12, *Creating and Installing Packages*
> This chapter describes the native package formats used by Mac OS X, as well as some other packaging options you can use to distribute applications.

Part IV, *Serving and System Management*

This part of the book talks about using Mac OS X as a server, as well as system administration.

Chapter 13, *Using Mac OS X as a Server*

In this chapter, you'll learn about setting up your Macintosh to act as a server, selectively letting traffic in (even through a Small Office/Home Office firewall such as the one found in the AirPort base station), and setting up Postfix.

Chapter 14, *MySQL and PostgreSQL*

This chapter explains how to set up and configure MySQL and PostgreSQL.

Chapter 15, *System Management Tools*

This chapter describes commands for monitoring system status and configuring the operating system.

 The previous edition, *Mac OS X for Unix Geeks*, included a chapter on building the Darwin kernel. According to a post on the *darwin-kernel* list, there are "minor differences between the sources that Apple uses to build production Mac OS X kernels and the Darwin sources." We felt that unless we could assure you that the sources were identical, we couldn't recommend that you build your own kernel from the Darwin CVS sources. Nevertheless, we will post a PDF copy of the original chapter on the catalog page in case you want to venture into this territory.

Part V, *Appendixes*

The final part of the book includes miscellaneous reference information.

Appendix A, *The Mac OS X Filesystem*

Here you'll learn about the layout of the Mac OS X filesystem, with descriptions of key directories and files.

Appendix B, *Command-Line Tools: The Missing Manpages*

There are some great Mac OS X utilities that don't have manpages. This appendix provides them for you.

Appendix C, *Mac OS X's Unix Development Tools*

This appendix provides a list of various development tools, along with brief descriptions.

Xcode Tools

This book assumes that you have installed the Xcode Tools, which includes the latest version of *gcc*. If you bought the boxed version of Mac OS X, Xcode should be included on a separate CD-ROM. If you bought a new Macintosh that came with Mac OS X preinstalled, the installer is */Applications/Installers/Developer Tools/Developer.mpkg*. Failing either of those, or if you'd like to get the latest version of the tools, they are available to Apple Developer Connection (ADC) members at *http://connect.apple.com*.

Where to Go for More Information

Although this book will get you started with the Unix underpinnings of Mac OS X, there are many online resources that can help you get a better understanding of Unix for Mac OS X:

Apple's Open Source Mailing Lists
> This site leads to all the Apple-hosted Darwin mailing lists, and includes links to list archives.
>
> > *http://developer.apple.com/darwin/mail.html*

The Darwin Project
> Darwin is a complete Unix operating system for *x*86 and PowerPC processors. Mac OS X is based on the Darwin project. Spend some time at *http://developer.apple.com/darwin/* to peek as deep under Mac OS X's hood as is possible.
>
> > *http://developer.apple.com/darwin/*

Open Darwin
> The Open Darwin project was founded in 2002 by Apple Computer and the Internet Software Consortium, Inc. (ISC). It is an independent project with a CVS repository that is separate from Apple's Darwin project, but it aims for full binary compatibility with Mac OS X.
>
> > *http://www.opendarwin.org/*

Fink
> Fink is a collection of open source Unix software that has been ported to Mac OS X. It is based on the Debian package management system, and includes utilities to easily mix precompiled binaries and software built from source. Fink also includes complete GNOME and KDE desktop distributions.
>
> > *http://fink.sourceforge.net/*

DarwinPorts

DarwinPorts is a project of OpenDarwin that provides a unified porting system for Darwin, Mac OS X, FreeBSD, and Linux. At the time of this writing, it includes several hundred applications, including the GNOME desktop system.

http://darwinports.opendarwin.org/

GNU-Darwin

Like Fink, GNU-Darwin brings many free Unix applications to Darwin and Mac OS X. GNU-Darwin uses the FreeBSD ports system, which automates source code and patch distribution, as well as compilation, installation, and resolution of dependencies.

http://gnu-darwin.sourceforge.net/

Mac OS X Hints

Mac OS X Hints presents a collection of reader-contributed tips, along with commentary from people who have tried the tips. It includes an extensive array of Unix tips.

http://www.macosxhints.com/

Stepwise

Before Mac OS X, Stepwise was the definitive destination for OpenStep and WebObjects programmers. Now Stepwise provides news, articles, and tutorials for Cocoa and WebObjects programmers.

http://www.stepwise.com/

VersionTracker

VersionTracker keeps track of software releases for Mac OS X and other operating systems.

http://www.versiontracker.com

MacUpdate

MacUpdate also tracks software releases for Mac OS X.

http://www.macupdate.com

FreshMeat's Mac OS X Section

FreshMeat catalogs and tracks the project history of thousands of mostly open source applications.

http://osx.freshmeat.net

Conventions Used in This Book

The following typographical conventions are used in this book:

Italic

> Used to indicate new terms, URLs, filenames, file extensions, directories, commands and options, Unix utilities, and to highlight comments in examples. For example, a path in the filesystem will appear in the text as */Applications/Utilities*.

`Constant width`

> Used to show functions, variables, keys, attributes, the contents of files, or the output from commands.

`Constant width bold`

> Used in examples and tables to show commands or other text that should be typed literally by the user.

`Constant width italic`

> Used in examples and tables to show text that should be replaced with user-supplied values.

Menus/Navigation

> Menus and their options are referred to in the text as File → Open, Edit → Copy, etc. Arrows are also used to signify a navigation path when using window options; for example: System Preferences → Accounts → *username* → Password means that you would launch System Preferences, click the icon for the Accounts preference panel, select the appropriate *username*, and then click on the Password pane within that panel.

Pathnames

> Pathnames are used to show the location of a file or application in the filesystem. Directories (or *folders* for Mac and Windows users) are separated by a forward slash. For example, if you're told to "...launch the Terminal application (*/Applications/Utilities*)", it means you can find the Terminal application in the Utilities subfolder of the Application folder.

$, #

> The dollar sign ($) is used in some examples to show the user prompt for the *bash* shell; the hash mark (#) is the prompt for the *root* user.

 These icons signify a tip, suggestion, or a general note.

 These icons indicate a warning or caution.

Comments and Questions

Please address comments and questions concerning this book to the publisher:

> O'Reilly & Associates, Inc.
> 1005 Gravenstein Highway North
> Sebastopol, CA 95472
> (800) 998-9938 (in the U.S. or Canada)
> (707) 829-0515 (international/local)
> (707) 829-0104 (fax)

To comment or ask technical questions about this book, send email to:

> *bookquestions@oreilly.com*

We have a web site for the book, where we'll list examples, errata, and any plans for future editions. The site also includes a link to a forum where you can discuss the book with the author and other readers. You can access this site at:

> *http://www.oreilly.com/catalog/mpantherunix/*

For more information about books, conferences, Resource Centers, and the O'Reilly Network, see the O'Reilly web site at:

> *http://www.oreilly.com*

Acknowledgments from the Previous Edition

This book builds on *Mac OS X for Unix Geeks*, for which we had help from a number of folks:

- The folks at the ADC, for technical review and handholding in so many tough spots!
- Erik Ray, for some early feedback and pointers to areas of library linking pain.
- Simon St.Laurent for feedback on early drafts, and prodding me towards more Fink coverage.
- Chris Stone, for tech review and helpful comments on the Terminal application.
- Tim O'Reilly, for deep technical and editorial help.
- Brett McLaughlin, for lots of great technical comments as well as helpful editorial ones.

- Brian Aker, for detailed technical review and feedback on Unixy details.
- Chuck Toporek, for editing, tech review, and cracking the whip when we needed it.
- Elaine Ashton and Jarkko Hietaniemi, for deeply detailed technical review, and help steering the book in a great direction.
- Steven Champeon, for detailed technical review and help on Open Firmware and the boot process.
- Simon Cozens, for technical review and pushing me toward including an example of how to build a Fink package.
- Wilfredo Sanchez, for an immense amount of detail on everything, and showing me the right way to do a startup script under Jaguar. His feedback touched nearly every aspect of the book, without which there would have been gaping holes and major errors.

Acknowledgments from Brian Jepson

Thanks to Nathan Torkington, Rael Dornfest, and Chuck Toporek for helping shape and launch this book, and to Ernie Rothman for joining in to make it a reality. Thanks also to Leon Towns-von Stauber for contributing Appendix B. And thanks to Andy Lester, Chris Stone, and James Duncan Davidson for looking over parts of the book. I'd especially like to thank my wife, Joan, and my stepsons, Seiji and Yeuhi, for their support and encouragement through my late night and weekend writing sessions, my zealous rants about the virtues of Mac OS X, and the slow but steady conversion of our household computers to Macintoshes.

Acknowledgments from Ernest E. Rothman

I would first like to thank Brian Jepson, who conceived the book and was generous enough to invite me to participate in its development. I would like to express my gratitude to both Brian and Chuck Toporek for their encouragement, patience, stimulating discussions, and kindness. Thanks to Leon Towns-von Stauber for contributing Appendix B to this book. I am also grateful to reviewers for useful suggestions and insights, to visionary folks at Apple Computer for producing and constantly improving Mac OS X, and to developers who spend a great deal of time writing applications and posting helpful insights on newsgroups, mailing lists, and web sites. Finally, I am very grateful to my lovely wife, Kim, for her love, patience, and encouragement, and to my Newfoundland dogs, Max and Joe, for their unconditional love and affection.

## PART I

Getting Around

This part of the book orients you to Mac OS X's unique way of expressing its Unix personality.

- Chapter 1, *Inside the Terminal*
- Chapter 2, *Startup*
- Chapter 3, *Directory Services*
- Chapter 4, *Printing*
- Chapter 5, *The X Window System*
- Chapter 6, *Multimedia*
- Chapter 7, *Third-Party Tools and Applications*

Inside the Terminal

The Terminal application (*/Applications/Utilities*) is Mac OS X's graphical terminal emulator. Inside the Terminal, Unix users will find a familiar command-line environment. In this chapter we describe Terminal's capabilities and compare them to the corresponding *xterm* functionality when appropriate. We also highlight key features of two alternative Aqua-native terminal applications, GLterm and iTerm. The chapter concludes with a synopsis of the shell command, *open*, which you can use to launch GUI applications.

Mac OS X Shells

Mac OS X comes with the Bourne-again shell (*bash*) as the default user shell, and also includes the TENEX C shell (*tcsh*) and the Z shell (*zsh*). Both *bash* and *zsh* are *sh*-compatible. When *tcsh* is invoked through the *csh* link, it behaves much like *csh*. Similarly, */bin/sh* is a hard link to *bash*, which also reverts to traditional behavior when invoked through this link (see the *bash* manpage).

If you install additional shells, you should add them to */etc/shells*. To change the Terminal's default shell, see "Customizing the Terminal," later in this chapter. To change a user's default shell (used for both the Terminal and remote and console logins), see "Modifying a User" in Chapter 3.

The Terminal and xterm Compared

There are several important differences between Mac OS X's Terminal application and the *xterm* and *xterm*-like applications common to Unix systems running X Windows:

- You cannot customize the characteristics of the Terminal with command-line switches such as *-fn*, *-fg*, and *-bg*. Instead, you must use the Terminal's Show Info dialog.

- Unlike *xterm*, in which each window corresponds to a separate process, a single master process controls the Terminal. However, each shell session is run as a separate child process of the Terminal.

- The Terminal selection is not automatically put into the clipboard. Use ⌘-C to copy, ⌘-V to paste. Even before you press ⌘-C, the current text selection is contained in a selection called the *pasteboard*. One similarity between Terminal and *xterm* is that selected text can be pasted in the same window with the middle button of a three-button mouse. If you want to paste selected text into another window, you must drag and drop it with the mouse or use copy and paste. The operations described in "The Services Menu" section, later in this chapter, also use the pasteboard.

- The value of $TERM is xterm-color when running under Terminal (it's set to xterm under *xterm* by default).

- Pressing ⌘-Page Up or ⌘-Page Down scrolls the Terminal window, rather than letting the running program handle it.

- On compatible systems (generally, a system with an ATI Radeon or NVidia GeForce AGP graphics adapter), the Terminal (and all of the Aqua user interface) uses Quartz Extreme acceleration to make everything faster and smoother.

If you need an *xterm*, you can have it; however, you will first have to install the X Window System, which is bundled with Mac OS X Panther as an optional installation. See Chapter 5 for more information about the X Window System.

At least two other Aqua-native terminal applications are available. These include the shareware GLterm and the freeware iTerm. We'll have more to say about these programs later in this chapter.

Enabling the root User

By default, the Mac OS X *root* user account is disabled, so you have to use *sudo* to perform administrative tasks. Even the most advanced Mac OS X users should be able to get by with *sudo*, and we suggest that you do *not* enable the *root* user account. However, if you must enable the *root* user account, start NetInfo Manager (*/Applications/Utilities*), click the lock to authenticate yourself, and select Enable Root User from the Security menu.

Using the Terminal

The first order of business when exploring a new flavor of Unix is to find the command prompt. In Mac OS X, you won't find the command prompt in the Dock or on a Finder menu. The Terminal application is instead located in the */Applications/Utilities* directory. Don't open it just yet, though. First, drag the Terminal's application icon to the Dock so you'll have quick access to it when you need to use the Terminal. To launch the Terminal, click its icon in the Dock once, or double-click on its icon in the Finder view.

> The full path to the Terminal is */Applications/Utilities/Terminal.app*, although the Finder hides the *.app* extension. *Terminal.app* is not a binary file. Instead, it's a Mac OS X *package*, which contains a collection of files, including the binary and support files. You can Control-click (or right-click) on the Terminal in the Finder and select Show Package Contents to see what's inside. You can alternatively use the standard UNIX commands *ls* and *cd* to explore the directory */Applications/Utilities/Terminal.app/*.

After the Terminal starts, you'll be greeted by the banner message from */etc/motd* and a *bash* prompt, as shown in Figure 1-1.

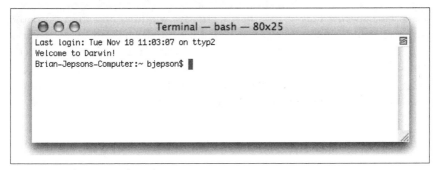

Figure 1-1. The Terminal window

Launching Terminals

One difference *xterm* users will notice is that there is no obvious way to launch a new Terminal window from the command line. For example, the Mac OS X Terminal has no equivalent to the following commands:

```
xterm &
xterm -e -fg green -bg black -e pine -name pine -title pine &
```

Instead, you can create a new Terminal window by typing ⌘-N or selecting File → New Shell from the menu bar.

 To cycle between open Terminals, you can use the same keystroke that most other Mac OS X applications use, ⌘-`. You can also switch between open Terminals by pressing ⌘-Right Arrow or ⌘-Left Arrow, using the Window menu, or by Control-clicking on the Terminal's Dock icon to reveal a context menu of open Terminals. You can also jump to a particular Terminal window with ⌘-*number* (see the Window menu for a list of numbers).

You can customize startup options for new Terminal windows by creating *.term* and *.command* files.

.term files

You can launch a customized Terminal window from the command line by saving some prototypical Terminal settings to a *.term* file, then using the *open* command to launch the *.term* file (see "The open Command" section, later in this chapter). You should save the *.term* file someplace where you can find it later: if you save it in *~/Library/Application Support/Terminal*, the *.term* file shows up in Terminal's File → Library menu.

To create a *.term* file, open a new Terminal window, and then open the Inspector (File → Show Info, or ⌘-I) and set the desired attributes, such as window size, fonts, and colors. When the Terminal's attributes have been set, save the Terminal session (File → Save, or ⌘-S) to a *.term* file, say named *proto.term*. If you save this file to *~/Library/Application Support/Terminal*, you'll be able to launch a new Terminal window with the *proto. term* file's special attributes from the File → Library menu.

Alternatively, you can launch such a Terminal window from the command line, by issuing the following command (depending on where you saved *proto.term*):

```
open ~/Library/Application\ Support/Terminal/proto.term
open ~/Documents/proto.term
```

 You can also double-click on *proto.term* in the Finder to launch a Terminal window.

The *.term* file is an XML property list (*plist*) that you can edit with a text editor like *vim* (it can be invoked with *vi*, which is a symbolic link to *vim)* or

with the *Property List Editor* application (*/Developer/Applications/Utilities*).*
By default, opening the *.term* file creates a new Terminal window. You can
configure the window so it executes a command by adding an *execution
string* to the *.term* file. When you launch the Terminal, this string is echoed
to standard output before it is executed. Example 1-1 shows an execution
string that connects to a remote host via *ssh* and exits when you log out.

Example 1-1. An execution string to connect to a remote host

```
<key>ExecutionString</key>
<string>ssh xyzzy.oreilly.com; exit</string>
```

.command files

Adding the *.command* extension to any executable shell script will turn it
into a double-clickable executable. The effect is similar to that of a *.term* file,
except that you can't control the Terminal's characteristics in the same way.
(A *.command* file will use the default Terminal settings.) However, you can
stuff the shell script full of *osascript* commands to set the Terminal characteristics after it launches. The *osascript* utility lets you run AppleScript from
the command line.† Example 1-2 is a shell script that sets the size and title of
the Terminal, and then launches the *pico* editor.

Example 1-2. Launching the pico editor

```
#!/bin/sh
# Script RunPico.command
osascript <<EOF
tell app "Terminal"
  set number of rows of first window to 34
  set number of columns of first window to 96
  set custom title of first window to "PICO Editor"
end tell
EOF
pico $@
```

If you don't want to give the shell a *.command* extension, you could also use
the Finder's Get Info option (File → Get Info, or ⌘-I) to choose which application will open the executable. To do this, perform the following steps:

1. Highlight the script's icon in the Finder.
2. Choose Get Info from the File menu (⌘-I).
3. In the Get Info dialog, choose Open with:.

---

* For more information on XML, see *Learning XML* (O'Reilly) or XML in a Nutshell (O'Reilly).

† To learn more about AppleScript, see *AppleScript: The Definitive Guide* (O'Reilly; 2004).

4. Click the drop-down menu and choose Other.

5. In the Choose Other Application dialog, select All Applications rather than Recommended Applications.

6. Find and choose the Terminal (*/Applications/Utilities*) application.

7. Click Add.

8. Close the Get Info window (⌘-W).

You can assign a custom-made icon to your shell scripts, and place them in the right section of the Dock. You can also drag the executable's icon to the lower section of the Places sidebar in the left column of the Finder, although this section of the Finder is intended primarily for quick access to frequently visited folders. To change an icon, use the following procedure:

1. Copy the desired icon to the clipboard.

2. Select your script in the Finder and open the Get Info window (⌘-I). The file's icon appears in the upper-left corner.

3. Click the current icon, and use the Paste option (Edit → Paste, or ⌘-V) to paste the new icon over it.

4. Close the Get Info window (⌘-W) to save the icon to the application.

To add the shell script application to the Dock, locate the application in the Finder and drag its icon to the Dock. Now you can click on the script's Dock icon to invoke the script.

Split Screen Terminal Feature

You can split a Terminal window into upper and lower sections by clicking on the small broken rectangle located just above the Terminal's scroll bar. The upper window contains the buffer (i.e., what you would see if you scrolled up in a non-split window), while the lower window contains your current Terminal section. This feature is useful for example, if you need to edit a file and copy and paste output from earlier in the Terminal session. Figure 1-2 shows a split Terminal window.

Contextual Menu

Users familiar with the X Window System know that right-clicking an *xterm* window opens a terminal-related contextual menu. Mac OS X's Terminal also has a contextual menu that can be accessed by Control-clicking (or right-clicking if you have a two- or three-button mouse). The Terminal contextual menu includes the choices: Copy, Paste, Paste Selection, Select All, Clear Scrollback, Send Break (equivalent to Control-C), Send Hard Reset, Send Reset, and Window Setting. Each of these items has keyboard shortcuts.

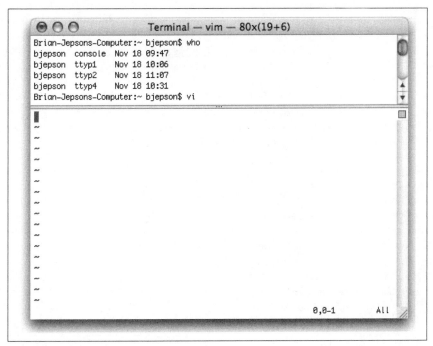

Figure 1-2. The Terminal's split screen

Customizing the Terminal

To customize the shell used by the Terminal, start by changing the Terminal's Preferences (Terminal → Preferences). In the Preferences pane, you can tell the Terminal to execute the default shell or a specific command (such as an alternative shell) at startup.* You can also declare the terminal type ($TERM), which is set as *xterm-color* by default. The other choices for the environment variable TERM are *ansi, rxvt, vt52, vt100, vt102,* and *xterm.* Among other things, the default setting for TERM allows you to take advantage of the support for color output in *ls* (via the *–G* option) and color syntax highlighting in the *vim* editor.

You can also adjust the Terminal's characteristics using Terminal → Window Settings (or ⌘-I), which brings up the Terminal Inspector, shown in Figure 1-3. Table 1-1 lists the available window settings. Changing these settings affects only the topmost Terminal window. If you want to change the default settings for all future Terminal windows, click the Use Settings As Defaults button at the bottom of the Terminal Inspector window.

---

* You can change the default shell in the Terminal preferences, but it will not affect the login shell used for remote or console logins. Changing a user's default shell is covered later in this chapter.

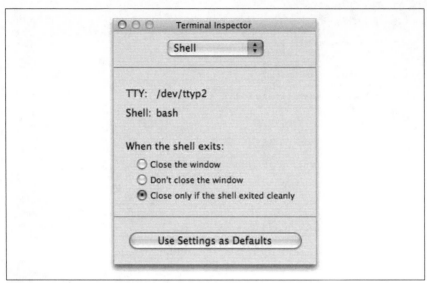

Figure 1-3. The Terminal Inspector

Table 1-1. Window settings

Pane	Description
Shell	Displays the shell used by the Terminal and lets you choose whether to close the Terminal window when the shell exits.
Processes	Displays the processes running under the frontmost window. You can also control whether Terminal will warn you if you try to close the window while you are running a program. You can disable this by choosing Never under "Prompt before closing window". You can also supply a list of commands that should be ignored, so if you're running a program (such as *vi* or *Emacs*) that's not in the list, the Terminal will warn you before closing the window.
Emulation	Controls the Terminal emulation properties.
Buffer	Sets the size and properties of the scrollback buffer.
Display	Changes the character set encoding, cursor style, font, and other attributes.
Color	Changes colors and transparency of the Terminal window.
Window	Controls window dimensions, title, and other settings.
Keyboard	Controls key mappings.

One useful option available in the Emulation tab is "Option click to position cursor". If you enable this feature, you will be able to Option-click with the mouse to position the cursor in Terminal applications such as *vim* or *Emacs* (this could save you many keystrokes when you need to move the insertion point). This option also works over a remote login session, assuming that this is supported by the remote host's terminal capabilities.

Customizing the Terminal on the Fly

You can customize the Terminal in shell scripts using escape sequences or AppleScript commands. *xterm* users may be familiar with using the following command to set the *xterm*'s title when using the *bash* shell:

```
echo -n -e "\033]0;My-Window-Title\007"
```

or the following when using *tcsh*:

```
echo '^[]2;My-Window-Title^G'
```

Mac OS X's Terminal accepts these sequences as well.

 ^[is the ASCII ESC character, and ^G is the ASCII BEL character. (The BEL character is used to ring the terminal bell, but in this context, it terminates an escape sequence.) The escape sequences described here are ANSI escape sequences, which differ from the shell escape sequences described earlier. ANSI escape sequences are used to manipulate a Terminal window (such as by moving the cursor or setting the title). Shell escape sequences are used to tell the shell to treat a metacharacter, such as |, as a literal character rather than an instruction to pipe standard output somewhere else.

To type the ^[characters in *bash*, use the key sequence Control-V Escape (press Control-V and release, then press the Escape key). To type ^G, use Control-V Control-G. The *vim* editor supports the same key sequence; *Emacs* uses Control-Q instead of Control-V.

You can capture the *bash* escape sequence in a function that you can include in your *.bash_profile* script:

```
function set_title ()
{
    case $TERM in
        *term | xterm-color | rxvt | vt100 | gnome* )
            echo -n -e "\033]0;$*\007" ;;
        *)  ;;
    esac
}
```

Then you can change the title by issuing the following command:

```
set_title your fancy title here
```

You may want to package this as a shell script and make it available to everyone who uses your system, as shown in Example 1-3.

Example 1-3. Setting the Terminal title in a shell script

```
#!/bin/bash
#
# Script settitle
# Usage:  settitle title
#
if [ $# == 0 ]; then
  echo "Usage:  settitle title"
else
    echo -n -e "\033]0;$*\007"
fi
```

You can also use *osascript* to execute AppleScript commands that accomplish the same thing:

```
osascript -e \
  'tell app "Terminal" to set custom title of first window to "Hello,
World"'
```

Working with File and Directory Names

Traditionally, Unix users tend to avoid spaces in file and directory names, sometimes by inserting hyphens and underscores where spaces are implied, as follows:

```
textFile.txt
text-file.txt
text_file.txt
```

However, most Mac users tend to insert spaces into file and directory names, and in a lot of cases, these names tend to be long and descriptive. While this practice is okay if you're going to work in the GUI all the time, it creates a small hurdle to jump over when you're working on the command line. To get around these spaces, you have two choices: escape them, or quote the file or directory name.

To escape a space on the command line, simply insert a backslash (\) before the space or any other special characters, such as a parenthesis. Because they have meaning to the shell, special characters that must be escaped are: * # ` " ' \ $ | & ? ; ~ ( ) < > ! ^. Here is an example of how to use a backslash to escape a space character in a file or directory name:

```
cd ~/Documents/Editorial\ Reports
```

Or you can use quotation marks around the file or directory name that contains the space, as follows:

```
cd ~/Documents/"Editorial Reports"
```

There is one other way to get around this problem, but it involves using the Finder in combination with the Terminal application. To launch a Classic (Mac OS 9 and earlier) application such as Word 2001, which probably lives on the Mac OS 9 partition of your hard drive, you could enter the path as follows, using escape characters:

```
open -a /Volumes/Mac\ OS\ 9/Applications\ \(Mac\ OS\ 9\)/Microsoft\ Office\↵
2001/Microsoft\ Word
```

Or you can enter the path using quotes:

```
open -a /Volumes/"Mac OS 9"/"Applications (Mac OS 9)"/"Microsoft Office↵
2001"/"Microsoft Word"
```

As you can see, neither way is very pretty, and both require you to know a lot of detail about the path. Now for the easy way:

1. Type *open –a,* followed by a space on the command line (don't press Return yet).

2. Locate Microsoft Word in the Finder and then drag its icon to a Terminal window to insert the path after the space. When you do this, the spaces and any other special characters will be escaped with backslashes, as follows:

```
open -a /Volumes/Mac\ OS\ 9/Applications\ \(Mac\ OS\ 9\)/Microsoft\↵
Office\ 2001/Microsoft\ Word
```

3. Press Return to invoke the command and launch Word 2001. If Classic isn't already running, Classic will start, too.

You can also drag and drop URLs from a web browser, which can be used with *curl –O* to download files from the command line. For example:

1. Open a new Terminal window and type *curl –O* , with a space after the switch.

2. Bring up your web browser and navigate to *http://www.oreilly.com.*

3. Drag the image at the top of the page to the Terminal window. You should now see the following in the Terminal window:

```
curl -O http://www.oreilly.com/graphics_new/header_main.gif
```

4. Press Enter in the Terminal window to download *header_main.gif* to your computer.

Tab completion

If you want to type a long pathname, you can cut down on the number of keystrokes needed to type it by using tab completion. For example, to type */Library/StartupItems,* you could type */Li<tab>,* which gives you */Library/.* Next, type *S<tab>.* This time, instead of completing the path, you're given a choice of completions: *Screen Savers, Scripts,* and *StartupItems.* Type a little bit more of the desired item, followed by a tab, as in *t<tab>.* The full key sequence for */Library/StartupItems* is */Li<tab>St<tab>.*

If you have multiple completions where a space is involved, you can type a literal space with *\<space>*. So, to get a completion for */System Folder* (the Mac OS 9 system folder), you should use */Sy<tab>\ <space><tab>.* It stops just before the space because */System* (Mac OS X's System folder) is a valid completion for the first three characters.

Changing Your Shell

Although other shells are available in Mac OS X, as we noted earlier, the default shell in Mac OS X Panther is *bash.* Earlier versions of Mac OS X shipped with *tcsh* as the default shell. Although you can change the default shell in the Terminal preferences, this does not affect the login shell used for remote or console logins. To change your default shell in a more pervasive manner, see "Modifying a User" in Chapter 3. If you install additional shells on the system, you'll need to add them to the */etc/shells* file to make Mac OS X aware that they are legitimate shells.

The Services Menu

Mac OS X's Services menu (Terminal → Services) exposes a collection of services that can work with the currently running application. In the case of the Terminal, the services operate on text that you have selected (the pasteboard). To use a service, select a region of text in the Terminal, and choose an operation from the Services menu. Mac OS X comes with several services, but third-party applications may install services of their own. When you use a service that requires a filename, you should select a fully qualified pathname, not just the filename, because the service does not know the shell's current working directory. (As far as the service is concerned, you are invoking it upon a string of text.) Here is a list of options available in the Services menu:

Finder
> The Finder Services menu allows you to open a file (Finder → Open), show its enclosing directory (Finder → Reveal), or show its information (Finder → Show Info).

Mail
> The Mail → Send To service allows you to compose a new message to an email address, once you have selected that address in the Terminal. You can also select a region of text and choose Mail → Send Selection to send a message containing the selected text.

Make New Sticky Note

This service creates a new Sticky (*/Applications/Stickies*) containing the selected text.

Open URL

This service opens the URL specified by the selected text in your default web browser.

Script Editor

This service gets the result of an AppleScript, makes a new AppleScript (in the Script Editor), or runs the selected text as an AppleScript.

Search with Google

This service searches for the selected text using *google.com* in your default web browser.

Send File to Bluetooth Device

This service sends the file specified by the selected text to a Bluetooth device.

Speech

The Speech service is used to start speaking the selected text. (Use Speech → Stop Speaking to interrupt.)

Summarize

This service condenses the selected text into a summary document. The summary service analyzes English text and makes it as small as possible while retaining the original meaning.

TextEdit

The TextEdit service can open a filename, or open a new file containing the selected text.

View in JavaBrowser

This service browses Java documentation for the selected class name. This is available whether the selected text is a real Java class name or not. (Garbage In, Garbage Out applies here.)

Alternative Terminal Applications

As noted earlier in this chapter, at least two other Aqua-native terminal applications are available: GLterm (shareware) and iTerm (freeware). Although Mac OS X's Terminal application is quite rich in useful features, GLterm and iTerm offer some interesting features that make these applications worthy of consideration as alternate comman. We won't cover these terminal emulation applications in great detail, but this section will focus on a few of their most interesting features.

Before getting into what makes these distinct, here are some similarities:

- One feature that each of these terminal applications share is that they use the same Services menu.

- Both iTerm and Terminal support transparency, language encodings, AppleScript, and have contextual menus that can be accessed by Control-clicking or right-clicking (if you have a two- or three-button mouse) in a window.

- Although GLterm lacks these features, it does have some unique features, such as the ability to set the refresh rate (i.e., how frequently it checks to see if there is something new to draw in the window).

GLterm

GLterm (*http://www.pollet.net/GLterm/*) was developed by Michael Pollet to use X11 *.bdf* fonts and render them using OpenGL, provided that it's run on a machine with a 3D accelerator supported by Mac OS X. GLterm supports ANSI color, vt102/xterm emulations, and DEC function keys.

The default behavior of GLterm is to use whatever shell is specified as the user's default in Directory Services (see Chapter 3). The shell for GLterm can be easily changed to any available shell in GLterm's preferences. The default value for the TERM environment variable is *xterm*, but this can be changed to an *xterm* color in the shell by setting the TERM environment variable.

If you find that the fonts used by the Terminal cannot handle some specialized graphics required by a particular terminal-based application, you may want to consider using GLterm on a regular basis.

iTerm

iTerm (*http://iterm.sourceforge.net*) was developed by Fabian and Ujwal S. Sathyam. Extensive documentation on iTerm is also available at its web site.

As with the Terminal, iTerm supports several language encodings, vt100/ANSI/xterm/xterm-color/rxvt emulations, and several GUI features. Particularly interesting features of iTerm include support for multiple tabbed terminal sessions within each window, bookmarks that allow you to open new iTerm sessions with preset terminal settings, and bookmarks for launching non-shell commands. The default value for TERM is xterm, but this can be changed either on the fly with the usual shell command, in the Configure menu or, if you want a global change, in iTerm's Preferences dialog.

The tabs feature will be familiar to GNOME users, since the *gnome-terminal* also supports this feature. Tabs in iTerm are designed to make efficient use of desktop space, much as they do in Safari and other popular web browsers. Figure 1-4 shows an iTerm window with two tabs.

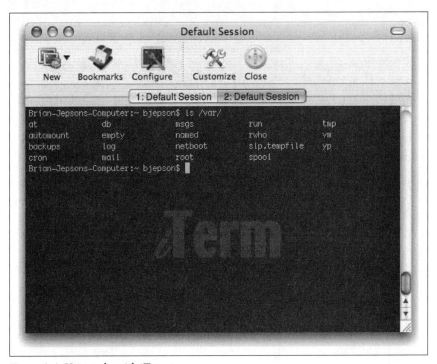

Figure 1-4. Using tabs with iTerm

The same *bash* (or *tcsh*) shell commands that can be used to customize the Terminal's titlebar work just as well with iTerm's titlebar. When used in iTerm, these commands also set the tab labels as shown in Figure 1-5.

iTerm's support for bookmarks should be familiar to KDE users, since the KDE Konsole terminal emulator supports a similar bookmark feature. Bookmarks are used to define iTerm sessions with preset terminal settings. For example, you can define the text color or font to use.

To define a bookmark, click the Bookmarks icon in iTerm's toolbar, highlight the Default Session, click Add, and then click Edit to open a Session Settings dialog for this bookmark. From the Sessions dialog, you can set various characteristics, including the session name, which will be used when you open a session from the New icon in iTerm's toolbar. Figure 1-6 shows a Bookmark dialog in which we have defined three bookmarks after the Default Session. The session named *bluetext* opens another login shell in a new tab, *OpenSafari* opens Safari, and *OpenSitesFolder* opens the *~/Sites* folder in the Finder.

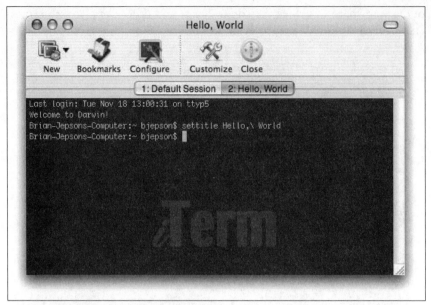

Figure 1-5. Customized tab labels in iTerm

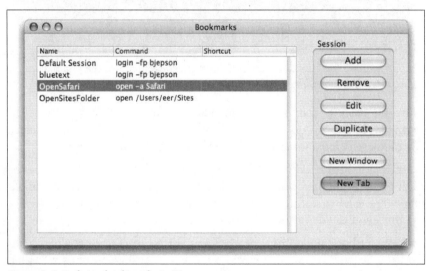

Figure 1-6. Defining bookmarks in iTerm

iTerm's contextual menu consists of the following items: New Tab (which allows you to choose a session from the bookmarks), Browser (which opens the selected URL in your default web browser), Mail (which opens a compose mail window with the selected email address as the recipient), Copy, Paste, Save, Print, Print Selection, Select All, Clear Buffer, Close, and Configure.

The open Command

The *open* shell command lets you open Finder windows and launch GUI applications. To open a directory in the Finder, use *open,* followed by the name of the directory. For example, to open a Finder window containing the current directory, type:

```
open .
```

To open your Public folder (*~/Public*):

```
open ~/Public
```

To open the */Applications* directory:

```
open /Applications
```

To open an application, you need only its name. For example, you can open Xcode (*/Developer/Applications*) with this command:

```
open -a Xcode
```

 You are not required to enter the path for the application, only its name—even if it is a Classic application. The only time you are required to enter the path is if you have two different versions of an application with similar names on your system.

You can also supply a filename argument with the *–a* option, which would launch the application and open the specified file with that application. You can use this option to open a file with something other than the application with which it's associated. For example, to open an XML file in Xcode instead of the default XML editor, the Property List Editor, you could use the following command:

```
open -a Xcode data.xml
```

To open multiple files, you can use wildcards:

```
open *.c
```

To force a file to be opened with TextEdit, use *–e*:

```
open -e *.c
```

The *–e* switch will only open files in the TextEdit application; it cannot be used to open a file in another text editor, such as BBEdit (however, you can use the command-line *bbedit* application to open a file with BBEdit). If you want to use TextEdit on a file that is owned by an administrator (or *root*), *open –e* will not work. You'll need to specify the full executable path, as in:

```
$ sudo /Applications/TextEdit.app/Contents/MacOS/TextEdit filename
```

CHAPTER 2
Startup

The most striking difference between Mac OS X and other flavors of Unix is in how Mac OS X handles the boot process. Gone are */etc/inittab*, */etc/init.d*, and */etc/rc.local* from traditional Unix systems. In their place is a BSD-like startup sequence sandwiched between a Mach* foundation and the Aqua user interface.

This chapter describes the Mac OS X startup sequence, beginning with the *BootX* loader and progressing to full multiuser mode, at which time the system is ready to accept logins from normal users. The chapter also covers custom startup items, network interface configuration, and Mac OS X's default *cron* jobs.

Booting Mac OS X

When the computer is powered up, the firmware is in complete control. After the firmware initializes the hardware, it hands off control to the *BootX* loader, which bootstraps the kernel. After a trip into Mach, the control bubbles up into the BSD subsystem, and eventually into the Aqua user interface.

By default, Mac OS X boots graphically. If you'd like to see console messages as you boot, hold down ⌘-V (the "V" stands for "verbose") as you start the computer. If you'd like to always boot in verbose mode, you can specify a flag in the boot arguments that are stored in your system's firmware. First, use the command nvram boot-args to make sure there aren't any flags already set (if there are, and you didn't set them, you probably should not change this setting). Set your boot arguments to -v with this command:

```
sudo /usr/sbin/nvram boot-args="-v"
```

---

* Mach is a microkernel operating system developed at Carnegie Mellon University. The Mac OS X kernel, *xnu*, is a hybrid of Mach and BSD.

The next time you boot the computer, it will boot in verbose mode. To turn this setting off, use the command:

```
sudo /usr/sbin/nvram boot-args=
```

To boot in single-user mode, hold down ⌘-S as you start the computer. In single-user mode, your filesystem will be mounted as read-only, and you will be limited in what you can do. Single-user mode should generally be used only to repair a system that has been damaged (for example, see "Restoring the Directory Services Database" in Chapter 3). Unlike with other Unix systems, we do not suggest that you use single-user mode to perform *fsck* repairs manually. Instead, boot from the Mac OS X install CD or DVD and run the Disk Utility (Installer → Open Disk Utility) to repair a problem disk volume.

The BootX Loader

BootX is located in */System/Library/CoreServices*. It draws the Apple logo on the screen and proceeds to set up the kernel environment. *BootX* first looks for kernel extensions (drivers, also known as *kexts*) that are cached in the *mkext cache*. If this cache does not exist, *BootX* loads only those extensions in */System/Library/Extensions* that have the *OSBundleRequired* key in their *Info.plist* file. Each extension lives in a folder (*ExtensionName.kext*), and the *Info.plist* file is an XML document that resides in its *Contents* subfolder. Example 2-1 is an excerpt from the */System/Library/Extensions/System.kext/Contents/Info.plist* file.

Example 2-1. A portion of a kernel extension's Info.plist file

```
<?xml version="1.0" encoding="UTF-8"?>
<!DOCTYPE plist PUBLIC "-//Apple Computer//DTD PLIST 1.0//EN"
        "http://www.apple.com/DTDs/PropertyList-1.0.dtd">
<plist version="1.0">
  <dict>
    <key>CFBundleDevelopmentRegion</key>
    <string>English</string>
    <!-- multiple keys and strings omitted -->
  </dict>
</plist>
```

After the required drivers are loaded, *BootX* hands off control to the kernel (*/mach_kernel*).

Initialization

The kernel first initializes all the data structures needed to support Mach and BSD. Next, it initializes the I/O Kit, which connects the kernel with the set of extensions that correspond to the machine's hardware configuration. Then, the kernel finds and mounts the *root* filesystem. The kernel next loads *mach_init*, which starts Mach message handling. *mach_init* then launches the BSD *init* process. In keeping with Unix conventions, *init* is process ID (PID) 1, even though it was started second. *mach_init* is given PID 2, and its parent PID is set to 1 (*init*'s PID).

The /etc/rc.boot Script

The *init* process launches the */etc/rc.boot* and */etc/rc* shell scripts to start the system. Both *rc* scripts (and all startup items) source the */etc/rc.common* script, which sets the initial environment, defines some useful functions, and loads the */etc/hostconfig* file, which controls the system services that will be started at boot. Example 2-2 is an excerpt from the *hostconfig* file.

Example 2-2. A portion of /etc/hostconfig

```
# Services
AFPSERVER=-NO-
CUPS=-YES-
```

This excerpt shows that Apple File Sharing and CUPS (Common Unix Printing System) will be launched at startup. See "The startup script," later in this chapter, for an explanation of how */etc/hostconfig* can be used to control services that you install yourself. Table 2-1 describes the default entries from */etc/hostconfig*.

Table 2-1. Default entries from the hostconfig file

Entry	Default value	Description
HOSTNAME	-AUTOMATIC-	Specifies a hostname. A setting of -AUTOMATIC- causes *configd* (described in Table 2-2) to use the value from the system configuration database.
ROUTER	-AUTOMATIC-	Description unavailable at time of printing. Please see the errata at *http://www.oreilly.com/catalog/mpantherunix/*.
AFPSERVER	-NO-	Controls whether Apple File Sharing (Personal File Sharing in System Preferences → Sharing) is enabled. This corresponds to the AppleShare startup item. (For information on startup items, see "SystemStarter", later in this chapter.)

Table 2-1. Default entries from the hostconfig file (continued)

Entry	Default value	Description
AUTHSERVER	-NO-	Specifies whether the NetInfo authentication server for legacy clients (*/usr/sbin/tim*) should be started. This corresponds to the AuthServer startup item.
AUTOMOUNT	-YES-	Determines whether the NFS automount daemon should be started. The NFS startup item consults this setting.
CUPS	-YES-	Controls whether Printing Services are started up. This corresponds to the PrintingServices startup item. However, this is not controlled by the Printer Sharing option in System Preferences → Sharing (that setting instead inserts the appropriate settings into the */etc/cups/cupsd.conf* file).
IPFORWARDING	-NO-	Determines whether the Network startup item enables IP forwarding.
IPV6	-YES-	Specifies whether the Network startup item should turn on IPv6 support.
MAILSERVER	-NO-	Controls whether the Postfix mail server is started. This corresponds to the Postfix startup item. If you want to enable Postfix, you will need to perform additional configuration. For more information, see "Postfix" in Chapter 13.
NETINFOSERVER	-AUTOMATIC-	Determines whether NetInfo should be started. A setting of -AUTOMATIC- causes Mac OS X to decide whether it is needed based on the current system configuration. This setting is consulted by the */etc/rc* script.
NFSLOCKS	-AUTOMATIC-	If your Mac is running as an NFS server, a setting of -AUTOMATIC- enables locking for NFS files. As an NFS client, a value of -YES- will enable locking, but -AUTOMATIC- will load the appropriate daemons (*rpc.statd* and *rpc.lockd*) so they are only used when needed. The NFS startup item consults this setting.
NISDOMAIN	-NO-	Specifies the NIS Domain that your Mac should participate in. Leave it set to -NO- to disable NIS, otherwise set it to the appropriate domain. The NIS startup item uses this setting.
RPCSERVER	-AUTOMATIC-	Determines whether the RPC server (*portmap*) should be started. A setting of -AUTOMATIC- causes Mac OS X to decide whether it is needed based on the current system configuration. This setting is consulted by the */etc/rc* script.
TIMESYNC	-YES-	Controls whether the network time daemon (*ntpd*) is started. You can configure these settings with System Preferences → Date & Time. This setting affects the NetworkTime startup item.

Table 2-1. Default entries from the hostconfig file (continued)

Entry	Default value	Description
QTSSERVER	-NO-	Specifies whether the QuickTime Streaming Server is started at boot time. Although it's not included with the desktop version of Mac OS X, you can download it from *http://developer.apple.com/darwin/projects/streaming/*.
WEBSERVER	-NO-	Controls whether the Apache web server (Personal Web Sharing in System Preferences → Sharing) is started. This corresponds to the Apache startup item.
SMBSERVER	-NO-	This setting has no effect. Previous versions of Mac OS X used it to control Samba, the Windows file sharing server. This setting can be toggled using Windows Sharing in System Preferences → Sharing, which toggles the disable setting in */etc/xinetd.d/smbd*.
DNSSERVER	-NO-	Determines whether the BIND DNS server (*named*) should be started. The default */etc/named.conf* file specifies a caching nameserver configuration. This corresponds to the BIND startup item.
COREDUMPS	-NO-	Specifies whether coredumps are enabled. This setting is consulted by the */etc/rc.common* script. You can override this in the shell with the *ulimit –c* command.
VPNSERVER	-NO-	Controls whether the Mac OS X VPN service (*vpnd*) is started. This service lets remote hosts tunnel into a network through your Mac. See the *vpnd* manpage for more information. The NetworkExtensions startup item consults this setting.

After *rc.boot* has loaded in values from */etc/rc.common* and */etc/hostconfig*, it sets the hostname to localhost (this will be changed later in the boot process) and then determines whether the system is booting from a CD. Next, *rc.boot* tests to see whether the system is booting in single-user mode. If the system is neither in single-user mode nor booting from a CD, *rc.boot* performs a check of the filesystem (*fsck*). If the *fsck* fails, *rc.boot* tries an *fsck –y*, which assumes a "Yes" answer to all the questions that *fsck* asks. If that fails, the system reboots (and may end up trying an *fsck –y* over and over again).

> If you find yourself in an *fsck* loop, you should boot from the Mac OS X installation CD. You can boot from a CD by holding down the C key at startup. When the Installer appears, choose Installer → Disk Utility from the menu bar and use it to inspect and repair the damaged disk.

The /etc/rc Script

If *rc.boot* succeeds, *init* drops into a shell (for single-user mode) or launches */etc/rc* (for installation or multiuser mode). In single-user mode, only the *root* user may log in. In multiuser mode, the system is fully functional and ready to accept logins from normal users.

If */etc/rc* determines that the system is booting from a CD, it starts the Mac OS X installation program. (If you booted from a CD in single-user mode, you'll get dropped into a shell and */etc/rc* won't get run.) Otherwise, */etc/rc* performs the following steps (among others, that is; this list describes the most significant):

Mounts local filesystems
> By this point, the root filesystem is already mounted, but the *rc* script now mounts any additional HFS+ and UFS volumes listed in */etc/fstab*, as well as the */dev* filesystem. This step does not, however, perform the automatic mounting of local volumes under the */Volumes* directory. This is handled by the disk arbitration daemon, which is started as a Mach bootstrap daemon (see Table 2-2).

Launches BootCacheControl
> The *rc* script initializes the boot-time performance cache (*BootCacheControl*), which implements intelligent read-ahead strategies for the boot volume.

Tunes the system
> Next, a series of *sysctl* calls tune kernel variables such as the maximum number of *vnodes* (data structures the kernel uses to represent files) and various shared memory settings.

Configures the loopback network interface
> At this step, the *ifconfig* utility configures and activates the loopback address, 127.0.0.1.

Starts the system log daemon
> The system log daemon (*syslogd*) starts running at this point. It logs most messages to */dev/console* (launch */Applications/Utilities/Console* or look in */Library/Logs/Console/$USER/console.log*) or */var/log/system.log*. See */etc/syslogd.conf* for complete details.

Starts kextd, the kernel extension daemon
> The kernel initially boots with the minimum set of extensions needed to mount the root filesystem on all supported hardware. Some of these extensions are not needed, so */etc/rc* starts the *kextd* daemon (*/usr/libexec/kextd*) to unload unnecessary extensions. For example, the *iPodDriver* includes the *OSBundleRequired* key to support booting from

your iPod. If you don't have your iPod plugged in, *kextd* can safely unload that driver. The *kextd* daemon is also responsible for loading and unloading extensions on demand for the duration of the system's uptime. Extensions live in the */System/Library/Extensions* directory.

Launches Mach bootstrap services

Next, the *rc* script runs *register_mach_bootstrap_servers* on all the services listed in */etc/mach_init.d*. That directory contains a collection of XML *.plist* files containing a description of services, the path to the corresponding executable, and whether the service should be loaded on demand. Table 2-2 describes the services started in this stage.

 Mac OS X Panther introduced Mach bootstrap services, a new approach for starting daemons.

Daemons can be loaded at two points: system startup (*/etc/mach_init.d*) and user login (*/etc/mach_init_per_user.d*), including local and remote (such as SSH) logins. Bootstrap daemons are identified to the system using the ServiceName in their *.plist* files, and the operating system can load that service on demand, if the OnDemand option is set to true (this is the default). The *mach_init* process will launch these services on demand or wake sleeping bootstrap services (when a bootstrap service goes unused for a period of time, it can sleep).

Launch the portmap daemon

If Mac OS X determines that the port mapper is necessary based on the settings in */etc/hostconfig* (see Table 2-1), it launches the *portmap* daemon here. For more information, see the *portmap* manpage.

Start NetInfo

NetInfo is a Directory Services database for standalone machines. See Chapter 3 for a complete discussion. In this step, the *rc* script creates a default NetInfo database (if none exists) and starts the daemon(s) that are needed for NetInfo to provide its services.

Updates the kernel extension cache

At this point, the *kextcache* utility updates the */System/Library/Extensions.mkext* extension cache, which is used at boot time (see "The BootX Loader," earlier in this chapter).

Starts the update process

This process flushes the filesystem buffers every 30 seconds.

Enables virtual memory

At this point, the *dynamic_pager* daemon starts running. This daemon manages swap files in the */var/vm/* subdirectory. The kernel uses these files to allocate virtual memory as it is needed.

Sets the system language

If this system is not fully configured (if the file */var/db/.AppleSetupDone* does not exist), the language chooser appears at this point and prompts the user to choose a default language for the system. Whether that chooser appears, the *rc* script reads in */var/log/CDIS.custom* and exports the variable it contains into subsequent environments.

After these steps are completed, */etc/rc* hands off control to */sbin/ SystemStarter.*

Table 2-2. Mach bootstrap services

Item	Description
ATSServer.plist	Launches the Apple Type Solution server.
configd.plist	Starts the Configuration server daemon. See "scutil" in Chapter 15 for information on working with the Configuration server's database.
coreservicesd.plist	Launches the Core Services daemon.
DirectoryService.plist	Starts The DirectoryService daemon. For more information, see Chapter 3, "Directory Services Utilities," and the *DirectoryService* manpage.
diskarbitrationd.plist	Launches the disk arbitration daemon, which coordinates the mounting of file-systems. For more information, see the *diskarbitrationd* manpage.
distnoted.plist	Starts the distributed notifications daemon.
fix_prebinding.plist	Launches the *fix_prebinding* daemon, which is invoked when the dynamic loader (dyld) comes across a binary that has not been through the prebinding process, or that has changed since prebinding was last run on it. The prebinding process creates hints for the dynamic loader that can make a binary load more quickly.
KerberosAutoConfig.plist	Configures the single sign-on service. See the *kerberosautoconfig* manpage .
kuncd.plist	Starts the Kernel-User Notification daemon, which kernel-level code can use to pop up dialogs when user action is needed. See the "Kernel-User Notification" topic in *Writing an I/O Kit Device Driver*, which you can find at *http://developer. apple.com/documentation/DeviceDrivers/*.
lookupd.plist	Starts *lookupd*, a thin layer that acts as a front-end to Directory Services. For more information, see the *lookupd* manpage and Chapter 3.
notifyd.plist	Description unavailable at time of printing. Please see the errata at *http://www. oreilly.com/catalog/mpantherunix/*
WindowServer.plist	Starts the Mac OS X WindowServer, the service that manages the screen and the windows drawn upon it.

SystemStarter

SystemStarter examines */System/Library/StartupItems* and */Library/StartupItems* for applications that should be started at boot time. */Library/StartupItems* contains items for locally installed applications; you can also put your own custom startup items there. */System/Library/StartupItems* contains items for the system. You should not modify these or add your own items here. Table 2-3 lists Mac OS X's available startup items.

Table 2-3. Mac OS X default startup items

Item	Description
AMD	Starts the NFS automounter, which mounts remote filesystems on demand. Enable this with the AMDSERVER entry in */etc/hostconfig*.
Accounting	Starts the *acct* daemon, which collects process accounting records.
Apache	Starts the Apache web server. Enable this with the WEBSERVER entry in */etc/hostconfig* or by turning on Web Sharing (System Preferences → Sharing).
AppServices	Starts the desktop database, input managers, and printing services.
AppleShare	Starts Apple file sharing. Enable this with the AFPSERVER entry in */etc/hostconfig* or by turning on File Sharing (System Preferences → Sharing).
AuthServer	Starts the authentication server. Enable this with the AUTHSERVER entry in */etc/hostconfig*.
BIND	Starts *named*, the Internet domain name server, if DNSSERVER is set to -YES- in */etc/hostconfig*.
ConfigServer	An empty startup script whose former role is now filled by the *configd.plist* item in *mach_init.d* (see Table 2-2).
CoreGraphics	Loads the QuartzDisplay bundle. Full description unavailable at time of printing. Please see the errata at *http://www.oreilly.com/catalog/mpantherunix/*
CrashReporter	Enables automatic crash report generation when an application crashes. Enable this with the CRASHREPORTER entry in */etc/hostconfig*.
Cron	Starts the *cron* daemon.
DirectoryServices	An empty startup script whose former role is now filled by the *lookupd.plist* item in *mach_init.d* (see Table 2-2).
Disks	Mounts local filesystems.
IPServices	Starts *xinetd* and, optionally, Internet address sharing.
KernelEventAgent	Description unavailable at time of printing. Please see the errata at *http://www.oreilly.com/catalog/mpantherunix/*
LDAP	Starts *slapd*, the standalone LDAP daemon. Enable this with the LDAPSERVER entry in */etc/hostconfig*.
LoginWindow	Does nothing except to note the point at which the system is ready to display the login window.
mDNSResponder	Starts the multicast DNS responder, which is used by Rendezvous for configuration.
NFS	Starts the NFS client. The NFS server is started if NetInfo or */etc/exports* has been configured to export one or more filesystems.

Table 2-3. Mac OS X default startup items (continued)

Item	Description
NIS	Starts the Network Information Service unless NISDOMAIN is set to -NO- in /etc/hostconfig.
NetInfo	An empty startup script whose former role is now filled by part of /etc/rc.
Network	Configures network interfaces and the hostname. If IPFORWARDING is enabled in /etc/hostconfig, this script also enables IP forwarding.
NetworkExtensions	Loads various networking extensions.
NetworkTime	Starts the NTP client. Enable this with the TIMESYNC entry in /etc/hostconfig or with System Preferences → Date & Time.
Portmap	An empty startup script whose former role is now filled by part of /etc/rc.
Postfix	Starts the Postfix mail server. If you want to enable Postfix, you will need to perform additional configuration. For more information, see Chapter 13.
PrintingServices	Starts the Common Unix Printing System (CUPS).
RemoteDesktopAgent	Starts the remote desktop server. Enable it with the ARDAGENT entry in /etc/hostconfig or by enabling Apple Remote Desktop in System Preferences → Sharing.
SNMP	Starts snmpd, the SNMP daemon. Enable it with the SNMPSERVER entry in /etc/hostconfig.
SecurityServer	Starts the security server, which provides keychain management
SystemLog	An empty startup script whose former role is now filled by part of /etc/rc.
SystemTuning	An empty startup script whose former role is now filled by part of /etc/rc.

The Login Window

Once *SystemStarter* is finished, control is returned to *init*, which launches *getty*. In */etc/ttys*, the console entry launches the Login Window (*/System/Library/CoreServices/loginwindow.app*). At this point, the system is fully functional and ready to accept logins.

Adding Startup Items

To automatically start applications, you have two choices: start them when a user logs in, or start them when the system boots up. On most Unix systems, startup applications either reside in the */etc/rc.local* script or the */etc/init.d* directory. Under Mac OS 9, you could add a startup item by putting its alias in *System Folder:Startup Items*. Mac OS X has a different approach, described in the following sections.

Login Preferences

To start an application each time you log in, use the Accounts panel of System Preferences and select the Startup Items tab. This is good for user applications, such as Stickies or an instant messenger program. For system daemons, you should set up a directory in *Library/StartupItems*, as described in the next section.

Startup Items

If you compile and install a daemon, you'll probably want it to start at boot time. For example, MySQL will build out of the box on Mac OS X (you can download it from *http://www.mysql.com*).

A startup item is controlled by three things: a folder (such as *Library/StartupItems/MyItem*), a shell script with the same name as the directory (such as *MyItem*), and a property list named *StartupParameters.plist*. The shell script and the property list must appear at the top level of the startup item's folder. You can also create a *Resources* directory to hold localized resources, but this is not mandatory.

To set up the MySQL startup item, create the directory *Library/StartupItems/MySQL*. Then, create two files in that directory, the startup script *MySQL* and the property list *StartupParameters.plist*. The *MySQL* file should be an executable since it is a shell script. After you set up these two files as directed in the following sections, *MySQL* will be launched at each boot.

The startup script

The startup script should be a shell script with StartService( ), StopService( ), and RestartService( ) functions. The contents of *Library/StartupItems/MySQL/MySQL* are shown in Example 2-3. The function call at the bottom of the script invokes the RunService( ) function from *rc.common*, which in turn invokes StartService( ), StopService( ), or RestartService( ), depending on whether the script was invoked with an argument of start, stop, or restart.

Example 2-3. A MySQL startup script

```
#!/bin/sh

# Source common setup, including hostconfig.
#
. /etc/rc.common

StartService( )
{
```

Example 2-3. A MySQL startup script (continued)

```
    # Don't start unless MySQL is enabled in /etc/hostconfig
    if [ "${MYSQL:=-NO-}" = "-YES-" ]; then
        ConsoleMessage "Starting MySQL"
        /usr/local/mysql/bin/mysqld_safe --user=mysql &
    fi
}

StopService( )
{
    ConsoleMessage "Stopping MySQL"
    /usr/local/mysql/bin/mysqladmin --password=password shutdown
}

RestartService( )
{
    # Don't restart unless MySQL is enabled in /etc/hostconfig
    if [ "${MYSQL:=-NO-}" = "-YES-" ]; then
        ConsoleMessage "Restarting MySQL"
        StopService
        StartService
    else
        StopService
    fi
}

RunService "$1"
```

 If you are using MySQL Version 3 (the older production release), replace */usr/local/mysql/bin/mysqld_safe* with */usr/local/mysql/bin/safe_mysqld*.

Because it consults the settings of the $MYSQL environment variable, the startup script won't do anything unless you've enabled MySQL in the */etc/hostconfig* file. To do this, add the following line to */etc/hostconfig*:

```
MYSQL=-YES-
```

Mac OS X does not recognize any special connections between *hostconfig* entries and startup scripts. Instead, the startup script sources the */etc/rc. common* file, which in turn sources *hostconfig*. The directives in *hostconfig* are merely environment variables, and the startup script checks the value of the variables that control its behavior (in this case, $MYSQL).

The property list

The property list can be in XML or NeXT format, and the list contains attributes that describe the item and determine its place in the startup sequence. The NeXT format uses NeXTSTEP-style property lists, as shown in Example 2-4.

Example 2-4. The MySQL startup parameters as a NeXT property list

```
{
  Description     = "MySQL";
  Provides        = ("MySQL");
  Requires        = ("Network");
  OrderPreference = "Late";
}
```

Over time, Apple will probably phase out legacy formats such as NeXT property lists, so it is best if you use XML property lists. The XML format adheres to the *PropertyList.dtd* Document Type Definition (DTD). You can use your favorite text editor or the *Property List Editor* (*/Developer/ Applications/Utilities*) to create your own property list. Example 2-5 shows the property list in XML.

Example 2-5. The MySQL startup parameters as an XML property list

```
<?xml version="1.0" encoding="UTF-8"?>
<!DOCTYPE plist
  SYSTEM "file://localhost/System/Library/DTDs/PropertyList.dtd">
<plist version="0.9">
<dict>
    <key>Description</key>
    <string>MySQL</string>
    <key>Provides</key>
    <array>
        <string>MySQL</string>
    </array>
    <key>Requires</key>
    <array>
        <string>Network</string>
    </array>
    <key>OrderPreference</key>
    <string>Late</string>
</dict>
</plist>
```

The following list describes the various keys you can use in a startup parameters property list:

Description
> This is a phrase that describes the item.

Provides
> This is an array of services that the item provides (for example, Apache provides *Web Server*). These services should be globally unique. In the event that *SystemStarter* finds two items that provide the same service, it will start the first one it finds.

`Requires`

> This is an array of services that the item depends on. It should correspond to another item's `Provides` attribute. If a required service cannot be started, the system won't start the item.

`Uses`

> This is similar to `Requires`, but it is a weaker association. If *SystemStarter* can find a matching service, it will start it. If it can't, the dependent item will still start.

`OrderPreference`

> The `Requires` and `Uses` attributes imply a particular order, in that dependent items will be started after the services they depend on. You can specify `First`, `Early`, `None` (the default), `Late`, or `Last` here. *SystemStarter* will do its best to satisfy this preference, but dependency orders prevail.

You can now manually start, restart, and stop MySQL by invoking System-Starter from the command line:

```
$ sudo SystemStarter start MySQL
$ sudo SystemStarter restart MySQL
$ sudo SystemStarter stop MySQL
```

Scheduling Tasks

Like other flavors of Unix, Mac OS X uses *cron* to schedule tasks for periodic execution. Each user's *cron* jobs are controlled by configuration files that you can edit with *crontab –e* (to list the contents of the file, use *crontab –l*).

Default cron Jobs

The global *crontab* file is contained in */etc/crontab*. It includes three *cron* jobs by default, which run the scripts contained in subdirectories of the */etc/periodic* directory: */etc/periodic/daily*, */etc/periodic/weekly*, and */etc/periodic/monthly*. Each of these directories contains one or more scripts:

```
/etc/periodic/daily/100.clean-logs
/etc/periodic/daily/500.daily
/etc/periodic/monthly/500.monthly
/etc/periodic/weekly/500.weekly
```

By default, */etc/crontab* runs them in the wee hours of the night:

```
15 3 * * *      root    periodic daily
30 4 * * 6      root    periodic weekly
30 5 1 * *      root    periodic monthly
```

So, if your Mac is not usually turned on at those times, you could either edit the /etc/crontab file or remember to run them periodically using the following syntax:

```
sudo periodic daily weekly monthly
```

As you'll see in Chapter 3, it is vitally important that you run these jobs to ensure that your local NetInfo database is backed up.

You should not modify these files, because they may be replaced by future system updates. Instead, create a /etc/daily.local, /etc/weekly.local, or /etc/monthly.local file to hold your site-specific cron jobs. The cron jobs are simply shell scripts that contain commands to be run as root. The local cron jobs are invoked at the end of the 500.daily, 500.weekly, and 500.monthly scripts found in the /etc/periodic subdirectory.

## CHAPTER 3

Directory Services

A *directory service* manages information about users and resources such as printers and servers. It can manage this information for anything from a single machine to an entire corporate network. The Directory Service architecture in Mac OS X is called *Open Directory*. Open Directory encompasses flat files (such as */etc/hosts*), NetInfo (the legacy directory service brought over from earlier versions of Mac OS X and NeXTSTEP), LDAPv3, and other services through third-party plug-ins.

This chapter describes how to perform common configuration tasks, such as adding a user or host on Mac OS X with the default configuration. If your system administrator has configured your Macintosh to consult an external directory server, some of these instructions may not work. If that's the case, you should ask your system administrator to make these kinds of changes anyhow!

Understanding Directory Services

In Mac OS X 10.1.*x* and earlier, the system was configured to consult the NetInfo database for all directory information. If you needed to do something simple, such as adding a host, you couldn't just add it to */etc/hosts* and be done with it. Instead, you had to use the NetInfo Manager (or NetInfo's command-line utilities) to add the host to the system.

However, as of Mac OS X 10.2 (Jaguar), NetInfo functions started to become more of a legacy protocol and were reduced to handling the local directory database for machines that did not participate in a network-wide directory, such as Active Directory or OpenLDAP. NetInfo is still present in Mac OS X Panther, but you can perform many configuration tasks by editing the standard Unix flat files. By default, Panther is configured to consult the local directory (also known as the NetInfo database) for authentication, which corresponds to */etc/passwd* and */etc/group* on other Unix systems. You can override this setting with the Directory Access application. For more information, see "Configuring Directory Services," later in this chapter.

For users whose network configuration consists of an IP address, a default gateway, and some DNS addresses, this default configuration should be fine. You'll need to tap into Open Directory's features for more advanced configurations, such as determining how a user can log into a workstation and find his home directory, even when that directory is hosted on a shared server.

In order to work with Mac OS X's Directory Services, you must first understand the overall architecture, which is known as Open Directory. Directory Services is the part of Mac OS X (and the open source Darwin operating system) that implements this architecture. Figure 3-1 shows the relationship of Directory Services to the rest of the operating system. On the top, server processes, as well as the user's desktop and applications, act as clients to Directory Services, which delegates requests to a directory service plug-in (see the "Configuring Directory Services" section, later in this chapter, for a description of each plug-in).

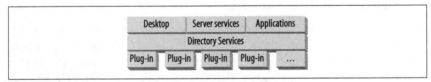

Figure 3-1. The Directory Services architecture

Programming with Directory Services

As a programmer, you frequently need to deal with directory information, whether you realize it or not. Your application uses Directory Services each time it looks up a host entry or authenticates a password. The Open Directory architecture unifies what used to be a random collection of flat files in */etc*. The good news is that the flat files still work. The other good news is that there is a brave new world just beyond those flat files. So, while all your old Unix code should work with the Open Directory architecture, you should look for new ways to accomplish old tasks, especially if you can continue writing portable code.

To get at directory information, Unix applications typically go through the C library using such functions as gethostent( ). The C library connects to *lookupd*, a thin shim that is the doorway to the *DirectoryService* daemon. The *DirectoryService* daemon consults the available plug-ins until it finds the one that can answer the directory query.

Working with Passwords

One traditional route to user and password information was through the getpw* family of functions. However, those functions are not ideal for working with systems that support multiple directories (flat files, NetInfo, LDAP, etc.). Also, in the interest of thwarting dictionary attacks against password files, many operating systems have stopped returning encrypted passwords through those APIs. Many Unix and Linux systems simply return an "x" when you invoke a function like getpwnam( ). However, those systems can return an encrypted password through functions like getspnam( ), which consult shadow password entries, and can generally be invoked by the root user only. Example 3-1 shows the typical usage of such an API, where the user enters her plaintext password, and the program encrypts it and then compares it against the encrypted password stored in the system.

Example 3-1. Using getpwnam( ) to retrieve an encrypted password

```
/*
 * getpw* no longer returns a crypted password.
 *
 * Compile with gcc checkpass.c -o checkpass
 * Run with: ./checkpass
 */

#include <pwd.h>
#include <stdio.h>
#include <stdlib.h>

int main(int argc, char *argv[])
{
  const char *user = NULL;
  struct passwd *pwd;

  /* Set the user name if it was supplied on the command
   * line.  Bail out if we don't end up with a user name.
   */
  if (argc == 2)
    user = argv[1];
  if(!user)
  {
    fprintf(stderr, "Usage: checkpass <username>\n");
    exit(1);
  }

  /* Fetch the password entry. */
  if (pwd = getpwnam(user))
  {
    char *password = (char *) getpass("Enter your password: ");
```

```
  /* Encrypt the password using the encrypted password as salt.
   * See crypt(3) for complete details.
   */
  char *crypted  = (char *) crypt(password, pwd->pw_passwd);

  /* Are the two encrypted passwords identical? */
  if (strcmp(pwd->pw_passwd, crypted) == 0)
    printf("Success.\n");
  else
  {
    printf("Bad password: %s != %s\n", pwd->pw_passwd, crypted);
    return 1;
  }
}
else
{
  fprintf(stderr, "Could not find password for %s.\n", user);
  return 1;
}
return 0;

}
```

As of Mac OS X Panther, your code no longer has a chance to look at an encrypted password. There are no functions such as getspnam( ), and if you invoke a function like getpwnam( ), you will get one or more asterisks as the result. For example:

```
$ ./checkpass bjepson
Enter your password:
Bad password: ******** != **yRnqib5QSRI
```

There are some circumstances where you can obtain an encrypted password, but this is not the default behavior of Mac OS X Panther. See the *getpwent(3)* manpage for complete details.

Instead of retrieving and comparing encrypted passwords, you should go through the Linux-PAM APIs. Since Linux-PAM is included with (or available for) many flavors of Unix, you can use it to write portable code. Example 3-2 shows a simple program that uses Linux-PAM to prompt a user for his password.

Example 3-2. Using Linux-PAM to authenticate a user

```c
/*
 * Use Linux-PAM to check passwords.
 *
 * Compile with gcc pam_example.c -o pam_example -lpam
 * Run with: ./pam_example <username>
 */
#include <stdio.h>
#include <pam/pam_appl.h>
#include <pam/pam_misc.h>

int main(int argc, char *argv[])
{

  int retval;
  static struct pam_conv pam_conv;
  pam_conv.conv = misc_conv;
  pam_handle_t *pamh = NULL;
  const char *user = NULL;

  /* Set the username if it was supplied on the command
   * line. Bail out if we don't end up with a username.
   */
  if (argc == 2)
    user = argv[1];
  if(!user)
  {
    fprintf(stderr, "Usage: pam_example <username>\n");
    exit(1);
  }

  /* Initialize Linux-PAM. */
  retval = pam_start("pam_example", user, &pam_conv, &pamh);
  if (retval != PAM_SUCCESS)
  {
    fprintf(stderr, "Could not start pam: %s\n",
        pam_strerror(pamh, retval));
    exit(1);
  }

  /* Try to authenticate the user. This could cause Linux-PAM
   * to prompt the user for a password.
   */
  retval = pam_authenticate(pamh, 0);
  if (retval == PAM_SUCCESS)
    printf("Success.\n");
  else
    fprintf(stderr, "Failure: %s\n", pam_strerror(pamh, retval));

  /* Shutdown Linux-PAM. Return with an error if
   * something goes wrong.
   */
  return pam_end(pamh, retval) == PAM_SUCCESS ? 0 : 1;
}
```

In order for this to work, you must create a file called *pam_sample* in */etc/pam.d* with the following contents (the filename must match the first argument to pam_start( )):

```
auth      required  pam_securityserver.so
account   required  pam_permit.so
password  required  pam_deny.so
```

Be careful when making any changes in the */etc/pam.d* directory. If you change one of the files that is consulted for system login, you may lock yourself out of the system. For more information on Linux-PAM, see the *pam(8)* manpage.

Configuring Directory Services

In order to configure Directory Services, use the Directory Access application (*/Applications/Utilities*), shown in Figure 3-2. You can enable or disable various directory service plug-ins, or change their configuration.

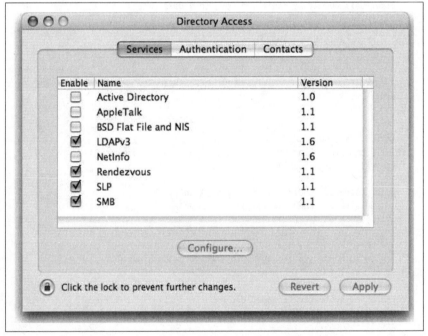

Figure 3-2. The Directory Access application shows the available plug-ins

Directory Access supports the following plug-ins:

Active Directory
This plug-in lets Mac OS X consult an Active Directory domain on a server running Windows 2000 or Windows 2003.

AppleTalk
This is the ultimate Mac OS legacy protocol. AppleTalk was the original networking protocol supported by Mac OS versions prior to Mac OS X. Linux and the server editions of Windows also support AppleTalk.

BSD Flat File and NIS
This includes the Network Information Service (NIS) and the flat files located in the */etc* directory, such as *hosts*, *exports*, and *services*. By default, this option is switched off. After you enable it, click Apply, switch to the Authentication tab, choose Custom Path from the search menu, click the Add button, choose */BSD/Local*, and click Apply again.

LDAPv3
This is the same version of LDAP used by Microsoft's Active Directory and Novell's NDS. In addition to the client components, Mac OS X includes *slapd*, a standalone LDAP daemon. Mac OS X's LDAP support comes through OpenLDAP (*http://www.openldap.org*), an open source LDAPv3 implementation.

NetInfo
This is a legacy Directory Services protocol introduced in NeXTSTEP. If the checkbox is off (the default), NetInfo uses the local domain but does not consult network-based NetInfo domains. If the checkbox is on, NetInfo will also look for and potentially use any network-based domains that it finds.

NetInfo and LDAP both use the same data store, which is contained in */var/db/netinfo/*. The data store is a collection of embedded database files.

Rendezvous
This is Apple's zero-configuration protocol for discovering file sharing, printers, and other network services. It uses a peer-to-peer approach to announce and discover services automatically as devices join a network.

SLP
This is the Service Location Protocol, which supports file and print services over IP.

SMB
This is the Server Message Block protocol, which is Microsoft's protocol for file and print services.

Under the Services tab, everything except NetInfo and BSD Configuration Files is enabled by default. However, if you go to the Authentication tab (Figure 3-3), you'll see that NetInfo is the sole service in charge of authentication (which is handled by */etc/passwd* and */etc/group* on other Unix systems).

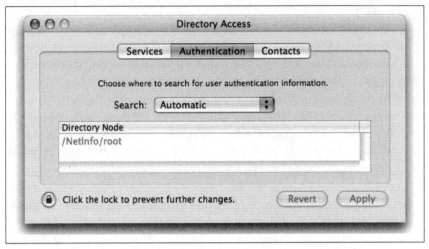

Figure 3-3. The Directory Access Authentication tab

By default, the Authentication tab is set to Automatic. You can set the Search popup to any of the following:

Automatic
> This is the default, which searches (in order): the local NetInfo directory, a shared NetInfo domain, and a shared LDAPv3 domain.

Local directory
> This searches only the local NetInfo directory.

Custom path
> This allows you to use BSD flat files *(/etc/passwd* and */etc/group)*. After you select Custom path from the pop up, click Add and select */BSD/ Local* (this option only appears in the list if you have enabled BSD Flat File and NIS on the Services tab and clicked Apply).

After you have changed the Search setting, click Apply. The Contact tab is set up identically to the Authentication tab and is used by programs that search Directory Services for contact information (office locations, phone numbers, full names, etc.).

Enabling BSD flat files does not copy or change the information in the local directory (the NetInfo database). If you want to rely only on flat files, you would need to find all the user entries from the local directory (you could use the command `nidump passwd .` to list them all) and add them to the password flat files (*/etc/passwd* and */etc/master.passwd*) with the *vipw* utility (do not edit either file directly). When you are done editing the password file, *vipw* invokes *pwd_mkdb* to rebuild the databases (*/etc/spwd.db* and */etc/pwd.db*) used for looking up usernames and passwords. Switching over to flat files would allow you to access encrypted passwords through `getpwnam( )` and friends, but would also mean you could no longer use the GUI tools to manage user accounts.

 If you change any settings in the Directory Access applications, you may find that some invalid credentials are temporarily cached by Directory Services. To clear out the cache immediately, run the command `lookupd –flushcache` as *root*.

NetInfo Manager

The local directory is organized hierarchically, starting from the *root*, which, like a filesystem's *root*, is called */*. However, this is not meant to suggest that there is a corresponding directory or file for each entry. Instead, the data is stored in a collection of files under */var/db/netinfo*.

You can browse or modify the local directory using NetInfo Manager, which is located in */Applications/Utilities*. Figure 3-4 shows NetInfo Manager displaying the properties of the *mysql* user.

Directory Services Utilities

This chapter demonstrates four Directory Services utilities: *dscl*, *nireport*, *nidump*, and *niload*. Table 3-1 describes these and other NetInfo utilities.

The *nidump* and *nireport* utilities display the contents of the local directory. *niload* loads the contents of flat files (such as */etc/passwd* or */etc/hosts*) into Directory Services. *niutil* directly manipulates the Directory Services database; it's the command-line equivalent of NetInfo Manager. To make changes, use *sudo* with these commands or first log in as the *root* user. The commands that can be performed as a normal user are shown without the *sudo* command in the examples that follow.

Unlike other *ni** utilities, *nicl* acts directly on the database files. Consequently, you can use *nicl* to modify the local directory even when Directory Services is not running (such as when you boot into single-user mode).

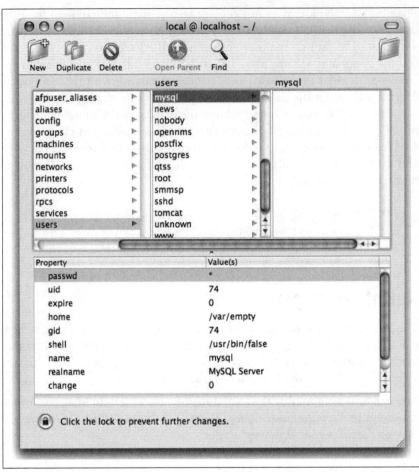

Figure 3-4. Browsing the local directory

Table 3-1. NetInfo tools

Tool	Description
dscl	Provides a command-line interface to Directory Services.
nicl	Provides a command-line interface to NetInfo.
nidump	Extracts flat file format data (such as */etc/passwd*) from NetInfo.
nifind	Finds a NetInfo directory.
nigrep	Performs a regular expression search on NetInfo.
niload	Loads flat file format data (such as */etc/passwd*) into NetInfo.
nireport	Prints tables from NetInfo.
niutil	NetInfo utility for manipulating the database.

When you use any of these utilities you are making potentially dangerous changes to your system. But even if you trash the local directory with reckless usage of these commands, you can restore the NetInfo database from your last backup. For more details, see the "Restoring the Directory Services Database" section, later in this chapter. To back up the local NetInfo database, use the command:

```
nidump -r / -t localhost/local > backup.nidump
```

Managing Groups

Directory Services stores information about groups in its */groups* directory. This is different from the */etc/group* file, which is consulted only in single-user mode.

To list all of the group IDs (GIDs) and group names for the local domain, invoke *nireport* with the NetInfo domain (., the local domain), the directory (*/groups*), and the properties you want to inspect—in this case, *gid* and *name*:

```
$ nireport . /groups gid name
-2      nobody
-1      nogroup
0       wheel
1       daemon
2       kmem
3       sys
4       tty
5       operator
6       mail
7       bin
20      staff
25      smmsp
26      lp
27      postfix
28      postdrop
31      guest
45      utmp
66      uucp
68      dialer
69      network
70      www
74      mysql
75      sshd
76      qtss
78      mailman
79      appserverusr
80      admin
81      appserveradm
99      unknown
```

Although the flat file format is called *group* (after the /etc/group file), the group directory is /groups. If you forget that last s, *nireport* will look for the wrong directory. However, if you want to dump the groups directory in the /etc/group file format, use the command `nidump group .` without that last s.

Creating a Group with niload

The *niload* utility can be used to read the flat file format used by /etc/group (`name:password:gid:members`). To add a new group, you can create a file that adheres to that format, and load it with *niload*. For ad hoc work, you can use a here document (an expression that functions as a quoted string, but spans multiple lines) rather than a separate file:

```
$ sudo niload group . <<EOF
> writers:*:1001:
> EOF
```

Creating a Group with dscl

To create a group with *dscl*, you'll need to create a directory under /groups and set the *gid* and *passwd* properties. An asterisk (*) specifies no password; be sure to quote it so that the shell does not attempt to expand it. The following creates a group named *writers* as GID 5005 with no password and no members:

```
$ sudo dscl . create /groups/writers gid 5005
$ sudo dscl . create /groups/writers passwd '*'
```

Adding Users to a Group

You can add users to the group by appending values to the *users* property with *dscl*'s *merge* command at the command line (or by using the *merge* command interactively; start *dscl* in interactive mode with `sudo dscl .`). If the *users* property does not exist, *dscl* creates it. If the users are already part of the group, they are not added to the list (contrast this with the *-append* command, which can result in the same user being added more than once if the command is invoked multiple times):

```
$ sudo dscl . merge /groups/writers users bjepson rothman
```

Listing Groups with nidump

Use *nidump* to confirm that the new group was created correctly. To list groups with *nidump*, pass in the format (in this case, the *group* file) and the domain (., the local domain):

```
$ nidump group . | grep writers
writers:*:5005:bjepson,rothman
```

Because you can use *nireport* to dump any directory, you could also use it to see this information:

```
$ nireport . /groups name passwd gid users | grep writers
writers *       5005    bjepson,rothman
```

Deleting a Group

To delete a group, use *dscl*'s *delete* command. Be careful with this command, since it will delete everything in and below the specified NetInfo directory:

```
$ sudo nicl / delete /groups/writers
```

Managing Users and Passwords

The Directory Services equivalent of the *passwd* file resides under the */users* portion of the directory. Although Mac OS X includes */etc/passwd* and */etc/master.passwd* files, they are consulted only while the system is in single-user mode, or if the system has been reconfigured to use BSD Flat Files (see the "Configuring Directory Services" section, earlier in this chapter).

To add a normal user to your system, you should use System Preferences → Accounts. However, if you want to bulk-load NetInfo with many users or create a user while logged in over *ssh*, you can use *dscl* or *niload*.

You can list all users with the *nireport* utility. Supply the NetInfo domain (., the local domain), the directory (*/users*), and the properties you want to inspect (*uid, name, home, realname,* and *shell*):

```
$ nireport . /users uid name home realname shell
-2  nobody   /var/empty          Unprivileged User       /usr/bin/false
0   root     /var/root           System Administrator    /bin/sh
1   daemon   /var/root           System Services         /usr/bin/false
99  unknown  /var/empty          Unknown User            /usr/bin/false
25  smmsp    /private/etc/mail   Sendmail User           /usr/bin/false
2   lp       /var/spool/cups     Printing Services       /usr/bin/false
27  postfix  /var/spool/postfix  Postfix User            /usr/bin/false
70  www      /Library/WebServer  World Wide Web Server    /usr/bin/false
71  eppc     /var/empty          Apple Events User       /usr/bin/false
74  mysql    /var/empty          MySQL Server            /usr/bin/false
```

```
75   sshd        /var/empty    sshd Privilege separation  /usr/bin/false
76   qtss        /var/empty    QuickTime Streaming Server /usr/bin/false
77   cyrus       /var/imap     Cyrus User                 /usr/bin/false
78   mailman     /var/empty    Mailman user               /usr/bin/false
79   appserver   /var/empty    Application Server         /usr/bin/false
```

Creating a User with niload

The *niload* utility understands the flat file format used by */etc/passwd* (name:
password:uid:gid:class:change:expire:gecos:home_dir:shell).   See   the
passwd(5) manpage for a description of each field. To add a new user, create a file that adheres to that format and load it with *niload*. You can use a
here document rather than a separate file. This example creates a user for
Ernest Rothman with a UID of 701 and membership in the group num-
bered 701, which you'll create next:

```
$ sudo niload passwd . <<EOF
> rothman:*:701:701::0:0:Ernest Rothman:/Users/rothman:/bin/bash
> EOF
```

Next, create a group with the same name as the new user and a GID that
matches his UID (as of Mac OS X 10.3, users are given their own groups):

```
$ sudo niload group . <<EOF
> rothman:*:701:
> EOF
```

As you can see from the example, we set the user's password field to *,
which disables logins for that account. To set the password, we'll use the
passwd command:

```
$ sudo passwd rothman
Changing password for rothman.
New password: ********
Retype new password: ********
```

If you *niload* a user that already exists, that user's entry will be updated with
the new information. Before the user can log in, you must create her home
directory (see the "Creating a User's Home Directory" section, later in this
chapter).

Creating a User with dscl

To create a user with *dscl*, you'll need to create a directory under */users*, and
set the *uid*, *gid*, *shell*, *realname*, and *home* properties.

The following commands will create the same user shown in the previous
section, "Creating a User with niload":

```
$ sudo dscl . create /users/rothman uid 701
$ sudo dscl . create /users/rothman gid 701
```

```
$ sudo dscl . create /users/rothman shell /bin/bash
$ sudo dscl . create /users/rothman home /Users/rothman
$ sudo dscl . create /users/rothman realname "Ernest Rothman"
$ sudo dscl . create /users/rothman passwd \*
$ sudo dscl . create /groups/rothman gid 701
$ sudo dscl . create /groups/rothman passwd \*
```

Be sure to quote or escape the asterisk (*) in the passwd entries. After you create the user, you should set the password as shown in the previous section.

Creating a User's Home Directory

One thing that NetInfo can't do for you is create the user's home directory. Mac OS X keeps a skeleton directory under the */System/Library/User Template* directory. If you look in this directory, you'll see localized versions of a user's home directory. To copy the localized English version of the home directory, use the *ditto* command with the *--rsrc* flag to preserve any resource forks that may exist:

```
$ sudo ditto --rsrc \
    /System/Library/User\ Template/English.lproj /Users/rothman
```

Then, use *chown* to recursively set the ownership of the home directory and all its contents (make sure you set the group to a group of which the user is a member):

```
$ sudo chown -R rothman:rothman /Users/rothman
```

This change makes the new user the owner of his home directory and all its contents.

Granting Administrative Privileges

To give someone administrative privileges, add that user to the *admin* group (*/groups/admin*). This gives him or her the ability to use *sudo* and run applications (such as software installers) that require such privileges:

```
$ sudo dscl . merge /groups/admin users rothman
```

If you want this setting to take place immediately, you can run the command *sudo lookupd –flushcache* to flush any cached credentials.

Modifying a User

You can change a user's properties by using the *create* command, even if that property already exists. For example, to change *rothman*'s shell to *zsh*, use:

```
$ sudo dscl . -create /users/rothman shell /bin/zsh
```

You can also modify most user settings with System Preferences → Accounts. If you want to do things the traditional Unix way, Mac OS X includes *chsh*, *chfn*, and *chpass* as of Version 10.3.

Listing Users with nidump

Use *nidump* to confirm that *rothman* was added successfully. To list users with *nidump*, pass in the format (in this case, the *passwd* file) and the domain (use . for the local domain):

```
$ nidump passwd . | grep rothman
rothman:********:701:701::0:0:Ernest Rothman:/Users/rothman:/bin/zsh
```

Deleting a User

To delete a user, use *dscl*'s *delete* command. Since *delete* recursively deletes everything under the specified directory, use this command with caution:

```
$ sudo dscl . delete /users/rothman
```

If you want to also delete that user's home directory, you will have to do it manually.

Managing Hostnames and IP Addresses

Mac OS X consults both the */etc/hosts* file and the */machines* portion of the local directory. For example, the following entry in */etc/hosts* would map the hostname *xyzzy* to 192.168.0.1:

```
192.168.0.1    xyzzy
```

Creating a Host with niload

The *niload* utility understands the flat file format used by */etc/hosts* (*ip_address name*). See the *hosts(5)* manpage for a description of each field. To add a new host, create a file using that format and load it with *niload*. This example adds the host *xyzzy*:

```
$ sudo niload hosts . <<EOF
> 192.168.0.1 xyzzy
> EOF
```

If you add an entry that already exists, it will be overwritten.

The */etc/hosts* file takes precedence over the local directory, so if you enter the same hostname with different IP addresses in both places, Mac OS X uses the one in */etc/hosts*.

Exporting Directories with NFS

You can use the */etc/exports* file to store folders that you want to export over NFS. For example, the following line exports the */Users* directory to two hosts (192.168.0.134 and 192.168.0.106):

```
/Users  -ro 192.168.0.134 192.168.0.106
```

The NFS server will start automatically at boot time if there are any exports in that file. After you've set up your exports, you can reboot, and NFS should start automatically. NFS options supported by Mac OS X include the following (see the *exports(5)* manpage for complete details):

`-maproot=user`

Specifies that the remote *root* user should be mapped to the specified user. You may specify either a username or numeric user ID.

`-maproot=user:[group[:group...]]`

Specifies that the remote *root* user should be mapped to the specified user with the specified group credentials. If you include the colon with no groups, as in `-maproot=username:`, it means the remote user should have no group credentials. You may specify a username or numeric user ID for *user* and a group name or numeric group ID for *group*.

`-mapall=user`

Specifies that all remote users should be mapped to the specified user.

`-mapall=user:[group[:group...]]`

Specifies that all remote users should be mapped to the specified user with the specified group credentials. If you include the colon with no groups, as in `mapall=username:`, it specifies that the remote user should be given no group credentials.

`-kerb`

Uses a Kerberos authentication server to authenticate and map client credentials.

`-ro`

Exports the filesystem as read-only. The synonym `-o` is also supported.

Flat Files and Their Directory Services Counterparts

As mentioned earlier, Directory Services manages information for several flat files in earlier releases of Mac OS X, including */etc/printcap*, */etc/mail/aliases*, */etc/protocols*, and */etc/services*. For a complete list of known flat file formats, see the *nidump* and *niload* manpages.

Although you can edit these flat files directly as you would on any other Unix system, you can also use Directory Services to manage this information. You can use *niload* with a supported flat file format to add entries, or you can use *dscl* or NetInfo Manager to directly manipulate the entries. Table 3-2 lists each flat file, the corresponding portion of the directory, and important properties associated with each entry. See the *netinfo(5)* manpage for complete details. Properties marked with (list) can take multiple values. (For an example, see the "Adding Users to a Group" section, earlier in this chapter.)

The "Flat files or local database?" column in Table 3-2 indicates whether Directory Services consults the flat file, the local database, or both. You can use Directory Access to modify the way information is looked up on your Macintosh.

Table 3-2. Flat files and their NetInfo counterparts

Flat file	NetInfo directory	Important properties	Flat files or local database?
/etc/exports	/exports	name, clients (list), opts (list)	Flat files
/etc/fstab	/mounts	name, dir, type, opts (list), passno, freq	Local database
/etc/group	/groups	name, passwd, gid, users (list)	Local database
/etc/hosts	/machines	ip_address, name (list)	Both; entries in /etc/hosts take precedence
/etc/mail/aliases	/aliases	name, members (list)	Flat files
/etc/networks	/networks	name (list), address	Flat files
/etc/passwd, /etc/ master.passwd	/users	name, passwd, uid, gid, realname, home, shell	Local database
/etc/printcap	/printers	*name*, and various *printcap* properties (see the *printcap(5)* manpage)	Flat files
/etc/protocols	/protocols	name (list), number	Flat files
/etc/rpc	/rpcs	name (list), number	Flat files
/etc/services	/services	name (list), *port*, *protocol* (list)	Flat files

Restoring the Directory Services Database

If the local directory database is damaged, boot into single-user mode by holding down ⌘-S as the system starts up. Next, check to see if you have a backup of the NetInfo database. The */etc/daily* cron job backs up the database each time it is run. You can find the backup in */var/backups/local. nidump*. If you don't have a backup, you won't be able to restore. The *local. nidump* file is overwritten each time the *cron* job runs, so make sure you back it up regularly (preferably to some form of removable media).

If your computer is generally not turned on at 3:15 a.m. (the default time for the *daily cron* job), you'll never get a backup of your local directory. You can solve this problem by editing */etc/crontab* to run this job at a different time, or to run the job periodically with the command *sudo periodic daily*. See the "Default cron Jobs" section in Chapter 2 for more details.

After the system boots in single-user mode, you should:

1. Wait for the root# prompt to come up.

2. Fix any filesystem errors; if you are using a journaled filesystem, this step won't be necessary (and if you try to run this command, you'll get an error):

   ```
   # /sbin/fsck -y
   ```

3. Mount the *root* filesystem as read/write:

   ```
   # /sbin/mount -uw /
   ```

4. Change directories and go to the NetInfo database directory:

   ```
   # cd /var/db/netinfo/
   ```

5. Move the database out of the way and give it a different name:

   ```
   # mv local.nidb/ local.nidb.broken
   ```

6. Start enough of the system to use NetInfo (each of these commands may take several seconds or more to complete; the last message you see should be "Startup complete."):

   ```
   # /usr/libexec/kextd
   # /usr/sbin/configd
   # /sbin/SystemStarter
   ```

7. Create a blank NetInfo database and start NetInfo (be sure you are still in the */var/db/netinfo* directory from step 4):

   ```
   # /usr/libexec/create_nidb
   # /usr/sbin/netinfod -s local
   ```

8. Load the backup into NetInfo:

   ```
   # /usr/bin/niload  -d -r / . < /var/backups/local.nidump
   ```

After you have completed these steps, reboot the system with the *reboot* command.

 If you totally mess up and find that you forgot to backup your NetInfo database, you can stop at step 8, and issue the command *rm /var/db/.AppleSetupDone*. This makes Mac OS X think that it's being booted for the first time next time you reboot, and will run the setup assistant so you can create the initial user for the system, bringing your system to a usable state for further repairs.

CHAPTER 4

Printing

Mac OS X offers a rich and flexible set of tools for administering and using a wide variety of printers. Unix and Linux users will find tools that are familiar, as well as a few new ones. In this chapter we will first discuss basic use of the Printer Setup Utility found in the */Applications/Utilities* folder. We will then discuss the Mac OS X implementations of the printing tools most Unix and Linux users will find familiar. In particular, we will discuss the Common Unix Printing System (CUPS), GIMP-print, HP InkJet Server (HPIJS), and Samba Printing.

Printer Setup Utility

If you're using a popular USB printer under Mac OS X, it is likely that all you'll need to do is connect it to the USB port and choose this printer in the Print dialog when you want to print a document. However, there are some circumstances where it's not so simple:

- Perhaps your USB printer does not automatically show up as an available printer in the Print dialog
- Maybe you want to share your printer with other computers on your LAN
- Perhaps you want to use a network printer such as one listed in Open Directory, an AppleTalk printer, or one for which all you have is an IP address

If you haven't already set up a printer using the Printer Setup Utility, there are three ways to add a new printer in Mac OS X:

Add a printer automatically
> Attempting to print a document from virtually any application automatically launches the Printer Setup Utility: Mac OS X first informs you that

you have no printers available, and asks if you'd like to add a printer. Click on the Add button to start the setup procedure.

Launch Print Center

You can also add a new printer by double-clicking the Printer Setup Utility icon in the */Applications/Utilities* folder and clicking the Add button. The */Applications/Utilities* folder also contains an icon for Print Center. In Panther, the Print Center is provided as an alias to Printer Setup Utility, to maintain backward compatibility with earlier versions of Mac OS X.

Use System Preferences

Open System Preferences, choose Print & Fax → Printing → Set Up Printers, and click Add when the Printer Setup Utility appears. You can share your printers with other computers by opening System Preferences and selecting Print & Fax and clicking "Share my printers with other computers."

Whichever way you end up clicking the Add button, Printer Setup Utility automatically searches for Rendezvous-enabled printers on your network. If a Rendezvous-enabled printer is found, you can easily add this printer and you'll be ready to use it immediately. If a Rendezvous-enabled printer is not found, you can select one of several alternatives from the pop-up menu as shown in Figure 4-1.

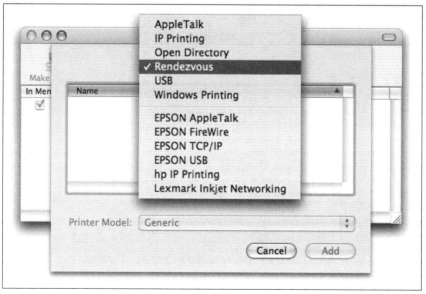

Figure 4-1. Specifying the printer type in the Printer Setup Utility

Adding an IP Printer

If you have a printer on your network that is not Rendezvous-enabled, you'll need to have some information about it on hand:

- The printer's IP address or hostname.
- The manufacturer and model of the printer.

 If you don't know the exact model of the printer, you may be able to set up the printer, albeit with reduced functionality. For example, if all you know is that you've got some kind of HP DeskJet, you could configure the printer as a generic DeskJet by selecting ESP → HP New DeskJet Series CUPS from the Printer Model options when you are adding the printer. However, knowing the exact model will probably let you take advantage of special printing features such as duplex printing.

To set up an IP printer, change the Rendezvous selection in Printer Setup Utility to "IP Printing" as shown in Figure 4-2.

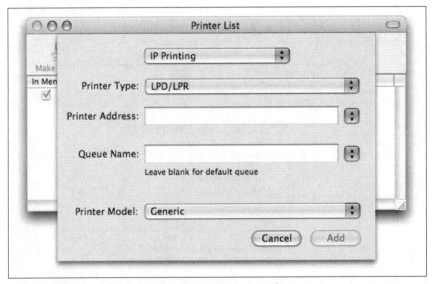

Figure 4-2. Setting up IP Printing in the Printer Setup Utility

You need to select a Printer Type from the following choices:

- Rendezvous
- LPD/LPR
- Internet Printing Protocol
- Socket/HP Jet Direct

For example, suppose you have a Tektronix Phaser 740 on your LAN and that its IP address is 192.168.0.77. In this case, you would select LPD/LPR as the Printer Type, enter 192.168.0.77 as the Printer Address, specify a Queue Name if required (otherwise it will be called "default"), and select the Tektronix Phaser 740 under Printer Model. Click the Add button and you'll be ready to print.

If you can't find your printer model, you can try selecting Generic; in most instances, that should work.

Setting up an LPD/LPR printer in this manner allows you to print documents not only by selecting Print from GUI-based applications, but also manipulate the print queue from the Terminal using the CUPS *lp*, *lpstat*, and *cancel* shell commands.

Modifying a Printer's Settings

Once your printer has been added, you can change some of its settings (location, printer model, and any installable options) using the Printer Setup Utility. To do this, open the Printer Setup Utility, highlight the printer whose settings you want to change, and click the Show Info icon in the toolbar; this opens the Printer Info window, which you can use to make the changes. Click Apply Changes to make your changes take effect.

Creating a Desktop Icon for a Printer

You can use the Printer Setup Utility to create desktop icons for printers. To do this, open Printer Setup Utility, highlight the printer in the list, and choose Printers → Create Desktop Printer from the menu bar. You can save the printer's desktop icon to the desktop or to any folder in which you have write permission. You can also place the printer's desktop icon in the left section of the dock with icons of applications or in the lower section of the Finder's Places sidebar. In each case, you'll be able to print a document by dragging its icon to the printer's icon.

Printer Sharing

Printers with a network adapter are not necessarily the only printers available on your LAN. You can share a printer that's connected to your computer with other computers. For example, you can share your USB printer with all the computers on your LAN by opening Preferences → Sharing, clicking the Services tab, and enabling Printer Sharing.

When you change a system preference you may need to click the lock in the lower left corner to authenticate yourself as an administrative user before you make any changes.

If you've activated the firewall, enabling Printer Sharing will open up ports 631 (Internet Printing Protocol) and 515 (lpd). Once you've shared your printer, other Macs on your subnet should automatically see your printer in their Print dialogs. If a user is on your local network, but not on your subnet, she can connect to your printer using the IP address or hostname of your Macintosh.

In addition to sharing your printer with Mac users, you can also share it with other Linux, Unix, and Windows users. If a Unix or Linux computer is on the same subnet as the computer sharing its printers and has CUPS installed, it will see the shared printer automatically. If not, you will need to provide the IP address of the computer sharing the printer (see "Printing from Remote Systems," later in this chapter).

To let Windows users connect to your printer, activate both Printer Sharing and Windows Sharing in the Sharing pane of System Preferences. Windows users on your network can now add the printer.

After you've activated sharing of your printer with other computers on your network, you may want to add some information about the physical location of the printer. You can do this by opening Printer Setup Utility, highlighting the shared printer, clicking the Show Info icon, and entering the location in the location field.

It is easy to print to a printer that is shared by a Windows computer. If your Mac is on the same subnet as the Windows machine, you will probably see it listed with other available printers in Printer Setup Utility. In this case, just check the In Menu box to the left of the printer name. Subsequently, this printer will be available in Print dialogs. If the Windows printer does not show up in the list, you can add it by clicking the Add icon, selecting Windows Printing in the pop-up dialog, and choosing the appropriate network workgroup. Once you've done this, any available Windows printers will appear in the Printer Setup Utility printer list; select the one that you'd like to use. For additional information, select Help → Printer Setup Utility Help and search for SMB (Server Message Block, the Windows networking protocol).

Common Unix Printing System (CUPS)

The Common Unix Printing System (CUPS), which is bundled with Mac OS X, is free open source software provided by Easy Software Products under the GNU General Public License and the GNU Lesser General Public License. It is a portable and extensible printing system for Unix based on the Internet Printing Protocol (IPP/1.1).

 Extensive documentation and source code is available at *http://www.cups.org*. As noted in online documentation, the goal of CUPS is "to provide a complete, modern printing system for Unix that can be used to support new printers, devices, and protocols while providing compatibility with existing Unix applications."

CUPS provides System V- and Berkeley-compatible command-line interfaces and a web-based interface to extensive documentation, status monitoring, and administration. This web-based administration interface is available only if Printer Sharing has been enabled in System Preferences → Sharing. To access it, point your web browser to *http://127.0.0.1:631*. The main page of the web-based administrative interface is shown in Figure 4-3.

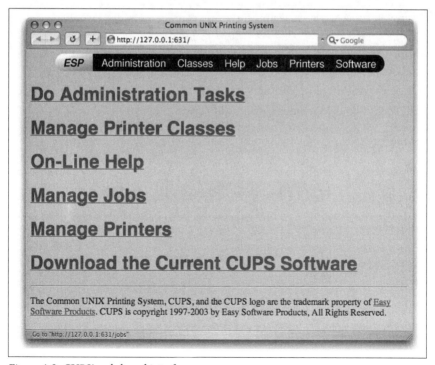

Figure 4-3. CUPS' web-based interface

Printing from Remote Systems

CUPS is available on a wide variety of Unix-based systems and makes both the administration and use of shared printers easy. For example, a shared USB printer connected to your Mac will immediately be visible to a Solaris-based SUN workstation running CUPS, provided the Solaris machine is on the same subnet (if not, remote users can connect to the printer by supplying your Mac's IP address or hostname). To connect to your Mac's printer from Mandrake Linux (other flavors of Linux will follow similar procedures), launch the Mandrake Control Center and select PrinterDrake. Next, select the tab labeled "Configured on other machines" (see Figure 4-4).

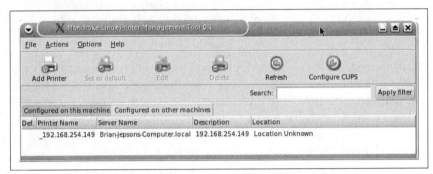

Figure 4-4. Using Mandrake Linux to browse printers hosted on other machines

If your Macintosh does not appear in this list, follow these steps:

1. Click Configure CUPS.

2. Select Additional CUPS Servers.

3. To add your Macintosh, click Add Server.

4. Specify your Mac's IP address and CUPS port (normally 631) as shown in Figure 4-5.

Figure 4-5. Specifying the IP address and port of your Macintosh's CUPS server

After you get your Mac and its printer to appear in the list, you don't need to do any further configuration. To print from an application such as Konqueror (the KDE web browser), select the Print option from the application's main menu. Your Mac's printer should appear in the Print dialog, as shown in Figure 4-6.

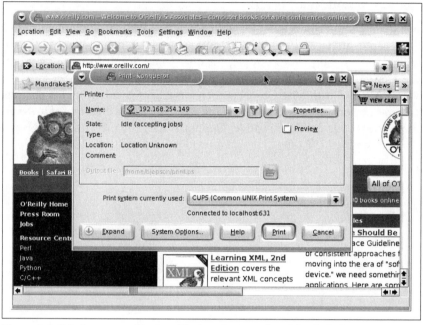

Figure 4-6. Printing to your Macintosh's shared printer from Mandrake Linux

Gimp-Print

Gimp-Print (*http://gimp-print.sourceforge.net*) is a package of printer drivers for a wide variety of printers that is bundled with Mac OS X Panther. There is a Mac OS X specific GIMP-Print web site located at *http://gimp-print.sourceforge.net/MacOSX.php3* (if you are using a version of Mac OS X prior to Panther, you will need to download the drivers from that site). The Gimp-Print drivers support printers from Epson, Canon, Lexmark, HP, and others. In many cases, drivers for these printers are not available from the printer manufacturer themselves. Even if drivers are available, the Gimp-Print drivers are often of better quality than those offered by the manufacturer.

HP InkJet Project (HPIJS)

The Hewlett-Packard InkJet Project (HPIJS) is a collection of drivers from Hewlett-Packard that has been released as open source software. Although HPIJS was originally targeted for Linux, it has been ported to Mac OS X (*http://www.linuxprinting.org/macosx/hpijs/*). HPIJS supports over 200 Hewlett-Packard printer models.

Although Gimp-Print is included with Mac OS X Panther, if you find both a Gimp-Print driver and the HPIJS driver we suggest that you try both and compare the quality. For example, the only Gimp-Print driver we found for the Hewlett-Packard OfficeJet d135 was the HP New DeskJet Series CUPS v1.1 that came with Mac OS X Panther. It supports neither duplex printing nor the higher resolutions that this printer model is capable of. However, the HPIJS OfficeJet D135 driver supports these higher resolutions and duplex printing.

## CHAPTER 5

The X Window System

Although the X in "Mac OS X" is not the same X as in "The X Window System," you can get them to play nice together.

Most Unix systems use the X Window System as their default GUI. (We'll refer to the X Window System as X11 instead of X, to avoid confusion with Mac OS X.) X11 includes development tools and libraries for creating graphical applications for Unix-based systems. Mac OS X does not use X11 as its GUI, relying instead on Quartz (and, on compatible hardware, Quartz Extreme), a completely different graphics system. However, Apple's own implementation of X11 for Mac OS X, based on the open source XFree86 Project's X11 (*http://www.xfree86.org/*), was initially released as a beta for Jaguar and is now bundled with Mac OS X Panther as an optional installation. Apple also provides an X11 software development kit (the X11 SDK) on the Xcode Tools CD that ships with Panther.

This chapter highlights some of the key features of Apple's X11 distribution and explains how to install Apple's X11 and the X11 SDK. It also explains how to use X11 in both rootless and full-screen modes (using the GNOME and KDE desktops). You'll also learn how to connect to other X Window systems using Virtual Network Computer (VNC), as well as how to remotely control the Mac OS X Aqua desktop from other X11 systems.

From Aqua to X11, there's no shortage of graphical environments for Mac OS X. The operating system's solid Unix underpinnings and powerful graphics subsystem make it possible for developers to support alternative graphical environments. For this reason, a humble iBook can make a fine cockpit for a network of heterogeneous machines!

About Apple's X11

As noted earlier, Apple's X11 distribution is based on the open source XFree86 Project's XFree86, Version 4.3. The X11 package has been optimized for Mac OS X and has the following features:

- X11R6.6 window server
- Support for the RandR (Resize and Rotate) extension
- Strong integration with Mac OS X environment
- A Quartz window manager that provides Aqua window decorations, ability to minimize windows to the Dock, and pasteboard integration
- Can use other window managers
- Compatible with Expose
- Supports rootless and full-screen modes
- Customizable Application menu, which allows you to add applications for easy launching and to map keyboard shortcuts
- Customizable Dock menu, which allows you to add applications for easy launching, to map keyboard shortcuts, and to list all open windows
- Finder integration, which supports auto-detection of X11 binaries and double-clicking to launch X11 binaries, starting the X server if it is not already running
- Preference settings for system color map, key equivalents, system alerts, keyboard mapping, and multi-button mouse emulation
- Hardware acceleration support for OpenGL (GLX) and Direct CG (AIPI)

Installing X11

Apple's X11 for Mac OS X is available as an optional installation bundled with Mac OS X. To install it when you first install (or upgrade an existing installation of) Mac OS X Panther, you must customize the installation (in the Selection Type phase) and select the X11 checkbox. If you don't install X11 during the Mac OS X installation, you can install it later by inserting the Install Mac OS X Disc 3 CD, then finding and double-clicking the *X11User.pkg* package in the Packages folder.

The installation places the double-clickable X11 application in the */Applications/Utilities* folder. If you're going to build X11-based applications, you'll need to install the X11SDK, which is located as an optional package on the Xcode Tools CD (*/Developer Tools/Packages/X11SDK.pkg*). Instructions for building X11 applications are included in Chapter 8; this chapter simply focuses on using X11.

Running X11

X11 can be run in two modes: *full screen* or *rootless* (the default). Both of these modes run side-by-side with Aqua, although full-screen mode hides the Finder and Mac OS X's desktop (to hide X11 and return to the Finder, press Option-⌘-A).

To launch the X server, double-click the X11 application (in */Applications/ Utilities*). An *xterm* window that looks similar to a Mac OS X Terminal window opens, sporting Aqua-like buttons for closing, minimizing, and maximizing the window. Also, X11 windows minimize to the Dock, just like other Aqua windows. Figure 5-1 shows a Terminal window and an *xterm* window side-by-side.

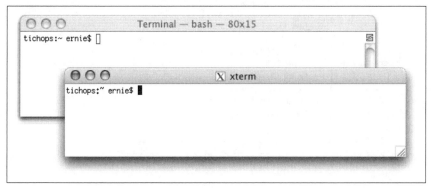

Figure 5-1. A Terminal and an xterm sporting the Aqua look

If you're using the default configuration, you'll also notice three obvious differences from a Terminal window. In particular:

- The *xterm* window has a titlebar that reads "xterm"
- The *xterm* window does not have vertical and horizontal scrollers
- The *xterm* window doesn't have a split window option

A less obvious difference between a Terminal window and an X11 *xterm* window is that Control-clicking (or right-clicking) in an *xterm* window does not invoke the same contextual menu that it does in a Terminal window. Control-clicking, Control-Option-clicking, and Control-⌘-clicking in an *xterm* invokes *xterm*-specific contextual menus, as shown in Figures 5-2, 5-3, and 5-4. If you have a three-button mouse, Control-clicking with the right mouse button does the same thing as Control-⌘-clicking; Control-clicking with the middle button does the same thing as Control-Option-clicking.

You can use Fink to install an *xterm* replacement such as *rxvt* or *eterm*. See Chapter 11 for more information on Fink.

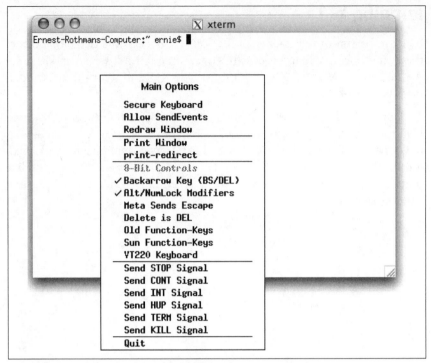

Figure 5-2. Control-click (or Control-left-click) in an xterm window

 Mac OS X emulates right-mouse clicks with Control-click. In X11, you can configure key combinations that simulate two- and three-button mice.

By default, Option-click simulates the middle mouse button, and ⌘-click simulates the right mouse button. You can use X11 → Preferences to enable or disable this, but you cannot change which key combinations are used (although you can use *xmodmap* as you would under any other X11 system to remap pointer buttons).

In rootless mode, X11 applications take up their own window on your Mac OS X desktop. In full-screen mode, X11 takes over the entire screen and is suitable for running an X11 desktop environment (DTE) like GNOME, KDE, or Xfce. If you want to run X11 in full-screen mode, you'll have to enable this mode in the X11 Preferences by clicking the Output tab and selecting the full-screen mode checkbox.

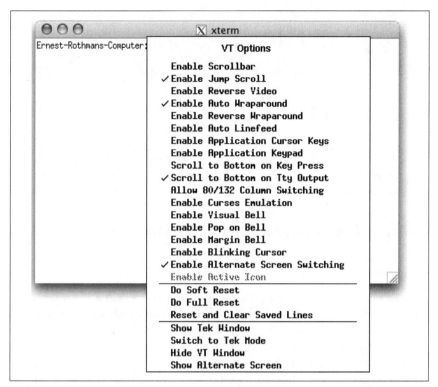

Figure 5-3. Control-Option-click (or Control-middle-click) in an xterm window

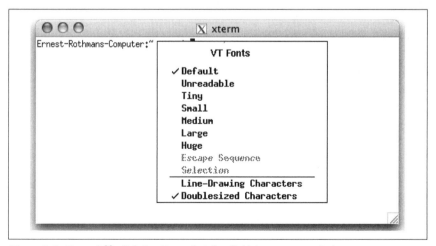

Figure 5-4. Control-⌘-click (or Control-right-click) in an xterm window

You can still access your Mac OS X desktop while in full-screen mode by pressing Option-⌘-A. To go back to the X11 desktop, bring X11 to the front by clicking its icon in the Dock or using ⌘-Tab, and press Option-⌘-A.

Customizing X11

There are a number of things you can customize in X11. For example, you can customize your *xterm* window, set X11 application preferences, customize the X11 application and Dock menus, and specify which window manager to use.

Dot-files, Desktops, and Window Managers

To customize X11, you can create an *.xinitrc* script in your *Home* directory. A sample *.xinitrc* script is provided in */etc/X11/xinit/xinitrc*.

Using the script as a starting point, you can specify which X11-based applications to start when X11 is launched, including which window manager you'd like to use as your default. The default window manager for X11 is the Quartz window manager (or *quartz-wm*). The tab window manager (or *twm*) is also bundled with X11, but many other window managers are available. You can visit the following web sites to get instructions and binaries for a wide variety of window managers and DTEs.

Fink
     http://fink.sourceforge.net

DarwinPorts
     http://darwinports.opendarwin.org

GNU-Darwin
     http://gnu-darwin.sourceforge.net

OroborOSX
     http://oroborosx.sourceforge.net

If you're going to use your own *.xinitrc* file and want to use the Quartz window manager, make sure you start the Quartz window manager with the command:

```
exec /usr/X11R6/bin/quartz-wm
```

Once you've installed X11, you will probably want to install additional X11 applications, window managers, and perhaps other DTEs (even if you are using Apple's window manager, you can still run most binaries from other DTEs such as GNOME and KDE even without using that DTE as your desktop). One of the easiest ways to install additional window managers is to use Fink. Table 5-1 lists some of the window managers and desktops that can be installed via Fink. (For information on installing and updating Fink, see Chapter 11.)

Table 5-1. Window managers available for Fink

Window manager/desktop	Fink package name
Blackbox	blackbox
Enlightenment	enlightenment
FVWM	fvwm, fvwm2
GNOME	bundle-gnome
IceWM	icewm
KDE	bundle-kde
mwm	lesstif
Oroborus	oroborus, oroborus2
PWM	pwm
Sawfish	sawfish
Window Maker	windowmaker
XFce	xfce

Fink has entire sections (*http://fink.sourceforge.net/pdb/sections.php*) devoted to GNOME and KDE, where you will find an extensive set of libraries, utilities, and plug-ins. Also included in the GNOME section are GTK+, *glib*, and Glade. Installing GNOME and KDE may be especially useful if you want to develop software for these desktops.

Fink installs everything in its */sw* directory. So, for example, if you've installed *lesstif* and want to use the *mwm* window manager, you must include */sw/bin* in your path, or include */sw/bin/mwm &* in your *.xinitrc* file to start the Motif window manager. However, if you've installed Fink according to its instructions, */sw/bin* will already be in your path (see Chapter 11).

You can customize the *xterm* window in Apple's X11 in the same way you would customize *xterm* on any other system running X11. You can, for example, set resources in an *.Xdefaults* file in your home directory or use escape sequences to set the title bar (see "Customizing the Terminal on the Fly" in Chapter 1).

X11 Preferences, Application Menu, and Dock Menu

You can also customize your X11 environment by setting X11's preferences via the X11 → Preferences window (⌘-,) and adding programs to its Application menu. X11's preferences are organized into three categories: Input, Output, and Security. The X11 preferences are described in Table 5-1 and have the following options:

Input

The following options are used for controlling how X11 interacts with input devices:

Emulate three-button mouse
> Determines whether Option-click and ⌘-click mimic the middle and right buttons.

Follow system keyboard layout
> Allows input menu changes to overwrite the current X11 keymap.

Enable key equivalents under X11
> Enabled menu bar key equivalents, which may interfere with X11 applications that use the Meta modifier.

By default, all three of these options are enabled.

Output

The following options are used for configuring X11's look and feel:

Colors
> This pop-up menu offers the following options:
> - From Display
> - 256 Colors
> - Thousands
> - Millions
>
> By default, the Color pop-up is set to "From Display"; if you change this setting to something else, you will need to relaunch X11 for the change to take effect.

Full-screen mode
> This option is unchecked by default. When unchecked, X11 runs in rootless mode, which means that X11 windows can reside side-by-side with Aqua windows. In full-screen mode, use Option-⌘-A to toggle full-screen X11 and Aqua.

Use system alert effect
> Determines whether X11's beeps will use the system alert, as specified in the Sound Effects System Preference. If unchecked, X11 windows will use a standard Unix system beep to sound an alert.

Security

The following options are used to configure X11's security features:

Authenticate connections
> Determines whether X11 creates Xauthority access-control keys. If the system's IP address changes, you should relaunch X11, since the old keys will become invalid.

Allow connections from network clients
> If you use this option, be sure to select Authenticate connections to ensure the security of your system. If this is disabled, remote applications won't be able to connect.

Both of these settings are checked by default. If you make any changes to these settings, you must quit and restart X11 for the change to take effect.

Customizing X11's Applications menu

X11's Applications menu can be used to quickly launch X11 applications, so you don't have to enter their command path. You can add other X11 applications to this menu and assign keyboard shortcuts by selecting Applications → Customize to bring up the X11 Application Menu dialog window, shown in Figure 5-5.

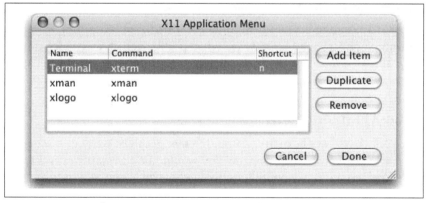

Figure 5-5. X11 Application Menu customization window

The same X11 Application Menu customization window can be opened by Control-clicking on X11's Dock icon and selecting Customize from the contextual menu. When you Control-click on X11's Dock icon, you will see that the applications shown in Figure 5-5 are listed there as well. X11's context menu allows you to quickly launch other X11 applications and to switch between windows of currently running X11 applications.

X11-based Applications and Libraries

You can use Fink to install many X11-based applications, such as the GNU Image Manipulation Program (GIMP), *xfig/transfig*, ImageMagick, *nedit*, and many others. Since Fink understands dependencies, installing some of these applications will cause Fink to first install several other packages. For example, since the text editor *nedit* depends on Motif libraries, Fink will first install *lesstif*. (This also gives you the Motif window manager, *mwm*.) Similarly, when you install the GIMP via Fink, you will also install the packages for GNOME, GTK+, and *glib* since Fink handles any package dependencies you might encounter.

You can also use Fink (see Chapter 11) to install libraries directly. For example, the following command can be used to install the X11-based Qt libraries:

```
$ fink install qt
```

This is an Aqua version of Qt for Mac OS X (available from Trolltech, *http://www.trolltech.com*); however, Qt applications won't automatically use the library. Instead, you'll need to recompile and link the application against the Aqua version of Qt, which may not always be a trivial task.

Another interesting development is the port of KDE to Mac OS X. As of this writing, Konqueror had been ported and a port of Koffice was underway. To keep abreast of developments pertaining to KDE on Mac OS X, see *http://ranger.befunk.com/blog/*.

Aqua-X11 Interactions

Since X11-based applications rely on different graphics systems, even when running XDarwin in rootless mode, you would not necessarily expect to see GUI interactions run smoothly between these two graphics systems. But actually, there are several such interactions that run very well.

First, it is possible to open X11-based applications from the Terminal application. To launch an X11-based application from the Terminal, use the *open-x11* command as follows:

```
$ open-x11 /sw/bin/gimp
```

You can also copy and paste between X11 and Mac OS X applications. For example, to copy from an *xterm*, select some text with your mouse and use the standard Macintosh keyboard shortcut to copy, ⌘-C. This places the selected text into the clipboard. To paste the contents of the clipboard into a Mac OS X application (such as the Terminal), simply press ⌘-V to paste the text.

To copy from a Mac OS X application, highlight some text and press ⌘-C. The copied text can be pasted into an *xterm* window by pressing the middle button of a three-button mouse or by Command-clicking in the X11 application.

Connecting to Other X Window Systems

You can connect from Mac OS X to other X Window systems using *ssh* with X11 forwarding. If you use OpenSSH (which is included with Mac OS X), you must use the –*X* option to request X11 forwarding (the –*2* option specifies the SSH Version 2 protocol, as opposed to the older Version 1 protocol). For example:

```
$ ssh -2 -X remotemachine -l username
```

As long as X11 is running, this can be entered in either an *xterm* window or in the Terminal. To have the X11 forwarding enabled in Terminal, you must have the DISPLAY variable set prior to making the connection. Under the *bash* shell (and other Bourne-compatible shells) use:

```
DISPLAY=:0.0; export DISPLAY
```

Under *csh* and *tcsh*, use:

```
setenv DISPLAY :0.0
```

It is also possible to create a double-clickable application that connects to a remote machine via SSH 2, with X11 forwarding enabled. For example, you can use the following script for this purpose:

```
#!/bin/sh
DISPLAY=:0.0; export DISPLAY
/usr/X11R6/bin/xterm -e ssh -2 -X remotemachine -l username
```

If you've installed the commercial version of SSH from *http://www.ssh.com*, the equivalent of the preceding script is as follows:

```
#!/bin/sh
DISPLAY=:0.0; export DISPLAY
/usr/X11R6/bin/xterm -e ssh2 remotemachine -l username
```

The X11 forwarding flag is +x with the commercial SSH, but it is enabled by default, so that you need not include it in the command.

Using Apple's X11, you can add an Application menu item to accomplish the same task. To do this, start by saving the above script to whatever you'd like to call this application. For example, suppose we want to connect to a remote machine named *mrchops* with a username of *eer*. We'll name the application *sshmrchops* and save it as *~/bin/sshmrchops.sh*. In X11, select Applications → Customize, and then click the Add Item button, as shown in Figure 5-6.

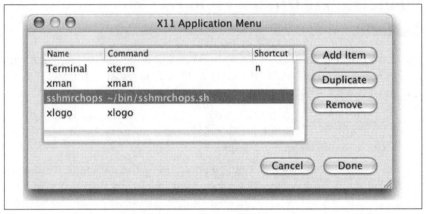

Figure 5-6. Adding an item to the X11 application menu

That's it! Now you'll be ready to launch the connection to the remote machine via the menu bar and the Dock. Once you've connected to a machine running X11, you can start X11-based applications on the remote machine and display them on your Mac OS X machine.

You can also do the reverse (SSH to your Mac and run X11 applications on the Mac, but display them on the local machine), but be sure to edit */etc/sshd_config* and change this line:

```
#X11Forwarding no
```

to this:

```
X11Forwarding yes
```

You will also need to stop and restart Remote Login using System Preferences → Sharing for this change to take effect.

OSX2X

These days, it's fairly common to find a Mac sitting next to as many as four Linux or Unix systems, each running an X11-based desktop. You may also have more than one Mac on your desk. In such situations, it would be convenient to use only one keyboard and mouse to control all of your Mac OS X and X11-based desktops, saving valuable desktop space. Enter Michael Dales' free BSD-licensed application *osx2x* (*http://opendarwin.org/projects/osx2x/*).

To use this handy little application, log into your Linux/Unix box running an X11 server, and enter the command:

```
xhost + mymachost
```

Then, double-click the *osx2x* application, and once the main window appears, click New Connection to open a drop-down window. In the drop-down window's Hostname field, supply the hostname or IP address of the Unix box running the X11 desktop, followed by either :0 or :0.0 (without any spaces), as in myhost:0.0. Next, select the Edge detection (East, West, North, or South), and the connection type X11. If, on the other hand, you are connecting your Mac to a machine running a VNC (Virtual Network Computer, described in the next section) server (for example, another Mac), select VNC as the Connection type rather than X11, and enter the VNC server password. You can switch back and forth between the Mac and the remote machine with Control-T, or you can enable edge detection and choose the position of your X11 system relative to your Mac. For example, if your Mac is to the left of your destination X11 machine, select East as illustrated in Figure 5-7.

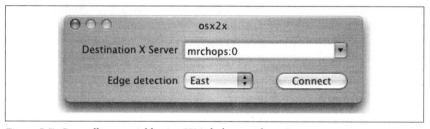

Figure 5-7. Controlling a neighboring X11 desktop with osx2x

In addition to using one keyboard and mouse to control up to four systems, you can use *osx2x* to copy text from an x11 clipboard using ⌘-C and paste on the Mac OS X side using ⌘-V.

Virtual Network Computer

One of the attractive features of Mac OS X is the ease with which you can integrate a Mac OS X system into a Unix environment consisting of multiple Unix workstations that typically rely on X11 for their GUI. In the previous section, for example, we explained how to log in to a remote Unix machine, launch an X11 application, and display the application on your Mac. The reverse process is also possible. You can log into a remote Mac OS X machine from another computer, launch an application on the remote Mac OS X machine, and have the application display on your local machine. The local machine, meanwhile, can be running the X Window System, Microsoft Windows, or any another platform supported by Virtual Network Computer (VNC).

VNC consists of two components:

- A VNC server, which must be installed on the remote machine
- A VNC viewer, which is used on the local machine to view and control applications running on the remote machine

The VNC connection is made through a TCP/IP connection.

The VNC server and viewer may not only be on different machines, but they can also be installed on different operating systems. This allows you to, for example, connect from Solaris to Mac OS X. Using VNC, you can launch and run both X11 and Aqua applications on Mac OS X, but view and control them from your Solaris box.

VNC can be installed on Mac OS X with the Fink package manager (look for the *vnc* package), but that version (the standard Unix version of the VNC server) only supports X11 programs, not Aqua applications. This standard Unix version of VNC translates X11 calls into the VNC protocol. All you need on the client machine is a VNC viewer. An attractive Mac-friendly alternative to the strictly X11-based VNC server is *OSXvnc* (*http://www. redstonesoftware.com/vnc.html*).

The standard Unix version of the VNC server is quite robust. Rather than interacting with your display, it intercepts and translates the X11 network protocol. (In fact, the Unix version of the server is based on the XFree86 source code.) Applications that run under the Unix server are not displayed on the server's screen (unless you set the DISPLAY environment variable to : 0.0, in which case it would be displayed only on the remote server, but not on your VNC client). Instead, they are displayed on an invisible X server that relays its virtual display to the VNC viewer on the client machine. OSX-vnc works in a similar manner except it supports the Mac OS X Aqua desktop instead of X11. With the *OSXvnc* server running on your Mac OS X system, you can use a VNC client on another system, for example, a Unix system, to display and control your Mac OS X Aqua desktop. You can even tunnel these VNC connections (both X11 and Aqua) through SSH.

Launching VNC

If you installed VNC on your Mac OS X system via Fink (or on any Unix system for that matter), you can start the VNC server by issuing the following command:

```
vncserver
```

If you don't have physical access to the system on which you want to run the VNC server, you can login into it remotely and enter the command before logging out:

```
nohup vncserver
```

This starts the VNC server, and *nohup* makes sure that it continues to run after you log out. In either case, the first time you start *vncserver*, you need to supply a password, which you need anyway when connecting from a remote machine. (This password can be changed using the command *vncpasswd*.) You can run several servers; each server is identified by its hostname with a *:number* appended. For example, suppose you start the VNC server twice on a machine named *abbott*; the first server will be identified as *abbott:1* and the second as *abbott:2*. You will need to supply this identifier when you connect from a client machine.

By default, the VNC server runs *twm*. So, when you connect, you will see an X11 desktop instead of the Mac OS X desktop. You can specify a different window manager in *~/.vnc/xstartup*. To terminate the VNC server, use the following command syntax:

```
vncserver -kill :display
```

For example, to terminate *abbott:1*, you would issue the following command while logged into *abbott* as the user who started the VNC server:

```
vncserver -kill :1.
```

VNC and SSH

VNC passwords and network traffic are sent over the wire as plaintext. However, you can use SSH with VNC to encrypt this traffic.

There is a derivative of VNC, called TightVNC, which is optimized for bandwidth conservations. (If you are using Fink, you can install it with the command *fink install tightvnc*). TightVNC also offers automatic SSH tunneling on Unix and backward compatibility with the standard VNC.

If you want to tunnel your VNC connection through SSH, you can do it even without TightVNC. To illustrate this process, let's consider an example using a SUN workstation running Solaris named *mrchops* and a Power-Book G4 named *tichops* running Panther. In the following example, the VNC server is running on the Solaris machine and a VNC client on the Mac OS X machine. To display and control the remote Solaris GNOME desktop on your local Mac OS X system, do the following:

1. Log into the Solaris machine, *mrchops*, via SSH if you need login remotely.

2. On *mrchops*, enter the following command to start the VNC server on *display :1*:

   ```
   nohup vncserver :1
   ```

3. In your *~/.vnc* directory, edit the *xstartup* file so that the *gnome* will start when you connect to the VNC server with a VNC client. In particular, your *xstartup* file should look like this:

   ```
   #!/bin/sh
   xrdb $HOME/.Xresources
   xterm  -geometry 80x24+10+10 -ls -title "$VNCDESKTOP Desktop" &

   exec /usr/bin/gnome-session &
   ```

4. Logout from the Solaris box, *mrchops*.

5. From a Terminal window (or *xterm*) on your Mac OS X machine, log into *mrchops* via *ssh:*

   ```
   ssh -L 5902:localhost:5901 mrchops
   ```

   Any references to *display :2* on your Mac will connect to the Solaris machine's *display :1* through an SSH tunnel (*display :1* uses port 5901, *display :2* uses 5902). You may need to add the *–l* option to this command if your username on the Solaris machine is different from the one you're using on your Mac OS X machine. For example, say your username on *mrchops* is *brian,* but on *tichops* it's *ernie.* The following command would be issued instead of the one above:

   ```
   ssh -L 5902:localhost:5901 mrchops -l brian
   ```

   Additionally, you may need to open ports through any firewalls you may have running. Open ports 5900-5902 for VNC, and 22 for *ssh.*

6. On your Mac, you can either start X11 or run *vncviewer* from the command line:

   ```
   vncviewer localhost:2
   ```

   You can also run an Aqua VNC client like *VNCDimension* (*http://www. mdimension.com/*) or *Chicken of the VNC* (*http://sourceforge.net/projects/ cotvnc/*). Figure 5-8 shows a VNCDimension connection to a Solaris GNOME desktop.

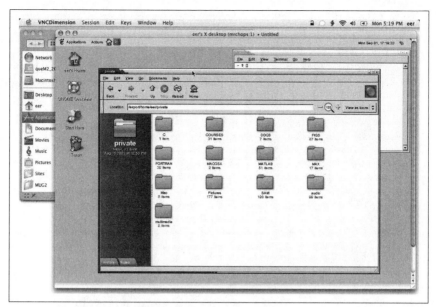

Figure 5-8. VNCDimension displaying a remote GNOME desktop

Connecting to the Mac OS X VNC Server

To connect to a Mac OS X machine that is running a VNC server, you will need a VNC viewer. We mentioned two Mac OS X viewers (*VNCDimension* and *Chicken of the VNC*) earlier, and additional Mac OS X viewers can be found on Version Tracker or MacUpdate (*http://www.versiontracker.com/macosx/* or *http://www.macupdate.com*) by searching for "VNC". VNC or TightVNC provide viewers for Unix systems. These viewers can be used to display and control the Mac OS X Aqua desktop.

To connect, start your viewer and specify the hostname and display number, such as *chops:1* or *chops:2*. If all goes well, you'll be asked for your password and then be connected to the remote Mac OS X desktop. VNC connections to Mac OS X Aqua desktops can be established through SSH tunnels.

To illustrate this process, let's do the reverse of what we did in our last example; let's make an SSH-secured connection from a Solaris machine to the Mac OS X machine running the VNC server. Again, let's assume that the name of the Solaris machine is *mrchops* and the Mac OS X machine has a hostname of *tichops*.

1. On *tichops* double-click the *OSXvnc* application. Select a display number (we've selected 1 in this example). The port number will be filled in automatically once you've selected the display number. Next, enter a password that will be used to connect to the VNC server and click the Start Server button. This step is illustrated in Figure 5-9.

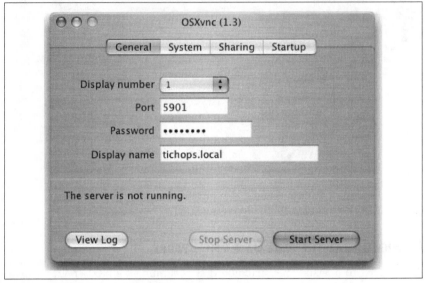

Figure 5-9. Starting the OSXvnc server

You can also *ssh* to *tichops* and start *OSXvnc* from the command line. For a list of command-line options enter:

```
/Applications/OSXvnc.app/OSXvnc-server -help
```

2. On the Solaris machine, *mrchops*, enter:

```
ssh -L 5902:localhost:5901 tichops
```

3. In another *xterm* window on *mrchops*, enter:

```
vncviewer localhost:2
```

4. The resulting VNC connection is shown in shown in Figure 5-10.

 Although we were able to control the Mac OS X desktop from the SUN Solaris machine, the image quality of the Mac OS X desktop shown in Figure 5-10 is rather poor on the systems that we used (SUN Ultra 10-440 running Solaris 8 and a PowerBook G4 running Mac OS X Panther).

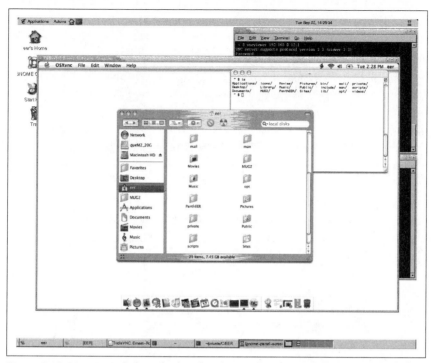

Figure 5-10. Mac OS X desktop displayed and controlled on a Solaris GNOME desktop

A wrapper application for OSXvnc, Share My Desktop (SMD), is available from Bombich Software (*http://www.bombich.com/software/smd.html*) and is licensed under the GNU General Public License. This handy little application reduces launching the OSXvnc server to a one-click operation. To start the VNC server, just launch the SMD application and click the "Start Sharing" button as shown in Figure 5-11. A random password and port for the VNC server is automatically chosen. You can modify the default setting in SMD's Preferences. In particular, you can keep the password private (it is displayed as asterisks in the SMD main window), and either generate a random password (default) or specify your own password. Additionally, you can select two energy saving settings: allow the screen to dim, and allow the computer to sleep.

If you want the VNC server to run whenever the Mac OS X system is running, SMD provides a way to install and configure a system-wide VNC server that will, optionally, start on when you boot up your Mac OS X system. To take advantage of this feature, you'll need to be logged in as an administrative user. Assuming this is the case, open the SMD application, and select File → Manage System VNC Server to open the dialog window as shown in Figure 5-12.

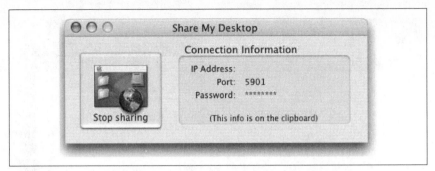

Figure 5-11. Share My Desktop's one click to start/stop the VNC server

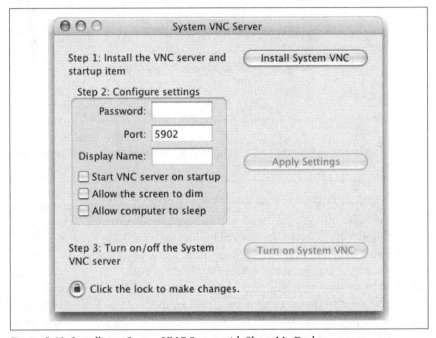

Figure 5-12. Installing a System VNC Server with Share My Desktop

Click the lock to make changes and supply your administrative password (you must be an administrative user to do this). This pop-up window will allow you to install the VNC server and startup item, configure settings (password, port, display name, start VNC server on startup, allow the screen to dim, allow the computer to sleep), and to turn on/off the System VNC Server. If you click the Install System VNC button, the *OSXvnc-server* and *storepasswd* binaries will be installed in */usr/local/bin* and a startup item in */Library/StartupItems/*. A backup of the */etc/hostconfig* file is also made, in case you later want to uninstall the system-wide VNC server and return to the settings you had prior to the installation of the system VNC.

The settings for the system-wide VNC server are stored in */etc/vnc_settings*, and the password is stored in */etc/vnc_pass*. Changing the "Start VNC server on startup" option resets the value of VNCSERVER in the */etc/hostconfig* file. If you've installed the system-wide VNC server using this procedure, you can uninstall it (along with its configuration files) by clicking the "Uninstall System VNC" button in the same Manage System VNC Server pop-up window. This uninstall procedure will also restore the */etc/hostconfig*, which was backed up when you installed VNC server. Since this can overwrite system configuration changes you've made since installing VNC, we suggest that you instead edit the VNCSERVER line so that it is set to -NO- instead of -YES- and restart (see Chapter 2 for more information on the *hostconfig* file).

VNC clients and servers are available for Windows machines, so Windows clients can connect to Mac OS X and other UNIX VNC servers. Mac OS X clients can also connect to and control Windows VNC servers. (See *http://www.realvnc.com/*.) As an alternative to VNC, you can use Microsoft's free Remote Desktop Client (RDC, available at *http://www.microsoft.com/mac/otherproducts/otherproducts.aspx?pid=remotedesktopclient*) to remotely control a Windows desktop from a Mac OS X machine.

CHAPTER 6

Multimedia

Since its introduction, the Macintosh has earned a reputation as a strong computing platform for multimedia applications. With the maturation of Mac OS X and its support for open source applications, coupled with Apple's Digital Hub strategy, the Macintosh has become an even better choice for multimedia applications.

This chapter highlights a few multimedia applications that may be especially interesting to those Mac OS X users who have used similar (and in some cases, the same) applications in Linux and/or various flavors of Unix. We begin with a brief discussion on how to burn CDs in Mac OS X, both using GUI and command-line tools. The chapter then moves on to discuss some familiar (to Linux/Unix users) open source and bundled applications for playing videos, image editing, and 3D modeling.

Burning CDs

There are several ways to burn CDs in Mac OS X. Which method of CD-burning you should use depends largely on what kind of data you are burning to the CD. Let's consider an example in which we'll use a CD-R to backup ~/Library/Mail, which is where your mailboxes are stored if you use the Mac OS X Mail application. The same procedure can be applied to other data. We'll discuss how to accomplish this task with the GUI-based Disk Utility application located in /Applications/Utilities and by using the command line in Terminal. In either case, you should make a disk image before burning your data to a CD-R.

To make a disk image of ~/Library/Mail using Disk Utility, first make sure that no existing disk is selected, then select ~/Library/Mail in Disk Utility's Images → New → Image From Folder menu. A Convert Image pop-up window will prompt you to enter the name of the image you want to save, where you want to save the disk image and in what format, and whether you want to encrypt the disk image. This is illustrated in Figure 6-1, where we've chosen to save the disk image as *backupmail2* (it will automatically be saved as *backupmail2.dmg*) to the Desktop in read-only format and without encryption.

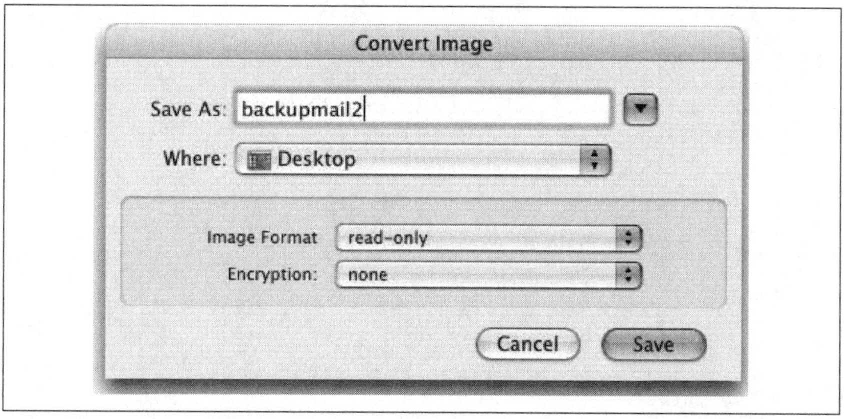

Figure 6-1. Creating a disk image with the Disk Utility

When the disk image has been created, it will appear in the left segment of the Disk Utility window. To burn this image to a CD-R, select the disk image in the Disk Utility window and click on the Burn icon in the toolbar. You will be prompted to insert a disc and to select some options for burning the CD, as shown in Figure 6-2.

The same task can be accomplished from Terminal using the commands, *hdiutil* and *ditto*. For example:

```
hdiutil create -fs HFS+ -volname BackupMail -size 200m ~/Desktop/backupMail.dmg
```

This creates a blank HFS+ disk image of size 200 MB named *backupMail.dmg* on your Desktop. Next, enter:

```
ditto -rsrc ~/Library/Mail /Volumes/BackupMail
```

This copies your Mail folder (along with all its mailboxes), which is located in *~/Library/Mail*, to the disk image. Use the command *ditto* with the *−rsrc* option to copy resource forks and metadata.

Once this command has completed, enter the following command to unmount the disk image:

```
hdiutil unmount /Volumes/BackupMail
```

Finally, use the following command to burn the disk image to CD:

```
hdiutil burn ~/Desktop/backupMail.dmg
```

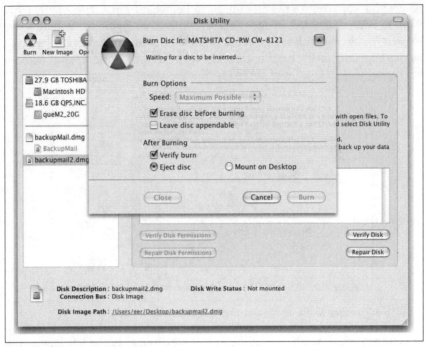

Figure 6-2. Burning a disk image with the Disk Utility

Video

You can install any of several X11-based open source applications for viewing various formats of video by using the Fink package manager (see Chapter 11). These applications will run under Apple's X11 environment. Also, some open source video applications have been ported to Mac OS X using Aqua, rather than relying on X11.

Open Source Video Players

MPlayer (*http://www.mplayerhq.hu*), a popular audio/video player among Linux/Unix users, can be run under Mac OS X. In addition to being among many packages that are being ported to Mac OS X by the Fink Project, a Mac OS X binary distribution of MPlayer, MPlayerOSX, is available at *http://mplayerosx.sourceforge.net/* and sports an Aqua GUI.

After you've downloaded and mounted the disk image, drag the MPlayer OS X application to your */Applications* folder, and then unmount and trash the disk image if you don't plan to install it anywhere else.

To play videos with MPlayer OS X (shown in Figure 6-3), you can drag and drop a video file on the MPlayer OS X icon in the Finder, or select a video from the MPlayer OS X menu bar by using File → Open.

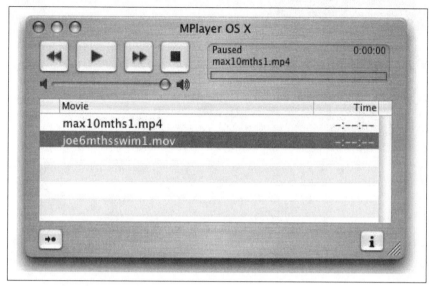

Figure 6-3. MPlayer OS X

Another popular open source, cross-platform multimedia player, VLC (shown in Figure 6-4), has been ported to Mac OS X and sports an Aqua-native GUI. VLC, distributed by the VideoLAN project (*http://www.videolan.org/*), supports a wide variety of video and audio formats. To play a video using VLC, choose either File → Open from the menu bar or drag and drop the video file onto the VLC icon in the Finder.

VideoLAN supports some formats that Apple's QuickTime Player does not. If you find that QuickTime does not support a particular file, you may want to try installing VLC or MPlayer OS X.

In some cases, a QuickTime component or plug-in may be available to allow QuickTime Player to handle a codec that it does not ordinarily support. For example, unlike QuickTime Player, VLC supports the audio codec Ogg Vorbis right out of the box. However, in this case, a QuickTime component is available at *http://qtcomponents.sourceforge.net/*. Once you download the component, you just need to drop the file *OggVorbis.component* in your */Library/QuickTime* (or *~/Library/QuickTime*) folder.

Figure 6-4. VLC

Image Editing

The GIMP (*http://www.gimp.org*) is one of the best-known open source image manipulation programs. You can get a build for Mac OS X from Fink (see Chapter 11). With the GIMP, you can create drawings, touch up photographs you've taken, convert images, and do much more.

You can even use the GIMP as iPhoto's default image editor. To do this, use the Script Editor (*/Applications/AppleScript*) to create the following Apple-Script, and save it as an Application named */Applications/LaunchGIMP*:

```
on open all_images
  repeat with image in all_images

    (* replace colons with slashes, prefix path with /Volumes *)
    do shell script "perl -e '$f=shift; $f =~ s/:/\\//g;  " & ¬
      "print \"/Volumes/$f\";' \"" & image & "\""
    set image to the result

    (* set the X11 DISPLAY variable, and launch gimp-remote *)
    do shell script "DISPLAY=:0.0; export DISPLAY;  " & ¬
      "/sw/bin/gimp-remote -n \"" & image & "\""

  end repeat
  tell application "X11" to activate
end open
```

Next, go to iPhoto's Preferences window (iPhoto → Preferences, or ⌘-,) and follow these steps:

1. In the Double-Click section, click on the radio button next to "Opens in other".
2. Click on the Select button.
3. Choose *LaunchGIMP* as the application.
4. Close the Preferences window (⌘-W).
5. Quit iPhoto (⌘-Q).

When you relaunch iPhoto, you will be able to use the GIMP as your image editing tool the next time you select an image file for editing.

Although gimp-remote's -n option is supposed to launch a new GIMP session if one is not already running, we got a spurious error message indicating the iPhoto image file was not found.

However, if GIMP was already running when we double-clicked the image, this script worked just fine. So, if you want to use GIMP as your iPhoto photo editor, be sure to launch GIMP before you start iPhoto.

There is a modified version of the GIMP, CinePaint (*http://cinepaint. sourceforge.net/*) that is designed to meet the needs of film professionals. It has been used in the *Harry Potter* movies, *Scooby Doo*, and other movies. CinePaint was originally known as Film GIMP, and an earlier version was available through Fink at the time of this writing. Check out the CinePaint web site for the latest version.

3D Modeling

Blender is a popular cross-platform, open source, integrated 3D graphics package for modeling, animation, rendering, post-production, real-time interactive 3D, and game creation and playback. A complete list of features can be found on Blender's web site (*http://www.blender3d.com/*). In addition to source code, binaries are available for a variety of platforms, including Mac OS X.

To install Blender on Mac OS X, download the appropriate disk image from Blender's site and, after it has mounted, copy Blender to your Applications folder. To run Blender, double-click its icon.

As you can see in Figure 6-5, the look and feel of Blender on Mac OS X is different from most standard Aqua applications. The reason is that OpenGL is used to draw Blender's interface.

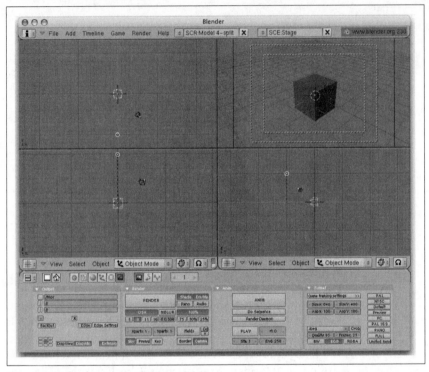

Figure 6-5. Blender, running on Mac OS X

Since Blender makes extensive use of OpenGL, you'll find that drawing images in large windows can be slow if your Mac's graphics card does not have sufficient memory. In this case, you can switch to fewer screen colors in System Preferences → Displays, and then click on the Display button and choose the Thousands option as the number of colors to display onscreen.

Although Blender is designed for use with a three-button mouse, the standard single-button Apple mouse can also be used in combination with various keystrokes.

- The left button of a three-button mouse is used to activate screen menus and buttons in the GUI, to resize subwindows, and to set the 3D cursor. The same effect can be achieved with the single button of a standard one-button Apple mouse.

- The middle button of a three-button mouse is used to move, rotate, and zoom the 3D views. To access this functionality with a one-button mouse, simultaneously press the Shift-Control-Option keys with the mouse button.

- The right button is used to select 3D objects. The right mouse button effect can be achieved by Control-clicking.

There are more Mac OS X-specific details to be aware of when using Blender. For example, on other platforms, the F12 key is used to render an image in Blender; however, on Mac OS X, you must press either Control-F12 or Option-F12 to render an image. This is because the F12 key is used on a Mac to eject a CD or DVD.

CHAPTER 7

Third-Party Tools and Applications

Although Apple ships Mac OS X with an impressive number of applications, including iPhoto, iMovie, iCal, Address Book, Mail, Safari, and an extensive set of developer tools (to name just a few), there are many third-party freeware and shareware applications available for Mac OS X that further enrich the Mac OS X experience. This chapter provides an overview of a few applications that we feel will interest Unix aficionados.

Virtual Desktops and Screens

One desktop feature that has long been a staple of the Unix world is the virtual desktop. For example, if you've used GNOME or KDE, you are probably accustomed to having multiple workspaces in which to run various applications, or open different sets of windows. Nearly all Unix/Linux desktop environments have this feature, and yet Mac OS X does not.

Although Mac OS X's desktop does not include virtual desktops or workspaces, it does include several desktop real estate-saving features. Moreover, virtual desktops (or screens) are available as third-party applications.

The primary desktop real estate-saving features of Aqua are provided by options on the application menu (the leftmost menu that has the same name as the frontmost application), Exposé, and third-party applications, described in the following sections.

The Application Menu

The ability to *hide* an application is particularly useful for applications that you don't frequently need to interact with, such as the OSXvnc server. The Hide option, found in the application menu of most Mac OS X applications (for example, OSXvnc → Hide OSXvnc), can usually be invoked with the ⌘-H keyboard shortcut to hide the currently running application.

To un-hide the application, simply click on the application's Dock icon or use the application switcher (⌘-Tab) to locate the application. The Hide Others menu selection (sometimes available with the keyboard shortcut Option-⌘-H) hides all other open applications.

Finally, the Show All menu option, which is located in the application menu, brings all running applications out of hiding.

Exposé

Exposé found its way into Mac OS X Panther as a nifty hack by one of the Apple engineers. Exposé was previewed and quickly added to Mac OS X's codebase as a must-have for the Panther release. Exposé uses Quartz Extreme rendering to quickly give you access to all of the open windows for running applications, or to scoot them out of the way so you can quickly see what's on your Desktop.

Exposé can be activated in three ways:

- Function keys
- Hot corners (as defined in System Preferences → Exposé)
- By programming the buttons of a multi-button mouse, which can be defined in System Preferences → Keyboard & Mouse

By default, F9 tiles all open windows (as shown in Figure 7-1), F10 tiles all open windows of the current application, and F11 forces all open windows out of the way so you can see what's on the Desktop. In each case, pressing the given function key a second time reverses the effect of pressing it the first time. For example, if you press F11 to hide all open windows, pressing F11 again will undo this action and return all open windows to the Desktop.

Other tricks you can try with Exposé include:

- If you hold down the Shift key and press either of the F9, F10, or F11 keys, Exposé works in slow motion.
- If you've pressed F9 to separate the windows (as shown in Figure 7-1), you can use the arrow keys on your keyboard to highlight a particular window. The window is shaded light blue, and its filename is superimposed on the window.
- If you've pressed F10 to separate the windows for the current application, hit the Tab key to switch to another application and bring its windows—again, separated by Exposé—to the front. Also, Shift-Tab cycles backward through the window stack, so if you've gone too far with the Tab key, try hitting Shift-Tab to return to the application you need.

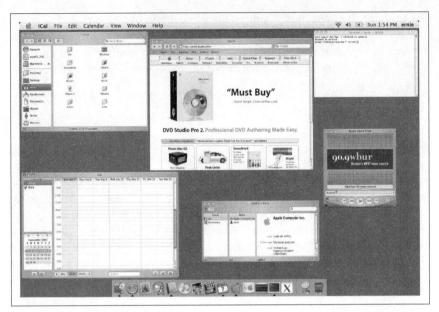

Figure 7-1. An Exposé-tiled desktop

- If you've done the last trick, combine that with the previous and use the arrow keys to highlight a window; pressing Return brings that window to the front of the stack.

- If you've used F11 to push the windows out of the way so you can see the Desktop, the window that previously had the focus is still active, even though it isn't really visible. For example, if you have a Terminal window open and you hit F11, try issuing a simple command like *ls*, then hit F11 to bring the windows back; you should see the output of *ls* in the Terminal window. (F9 and F10 take the focus away.)

Virtual Desktops

Although Exposé adds some useful and interesting features, it doesn't provide you with the virtual desktops that many X11 users are used to. Mac OS X users can, however, add this feature with one of at least two third-party applications. These third-party applications include:

- CodeTek's shareware VirtualDesktop (*http://www.codetek.com/php/ virtual.php*)

- Marco Coïsson's freeware Virtual Screens (*http://homepage.mac.com/ marco_coisson/VirtualScreens/VirtualScreensEn.html*)

In both cases, the Exposé feature is still available—these third-party applications add features to the Mac OS X desktop rather than replace them.

VirtualDesktop

VirtualDesktop from CodeTek is rich in features, customizable, and comes with extensive documentation. Unlicensed copies are fully functional, but only two virtual desktops are allowed. The two licensed versions, Pro and Lite, both allow up to 100 virtual desktops, and support Apple's X11, Exposé, and AppleScript, among other features. The Pro version includes several features not found in the Lite version, for example, desktop switching using the mouse. A detailed comparison of the Lite and Pro versions is available at *http://www.codetek.com*.

The default configuration of VirtualDesktop, shown in Figure 7-2, places a pager in the lower-left corner of the screen. This pager is used to switch to any available virtual desktop, or to drag a window from one virtual desktop to another. A menu bar tool is also added—you can use it to click on and select any available virtual desktop, a foreground application, or window in the selected virtual desktop. The menu bar tool also hides or shows the pager, and can open VirtualDesktop's preferences.

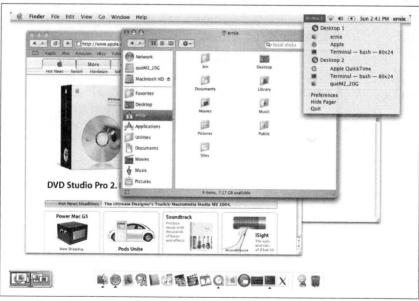

Figure 7-2. CodeTek VirtualDesktop

VirtualDesktop also allows you to open multiple windows of an application in more than one virtual desktop. This is useful in many situations, and especially convenient for X11 users accustomed to having at least one *xterm* window open in each virtual desktop. You can also assign particular applications to specific desktops and customize keyboard shortcuts in the application's preferences. There are many additional features of VirtualDesktop that we have not covered here; see the program's web site for more information.

Virtual Screens

Virtual Screens is similar to VirtualDesktop, but is not as rich in features and capabilities. Nevertheless, Virtual Screens is a useful product that allows up to 10 virtual screens in which to run different applications.

When you start the Virtual Screens application, it places a menu bar tool to the right of the system status menu bar. From this menu, you can set the number of screens from 1 to 10, configure screens (to specify which screen will own which application), and specify an exclusion list. For each user application that is running (and those that you've added manually), the exclusion list specifies whether an application will appear in each virtual screen or only on one screen. If an application is set to Yes in the exclusion list, all of its windows will appear in each virtual screen. Effectively, Virtual Screens hides applications. If you exclude an application, Virtual Screens will not hide that particular application.

A limitation of Virtual Screens is that you cannot have different windows open for a single application in different virtual screens, as you can with VirtualDesktop. For example, if you want a Terminal window open in each virtual screen, you must place the Terminal application in the exclusion list. Then you will have all open Terminal windows in every virtual screen. Clicking on a running application's icon in the Dock moves that particular application to the current virtual screen.

SSH GUIs

OpenSSH is a free version of the SSH suite of network connectivity tools that provides encrypted replacements for *telnet*, *ftp*, *rlogin*, *rcp*, and more. As noted earlier in the book, OpenSSH is bundled with Mac OS X. Although the SSH tools are fully functional from the command line, several GUIs are available for SSH. One such frontend, familiar to Unix/Linux users, is Brian Masney's GTK+/glib-based *gftp* (*http://www.gftp.org/*). *gftp* can be installed on Mac OS X using Fink.

Another option is Fugu (*http://rsug.itd.umich.edu/software/fugu/*), which is a graphical interface to the OpenSSH program bundled with Mac OS X. Fugu is developed and provided as freeware by the University of Michigan's

Research Systems Unix Group. As noted on its web site (which should always be consulted for the most up-to-date version and information), Fugu has many useful features including, but not limited to, the following:

- Drag and drop files on its interface to upload/download files
- External editor support
- Image previews
- Directory upload
- Permissions, owner and group modification
- Directory histories
- Unicode character support
- Support for connections to alternate ports
- Compression support
- Support for SSH command-line options
- SCP support
- Ability to create SSH Tunnels
- Keychain support
- Favorites list for frequently visited hosts

When Fugu is launched, you will be greeted with a dialog window that includes a file browser showing your local Home directory, and blank fields that you must fill in to make an *sftp* connection to a remote site, as illustrated in Figure 7-3.

To use Fugu, enter the IP address or domain name, remote username, port, and directory that you want to access. Under Advanced SFTP Options, you can enable features such as compression or enter additional SSH options. Once you've added this information, add the host to a list of Favorites so you can quickly connect to that site in the future, instead of entering all of its information each time.

Once you've entered this information as shown in Figure 7-3, click the Connect button. If you're connecting to this host for the first time, you'll be prompted to enter a password and add it to your Keychain. Click the Authenticate button and, if all goes well, the right column of Fugu's window displays the remote directory in its file browser.

You can now drag and drop to upload or download files. However, at the time of this writing, you could not use Fugu to drag and download directories with *sftp*. To download folders in Fugu, you must use *scp*.

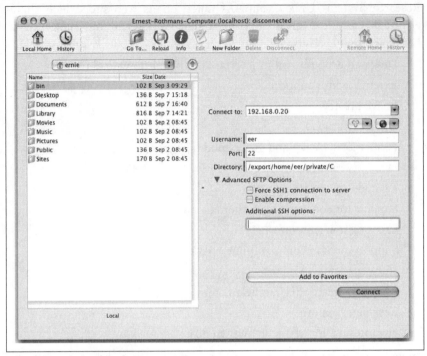

Figure 7-3. Fugu's sftp connection

As noted earlier, Fugu can be used to remotely delete files simply by selecting the filename and then clicking on the Delete icon. At the time of this writing, Fugu could not delete recursively. In other words, if you want to delete a directory and all of the files contained within it, you'll have to delete the files manually. Only then can you delete the empty directory.

You can also change certain attributes of a file, regardless of whether a file is local or remote, by selecting the file in Fugu's file browser and clicking the Get Info icon. In the resulting pop-up window, you'll be able to change, among other things, the file's permissions.

Two other freeware SSH frontends worth mentioning are:

- SSHTunnelManager (*http://projects.tynsoe.org/en/stm/*)
- SSH Agent (*http://www.phil.uu.nl/~xges/ssh/*)

SSHTunnelManager is designed to create SSH tunnels. Figure 7-4 illustrates how to use SSHTunnelManager to set up an SSH tunnel for the purpose of making a secure connection to a VNC server.

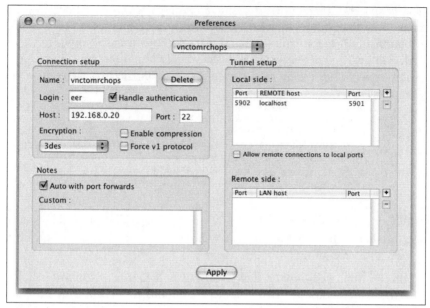

Figure 7-4. Setting up an SSH tunnel to a VNC server with SSHTunnelManager

SSH Agent can be used to (among other things) start an SSH-agent, generate identities, add identities to agents, and establish a secure tunnel. Figure 7-5 illustrates how to use the SSH Agent to set up an SSH tunnel in order to make a secure connection to a VNC server.

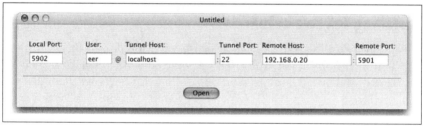

Figure 7-5. Setting up an SSH tunnel to a VNC server with SSH Agent

LaTeX

TeX was developed by computer scientist Donald Knuth as a special programming language used to typeset mathematical and scientific publications. LaTeX, developed by Leslie Lamport and subsequently further developed by Frank Mittelbach among others, is essentially a rather large set of macros built on top of TeX.

The TeX Users Group (TUG) web site (*http://www.tug.org/*) contains an enormous amount of information on TeX-related projects and resources. One distribution of TeX for Unix systems, teTeX (*http://www.tug.org/teTeX/*), is provided by Thomas Esser. teTeX is commonly found on Unix- and Linux-based systems, especially those used by mathematicians, scientists, and engineers.

 The Mac-TeX web site (*http://www.esm.psu.edu/mac-tex*), maintained by Gary L. Gray and Joseph C. Slater, is devoted to tracking TeX developments for the Mac platform. This site is a must-visit if you're interested in using TeX on Mac OS X.

teTeX can be installed on a Mac OS X system with Fink. You could also use the installation provided by Gerben Wierda's i-Installer to install TeX Live-teTeX, a superset of teTeX.

In this section, we'll discuss how to install TeX Live-teTeX with i-Installer and then briefly describe two graphical frontends to LaTeX: TeXShop and iTeXMac. TeXShop and iTeXMac are actually more than frontends; they provide unified LaTeX environments, complete with editors and other tools. We'll round out this section with two more applications, Equation Service and LaTeX Equation Editor, which allow you to easily use your LaTeX installation to add mathematical typesetting capabilities to applications such as Mail and Keynote.

Installing TeX Live-teTeX

To install TeX Live-teTeX (*http://www.rna.nl/tex-org.html*), first download the i-Installer application from *ftp://ftp.nluug.nl/pub/comp/macosx/volumes/ii2/II2.dmg* and install it in */Applications/Utilities*. Once you've done this you will need to use it to install TeX. You may want to also install CM Super for TeX, Ghostscript 8, Freetype 2, wmf and iconv support, and ImageMagick. These last five packages are optional.

Double-click the i-Installer in the Finder, and then select i-Package → Known Packages i-Directory. A window listing many packages will open, as shown in Figure 7-6.

Double-click the TeX choice to open another pop-up window. In this new window, click Install & Remove, followed by Install. This downloads and installs the teTeX Foundation package in */usr/local/teTeX* with symbolic link */Library/teTeX* pointing to */usr/local/teTeX*. When installation of TeX nears completion, you'll be prompted to configure items such as language selection, paper size, and formats.

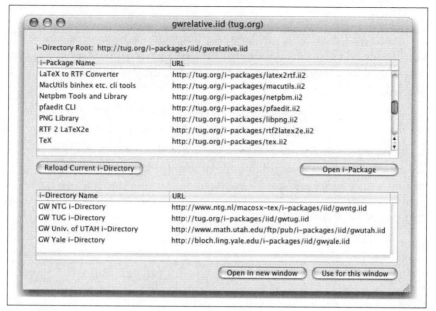

Figure 7-6. Known packages listed in the i-Directory window

Local system modifications, for example, addition of new LaTeX packages (i.e., **.sty* files) can be made to */usr/local/teTeX/share/texmf.local*. Modifications can also be made on a per-user basis by modifying *~/Library/texmf*. If you subsequently upgrade your LaTeX installation with i-Installer, these local modifications are not affected. The teTeX search order for files is:

1. *~/Library/texmf*
2. */usr/local/teTeX/share/texmf.local*
3. */usr/local/teTeX/share/texmf.gwtex*
4. */usr/local/teTeX/share/texmf.tetex*
5. */usr/local/teTeX/share/texmf*

Once the installation and configuration of TeX Live-teTeX is complete, you will be able to run *latex* from the command line. However, even the most hardcore command-line fanatics may find the available Aqua-based interfaces enticing.

Finally, Gerben Wierda's TeX Live-teTeX can coexist with a teTeX that you've installed using Fink. Fink, which installs software in */sw*, actually provides an option (install system-tetex) to place symbolic links in */sw* instead of installing a second version of teTeX. This method allows you to maintain only one version of teTeX and ensures that Fink is aware of it when checking dependencies.

TeXShop

To install TeXShop, go to its web site (*http://darkwing.uoregon.edu/~koch/texshop/texshop.html*) and download the *TeXShop.dmg* file. Mount the disk image by double-clicking on it, and then drag the TeXShop application to your */Applications* folder.

TeXShop includes a specialized editor with syntax highlighting, LaTeX macros accessible from a toolbar menu, and a previewer. The LaTeX macros can be used to insert LaTeX code into your document.

By default, TeXShop uses *pdftex* and *pdflatex* (part of standard teTeX distribution) to produce output in PDF instead of the more traditionally used DVI format. Figure 7-7 shows TeXShop's built-in editor, while Figure 7-8 shows TeXShop's previewer.

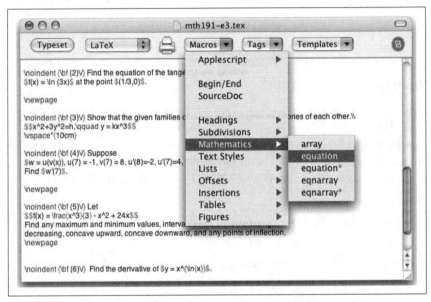

Figure 7-7. TeXShop editor with its LaTeX Macros menu

Among its many useful features, TeXShop supports AppleScript, and is highly configurable. In particular, you can configure the Latex Panel, Auto Completion, the Keyboard Menu Shortcuts, and the Macro menu. These user-level configurations are written to four *plist* files, stored in *~/Library/TeXShop*: *completion.plist*, *autocompletion.plist*, *KeyEquivalents.plist*, and *Macros.plist*. Figure 7-9 shows TeXShop's Macro Editor, which can be opened from the Macros toolbar. Select Window → LaTeX Panel to open the LaTeX Panel.

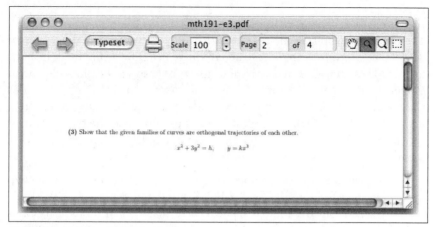

Figure 7-8. TeXShop's built-in previewer

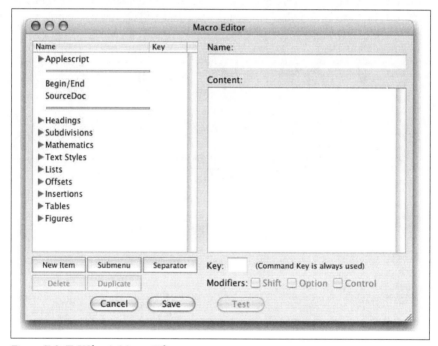

Figure 7-9. TeXShop's Macro Editor

TeXShop (together with TeX Live-teTeX) provides a highly customizable, complete, and unified LaTeX environment that is nicely integrated for Mac OS X.

iTeXMac

The iTeXMac application, a feature-rich alternative to TeXShop, can be downloaded from *http://itexmac.sourceforge.net/Download.html*. Installation involves dragging and dropping the iTeXMac application file to the */Applications* folder. You may also want to download *LaTeX.help* and *TeX Catalogue Online.help*, since both provide extensive help on LaTeX from within Mac OS X's Help Viewer. If you opt to download the two *.help* files, you must drop them in */Library/Documentation/Help* before you can view them in Apple's Help Viewer (*/Library/System/CoreServices*).

iTeXMac provides a customizable, integrated LaTeX environment, including a specialized editor with syntax highlighting and extensive LaTeX macros accessible from the toolbar menu. These macros can be used to insert LaTeX code into your document from a menu selection. While TeXShop also has this ability, iTeXMac comes with a larger selection of macros. Figure 7-10 shows iTeXMac's built-in editor and LaTeX macro menu.

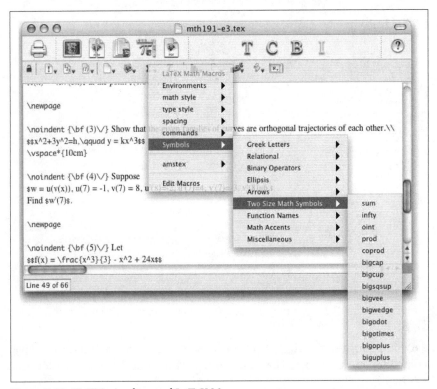

Figure 7-10. iTeXMac's editor and LaTeX Macro menu

Additional features of iTeXMac include:

- Customizable macros
- Customizable key bindings
- Extensive support for project design
- iTeXMac Help, LaTeX Help, and TeX Catalogue Online Help, each accessible from the Help Viewer
- AppleScript support
- Aside from PDF, iTeXMac's viewer can view PS, EPS, and DVI files, which are processed by iTeXMac to produce PDF output
- Extensive set of Dock menu items

Although iTeXMac is designed to use Gerben Wierda's TeX Live-teTeX distribution, you can use it with teTeX installed by Fink, provided that you enable Fink teTeX in iTeXMac's Preferences → teTeX Assistant menu.

iTeXMac and TeXShop share many of the same features. The differences between these two applications are essentially that iTeXMac has more features and those features are more extensively implemented. For example, the LaTeX macro menu in iTeXMac includes many more macros. On the other hand, it seems that (at least at the time of this writing, with iTeXMac at Version 1.3.1 and TeXShop at Version 1.30) TeXShop has a performance advantage when compiling large LaTeX files, as well as in viewing the resulting PDF files. Fortunately, these two very useful and well-designed applications can coexist. Since neither occupies a large amount of disk space, you may want to keep them both on hand in your */Applications* folder and perhaps even in your Dock.

An open source X11-based WYSIWYM (What You See Is What You Mean) document processor, LyX (*http://www.lyx.org/*), uses teTeX as a rendering engine and runs on most Unix/Linux systems, Windows OS/2, and Mac OS X. There are essentially two versions of LyX: one built on *xforms*, and another on *Qt*. Thanks to Qt/Mac (*http://www.trolltech.com/download/qt/mac.html*), an Aqua-native port of LyX, named LyX/Mac (*http://www.18james.com/lyx_on_aqua.html*), is available as a self-installing binary. To run LyX/Mac, however, you must first install teTeX using i-Installer or Fink.

LaTeX Services

A useful feature of Mac OS X is its ability to allow services via menu selection. For example, in the Mail application, you can select text in an email, then select Mail → Services → Speech → Start Speaking Text to hear your Mac read the selected text to you. There are at least two LaTeX-related applications that use *pdflatex* (included with teTeX) to produce small PDF images of LaTeX-processed code. One of these two applications creates a Services menu item that can be used with other applications.

Equation Service (*http://www.esm.psu.edu/mac-tex/EquationService/*) provides inline typesetting of LaTeX code. To install this service, download and install the Equation Service application in */Applications*. When you run it the first time, configuration files are placed in *~/Library/Application Support*. Equation Service is known to work with Mail.app, Keynote, TextEdit, Microsoft PowerPoint, OmniGraffle, and Stone Design's Create.

There two ways to use Equation Service: by highlighting LaTeX code in an application and selecting one of several choices from the Services menu or by creating and previewing equations in the Equation Service application's main window. To use Equation Services to typeset LaTeX within an application (for example, Mail), highlight LaTeX string in a compose (i.e., New Message) Mail window, and select Mail → Services → Equation Service → Typeset Equation. Figure 7-11 illustrates the result of this process.

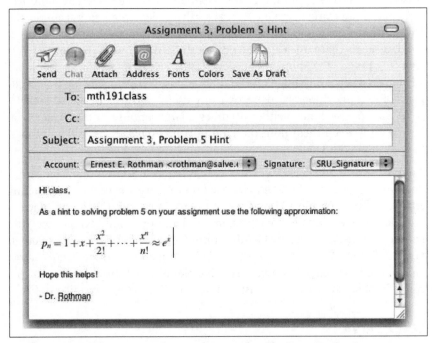

Figure 7-11. A Mail message with an equation rendered by Equation Service

LaTeX strings can also be typeset in the main window of Equation Service, as Figure 7-12 illustrates.

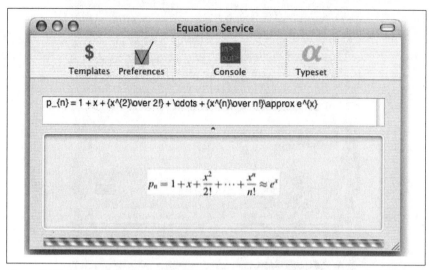

Figure 7-12. Typesetting an equation in Equation Service's main window

Once you've typeset an equation in the main window of Equation Service, you can drag and drop the resulting PDF image into a number of applications, such as Microsoft Office X or Apple's Keynote. There are several preferences you can set in Equation Service's preferences including font size, text color, and background color of the typeset equations.

LaTeX Equation Editor (*http://evolve.lse.ac.uk/software/EquationEditor/*) is similar to LaTeX Equation Service, but it operates in one mode only: you must create and preview equations in the application's main window. This application does not provide a Services menu selection to typeset LaTeX strings within other applications. Nevertheless, LaTeX Equation Editor is useful and easy to use, since it is a simple matter to drag and drop the small PDF image it produces into Mail and Keynote documents. Figure 7-13 shows LaTeX Equation Editor's typesetting of a simple LaTeX string.

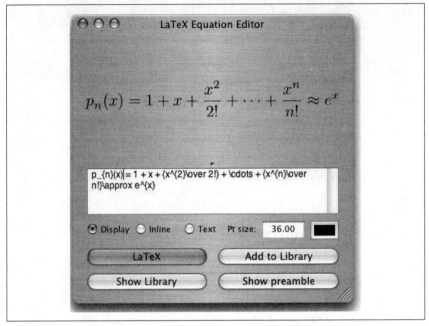

Figure 7-13. Typesetting an equation with LaTeX Equation Editor

RAqua

The open source statistical computing package R is a GNU project to develop a package similar to Bell Laboratories' S statistical package. R runs on a variety of platforms, including most X11-based systems and Windows. Although an X11-based version of R can be installed with Fink, another port of R that supports both X11 and Mac OS X, RAqua, has been developed by Stefano M. Iacus and others associated with the R-Core/R-Foundation. A binary distribution of RAqua is distributed through the Comprehensive R Network (CRAN; *http://cran.r-project.org/*).

The installer places an application named StartR in your Applications folder. Double-clicking the StartR icon opens an Aqua-based console window, which is divided into lower and upper subwindows. You can enter R commands in the lower subwindow, while the upper subwindow shows your command history, as shown in Figure 7-14.

Figure 7-15 shows an RAqua graphics window containing a histogram.

RAqua is AppleScriptable. Example 7-1 shows an AppleScript that instructs RAqua to store some values in a variable *x*, and display a histogram corresponding to these values.

```
000                          R Console
Type 'license()' or 'licence()' for distribution details.

R is a collaborative project with many contributors.
Type 'contributors()' for more information.

Type 'demo()' for some demos, 'help()' for on-line help, or
'help.start()' for a HTML browser interface to help.
Type 'q()' to quit R.

> x=scan()
1: 43.0 76.0 89.0 90.0 98.0 100.0 96.0 81.0 63.0 79.0 69.0 100.0 99.
14: 75.0 73.0 77.0 54.6 81.0 83.0
20:
Read 19 items
> hist(x)
> hist(x,probability=TRUE)
> rug(jitter(x))
>
```

Figure 7-14. RAqua's console

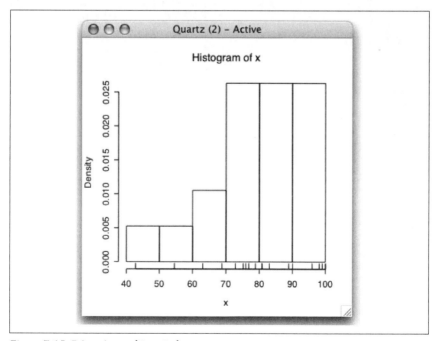

Figure 7-15. RAqua's graphics window

You can use X11 graphics with R from the Aqua R console or from a Terminal (or *xterm*) window. In either case you must start X11 before starting R. To use X11 graphics from the R console, you must first start X11. If you prefer to start R from the Terminal (or *xterm*), you should make a symbolic link in */usr/local/bin* and add this to your path before entering R at the command line:

```
sudo ln -s /Applications/StartR.app/RAqua.app/Contents/ /usr/local/lib/R
sudo ln /Applications/StartR.app/RAqua.app/Contents/MacOS/R /usr/local/bin/R
```

In this case, the *xterm* window is used to enter R commands, and the graphics are displayed using X11. Figure 7-16 shows the same histogram shown in Figure 7-15, but this time it's displayed in an X11 window.

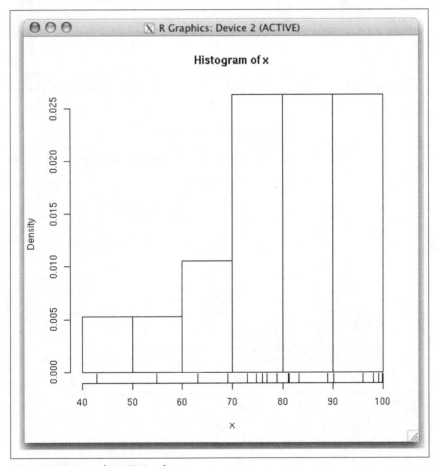

Figure 7-16. R graphics, X11 style

Example 7-1. AppleScript to interact with RAqua

```
try
    tell application "RAqua"
    activate
        with timeout of 1000 seconds
            cmd "x = c(77, 79, 90, 69, 75, 73, 71, 69, 84)"
            cmd "hist(x)"
            cmd "hist(x,probability=TRUE)"
            cmd "rug(jitter(x))"
        end timeout
    end tell
end try
```

We have presented a situation that corresponds to Release R-1.81, which was available at the time of this writing. Be sure to consult the CRAN web site for up-to-date information.

PART II
Building Applications

Although Apple's C compiler is based on the GNU Compiler Collection (GCC), there are important differences between compiling and linking on Mac OS X and on other platforms. This part of the book describes these differences.

- Chapter 8, *Compiling Source Code*
- Chapter 9, *Libraries, Headers, and Frameworks*
- Chapter 10, *Perl*

Compiling Source Code

The Xcode Tools that ship with Panther provide a development environment for building applications with Cocoa, Carbon, Java, and even AppleScript. Xcode Tools include utilities that should be familiar to any Unix developer who works with command-line compilers. For details about obtaining these tools, see the Xcode Tools section in the Preface. Xcode Tools includes all sorts of other goodies, including an advanced Integrated Development Environment (IDE), but coverage of those tools is beyond the scope and intent of this book. To learn more about the Xcode Tools, you can see */Developer/Documentation/DeveloperTools/Tools.html*.

The C compiler that comes with Xcode is based on the Free Software Foundation's GNU Compiler Collection, or GCC. Apple has added an Objective-C compiler, as well as various modifications to deal with the Darwin operating system. The development environment in Mac OS X includes:

AppleScript
> This is an English-like language used to script applications and the operating system. AppleScript is installed as part of the Mac OS X operating system and does not require Xcode. Instead, to write AppleScripts, use the Script Editor (*/Applications/AppleScript*).

AppleScript Studio
> This is a high-level development environment based on AppleScript that allows you to build GUI applications by hooking AppleScript into the Cocoa frameworks. If you plan to build AppleScript Studio applications, you will need to use the Xcode Tools instead of the Script Editor.

Compilers
> These compilers are based on GCC and provide support for C, C++, Objective-C, Objective-C++, and assembly. Apple's enhancements to GCC for Panther include support for the G5 (also known as the PowerPC 970) and 64-bit arithmetic, as well as the ability to generate optimized code to run on G5, G4, and G3 systems.

Compiler Tools

These include the Mac OS X Mach-O GNU-based assemblers, Mach-O static link editor, Mach-O dynamic link editor, and Mach-O object file tools, such as *nm* and *otool*.

Documentation

Extensive documentation for Xcode is available in both HTML and PDF formats in the */Developer/Documentation* directory. These documents are also available online from the Apple Developer Connection (ADC) web site (*http://developer.apple.com*).

After installing Xcode, you can access the local documentation for GCC at */Developer/Documentation/DeveloperTools/gcc-3.3/gcc/index.html*.

Debugger

The Apple debugger is based on GNU *gdb*.

Miscellaneous Tools

These include traditional development tools, such as *make* (both GNU, which is the default, and BSD) and GNU *libtool*, graphical and command-line performance tools, Xcode for WebObjects, parsing tools (such as *lex*, *flex*, *yacc*, and *bison*), standard Unix source code management tools (such as *CVS* and *RCS*), and an extensive set of Java development tools. There's also a frontend to GCC, *distcc*, which uses Rendezvous to distribute builds of C, C++, Objective-C, or Objective-C++ code across computers on a network.

Xcode

Formerly known as Project Builder, Xcode is an IDE for Mac OS X that supports Cocoa and Carbon programming with C, C++, Objective-C, and Java.

Interface Builder

This is a graphical user interface (GUI) editor for Cocoa and Carbon applications.

We do not address the complete Mac OS X development suite in this chapter. Instead, we focus on the command-line development tools and how they differ from the implementations on other Unix platforms.

Java programmers will find that the Mac OS X command-line Java tools (see "Java Development Tools" in Appendix C) behave as they do under Unix and Linux. Another resource for Java developers is *Mac OS X for Java Geeks* (O'Reilly).

Perl programmers coming from previous Macintosh systems will find that Mac OS X does not use MacPerl (*http://www.macperl.com*), but instead uses the standard Unix build of the core Perl distribution (*http://www.perl.org*). For additional information on using Perl under Mac OS X, see Chapter 10.

Compiler Differences

GCC is supported on a wide range of platforms, and it is the default compiler on Mac OS X. There are, however, some important differences between the version of GCC that ships with Mac OS X and that found on other Unix systems.

One difference that experienced GCC users may notice, particularly if they have dealt with a lot of mathematical and scientific programming, is that the Xcode Tools do not include FORTRAN. However, the Fink distribution (*http://fink.sourceforge.net*) includes *g77*, the GNU FORTRAN 77 compiler. Also, the Darwin archive includes the source code for *g77*, which you can use to compile FORTRAN code.

 Mac OS X's C compiler contains a number of Mac-specific features that have not been folded into the main GCC distribution. (It is up to the Free Software Foundation [FSF] to accept and merge Apple's patches.) For information on how Apple's compiler differs from the GNU version, see the *README.Apple* file in the Darwin CVS archive's *gcc3* subdirectory.

As of this writing, Apple's *cc* compiler is based on GCC 3.3. However, GCC 3.1 and 2.95 are also available as */usr/bin/gcc2*, and */usr/bin/gcc3*, respectively. By default, invoking *cc* or *gcc* invokes GCC 3.3; both */usr/bin/cc* and */usr/bin/gcc* are symbolic links to */usr/bin/gcc3.3*. You can change the default GCC to GCC 2.95 or GCC 3.1 by running the command *gcc_select 2*, or *gcc_select 3*, respectively. Similarly, you can change it back to GCC 3.3 with *gcc_select 3.3*. The *gcc_select* command (used with one of the options 2, 3, and 3.3) changes the symbolic links */usr/bin/cc* and */usr/bin/gcc* to point to the desired version of gcc. Since files in */usr/bin* are changed by this command, you must execute it with *sudo*.

You can see the current settings by running *gcc_select* with no arguments:

```
$ gcc_select
Current default compiler:
gcc version 3.3 20030304 (Apple Computer, Inc. build 1495)
```

 You can find the Mac OS X Compiler Release Notes on your system at */Developer/Documentation/ReleaseNotes/Compiler-Tools.html*. You should consult these release notes for details on the most current known problems, issues, and features.

AltiVec

The Motorola AltiVec Velocity Engine is also supported for G4 processors by the Mac OS X GCC implementation. The compiler flag *–faltivec* must be specified to compile code engineered to use the Velocity Engine. Inclusion of this command-line option to *cc* defines the preprocessor symbol _ _VEC_ _.

Compiling Unix Source Code

Many of the differences between Mac OS X and other versions of Unix become apparent when you try to build Unix-based software on Mac OS X. Most open source Unix software uses GNU *autoconf* or a similar facility, which generates a *configure* script that performs a number of tests of the system—especially of the installed Xcode Tools—and finishes by constructing one or more makefiles. After the *configure* script has done its job, you run the *make* command to first compile, and, if all goes well, install the resulting binaries.

> Most tarballs will include a *configure* script, so you do not need to generate it yourself. However, if you retrieve *autoconf*-managed source code from a CVS archive, you will have to run *autoconf.sh* manually to generate the *configure* file.

In most cases, it's pretty easy to compile a Unix application on Mac OS X. After unpacking the tarball and changing to the top-level source code directory, just issue the following three commands to compile the application:

```
./configure
make
make install
```

> Mac OS X web browsers are configured to invoke StuffIt Expander on compressed archives. So, if you click on a link to a tarball, you may find that it gets downloaded to your desktop and extracted there. If you'd prefer to manage the download and extraction process yourself, Control-click (or right-click) on the link so you can specify a download location.
>
> Also, because the Mac OS X HFS+ filesystem is case-insensitive, watch out for tarballs that have filenames differing in case only (as in *makefile* and *Makefile*). While it's unlikely to find filenames like this in a modern software package, it's not unusual in older tarballs.

The following sections deal with issues involved in successfully performing these steps. Determining how to improvise within this three-step procedure reveals some of the differences between Mac OS X and other Unix systems.

The First Line of Defense

Most tarballs include the following files in the top-level directory:

README
> This is an introduction to the application and source code. You'll often find copyright information in this document, notes about bug fixes or improvements made to different versions, and pointers to web sites, FAQs, and mailing lists.

INSTALL
> This document contains step-by-step installation instructions.

PORT or PORTING
> If present, one of these documents will include tips for porting the application to another Unix platform.

These files contain useful information that may help you get the application running on Mac OS X.

Host Type

One of the first difficulties you may encounter when running a *configure* script is that the script aborts with an error message stating that the host system cannot be determined.

Strictly speaking, the *host type* refers to the system on which software will run, and the *build type* refers to the system on which the software is being built. It is possible to build software on one system to run on another system, but to do so requires a cross-compiler. We will not concern ourselves with cross-compiler issues. Thus, for our discussion, both the host type and the build (and target) types are the same: powerpc-apple-darwin*VERSION*, where the *VERSION* denotes the particular version of Darwin. In fact, a *configure* script detects Mac OS X by the host/build type named *Darwin,* since Darwin is the actual operating system underlying Mac OS X. This can be verified by issuing the *uname -v* command, which tells you that you're running a Darwin kernel, the kernel version, and when it was last built.

Many *configure* scripts are designed to determine the host system, since the resulting makefiles differ depending on the type of system for which the software is built. The *configure* script is designed to be used with two files related to the host type, usually residing in the same directory as the *configure* script. These files are *config.guess*, which is used to help guess the host type; and *config.sub*, which is used to validate the host type and to put it into a canonical form (such as *CPUTYPE-MANUFACTURER-OS*, as in `powerpc-apple-darwin7.0.0`).

Although Mac OS X and Darwin have been around for a while now, you may still run across source code distributions containing older *config.** files that don't work with Mac OS X. You can find out if these files support Darwin by running the *./configure* script. If the set of *config.** files does not support Darwin, *./configure* will complain about an unknown host type.

In that case, you can replace the *config.guess* and *config.sub* files with the Apple-supplied, like-named versions residing in */usr/share/automake-1.6*. These replacement files originate from the FSF and include the code necessary to configure a source tree for Mac OS X. To copy these files into the *source* directory, which contains the *configure* script, simply issue the following commands from within the *sources* directory:

```
cp /usr/share/automake-1.6/config.sub .
cp /usr/share/automake-1.6/config.guess .
```

Macros

You can use a number of predefined macros to detect Apple systems and Mac OS X in particular. Table 8-1 lists the predefined macros available on Mac OS X.

Table 8-1. Mac OS X C macros

Macro	When defined
`__OBJC__`	When the compiler is compiling Objective-C *.m* files or Objective-C++ *.M* files. (To override the file extension, use *-ObjC* or *-ObjC++*.)
`__ASSEMBLER__`	When the compiler is compiling *.s* files.
`__NATURAL_ALIGNMENT__`	When compiling for systems that use natural alignment, such as *powerpc*.
`__STRICT_BSD__`	If, and only if, the *-bsd* flag is specified as an argument to the compiler.
`__MACH__`	When compiling for systems that support Mach system calls.
`__APPLE__`	When compiling for any Apple system. Defined on Mac OS X systems running Apple's variant of the GNU C compiler, and third-party compilers.
`__APPLE_CC__`	When compiling for any Apple system. Integer value that corresponds to the (Apple) version of the compiler.
`__VEC__`	When AltiVec support was enabled with the *-faltivec* flag.

Do not rely on the presence of the __APPLE__ macro to determine which compiler features or libraries are supported. Instead, we suggest using a package like GNU *autoconf* to tell you which features the target operating system supports. This approach makes it more likely that your applications can compile out-of-the-box (or with little effort) on operating systems to which you don't have access.

Supported Languages

When using the *cc* command, which supports more than one language, the language is determined by either the filename suffix or by explicitly specifying the language using the *–x* option. Table 8-2 lists some of the more commonly used filename suffixes and *–x* arguments supported by Apple's version of GCC.

Table 8-2. File suffixes recognized by cc

File suffix	Language	–x argument
.c	C source code to be preprocessed and compiled	c
.C, .cc, .cxx, .cpp	C++ source code to be preprocessed and compiled	c++
.h	C header that should neither be compiled nor linked	c-header
.i	C source code that should be compiled but not preprocessed	cpp-output
.ii	Objective-C++ or C++ source code that should be compiled but not preprocessed	c++-cpp-output
.m	Objective-C source code	objective-c
.M, .mm	Mixed Objective-C++ and Objective-C source code	objective-c++
.s	Assembler source that should be assembled but not preprocessed	assembler
.S	Assembler source to be preprocessed and assembled	assembler-with-cpp

Although the HFS+ filesystem is case-insensitive, the *cc* compile driver recognizes the uppercase C in a source file. For example, *cc foo.C* invokes *cc*'s C++ compiler because the file extension is an uppercase C, which denotes a C++ source file. (To *cc*, it's just a command-line argument.) So, even though HFS+ will find the same file whether you type *cc foo.c* or *cc foo.C*, what you enter on the command line makes all the difference in the world, particularly to *cc*.

Preprocessing

When you invoke *cc* without options, it initiates a sequence of four basic operations, or stages: preprocessing, compilation, assembly, and linking. In a multifile program, the first three stages are performed on each individual source code file, creating an object code file for each source code file. The final linking stage combines all the object codes that were created by the first three stages, along with user-specified object code that may have been compiled earlier into a single executable image file.

Apple's compiler provides two preprocessors. The default preprocessor for both C and Objective-C is the *precompilation preprocessor* written by Apple, named *cpp-precomp*. The standard GNU C preprocessor, named *cpp*, is also available and is the default for Objective-C++ code. *cpp-precomp* supports precompiled header files (for more information about *cpp-precomp* and general precompilation, see Chapter 9). *cpp-precomp* is faster than *cpp*, but some code may not compile with *cpp-precomp*. In that case, you should invoke *cpp* by instructing *cc* not to use *cpp-precomp*. For example, to compile the C program *myprog.c* using the standard GNU preprocessor, *cpp*, use the *-no-cpp-precomp* switch as follows:

```
cc -no-cpp-precomp myprog.c
```

 Earlier versions of the Xcode Tools (known as the Developer Tools) used the *–traditional-cpp* switch, but this switch had undesirable side effects and is deprecated.

Frameworks

In Mac OS X, frameworks are bundles that are named with a *.framework* extension. Before discussing the framework type of bundle, let's first briefly describe the notion of a bundle. A bundle is an important software packaging model in Mac OS X that consists of a directory that stores resources related to a given software package, or resources used by many software packages. Bundles, for example, can contain image files, headers, shared libraries, and executables. In addition to frameworks, there are at least two other types of bundles used in Mac OS X: applications (named with the *.app* extension), and loadable bundles including plug-ins (which are usually named with the *.bundle* extension).

- An *application bundle* contains everything an application needs to run: executables, images, etc. You can actually see these in the Finder if you Control-click on an application's icon, and select Show Package Contents.

- A *framework bundle*, on the other hand, is one that contains a dynamic shared library along with its resources, including header files, images, and documentation.

- A *loadable bundle* contains executables and associated resources, which are loaded into running applications; these include plug-ins and kernel extensions.

The application and plug-in type bundles are built and organized so that the top-level directory is named *Contents*. That is, the directory *Contents/* contains the entire bundle, including any file needed by the bundle. Take for example, Safari. If you Control-click on the Safari application in the Finder and select Show Package Contents, the *Contents/* directory will be revealed in the Finder. To see what's in the *Contents/* directory, quickly hit ⌘-3 to switch the Finder to Column View, and then hit the C key on your keyboard. You will see the typical contents of an application bundle. In particular, you will see:

- The required XML property list file named *Info.plist*, which contains information about the bundle's configuration

- A folder named *MacOS/*, which contains the executable

- A folder named *Resources/*, which contains, among other resources, image files

- Files named *version.plist* and *PkgInfo*

Applications can also contain application-specific frameworks. That is, frameworks that are not used by any other application or plug-in.

Framework structure

Frameworks are critical in Mac OS X. Cocoa, the toolkit for user interface development, consists of the Foundation and Application Kit (or AppKit) frameworks for Objective-C and Java. Frameworks use a *versioned* bundle structure, which allows multiple versions of the same information; for example, framework code and header files. They are structured in one of the following ways:

- Symbolic links are used to point to the latest version. This allows for multiple versions of the framework to be present.

- In the framework bundle structure, the top level directory is named *Resources*. The actual *Resources/* directory need not be located at the top level of the bundle; it may be located deeper inside of the bundle. In this case, a symbolic link pointing to the *Resources/* directory is located at the top level.

In either case, an *Info.plist* file describing the framework's configuration must be included in the *Resources/* directory. (Chapter 9 discusses how to create frameworks and loadable bundles. This chapter only describes how to use the frameworks.)

Before discussing how to use frameworks, let's look at the different kinds of frameworks. A *private framework* is one that resides in a directory named *PrivateFrameworks*, and whose implementation details are not exposed. Specifically, private frameworks reside in one of the following locations:

- *~/Library/PrivateFrameworks*
- */Library/PrivateFrameworks*
- */System/Library/PrivateFrameworks*

An *application-specific framework* can be placed within the given application's package. For example, consider the private framework, *Graphite. framework*, which is located in */System/Library/PrivateFrameworks*. This private framework consists of a directory named *Graphite.framework/*, which aside from symbolic links and subdirectories, contains the Graphite executable, and files named *Info.plist* and *version.plist*. No implementation details are revealed. The same is true for the *gdb* framework, also located in */System/Library/PrivateFrameworks*.

A *public framework*, on the other hand, is one whose API can be ascertained, for example, by viewing its header files. Public frameworks reside in appropriate directories named *Frameworks/*. For example, the OpenGL framework resides in */System/Library/Frameworks*. This public framework consists of the directory */System/Library/Frameworks/OpenGL.framework*, which contains (among other things) a subdirectory named *Headers*. Implementation details can be ascertained by examining the header files.

Precisely where a public framework resides depends on its purpose, and where it is placed. When you build an application, you can program the path of the framework. Later, when the application is run, the dynamic link editor looks for the framework in the path that was programmed into the application. If a framework cannot be found, the following locations are searched in the following order:

~/Library/Frameworks
    This is the location for frameworks used by a single user.

/Library/Frameworks
    Third-party applications that are intended for use by all users on a system should have their frameworks installed in this directory.

/Network/Library/Frameworks

Third-party applications that are intended for use by all users across a local area network (LAN), should have its frameworks installed in this directory.

/System/Library/Frameworks

The shared librares in these frameworks (for example, the Application Kit, or AppKit) are provided by Apple for use by all applications on the system.

There are three types of frameworks in */System/Library/Frameworks*:

Simple public framework

Apple defines a *simple framework* as one which is neither a subframework nor an umbrella framework, and has placed in this category only those frameworks that have been used in older versions of Mac OS X. One such example is AppKit, which is located in */System/Library/ Frameworks/AppKit.framework* and can be examined in the Finder.

Subframework

A subframework is public, but has a restriction in that you cannot link directly against it. Its API is exposed, however, through its header files, and subframeworks reside in umbrella frameworks. To use a subframework, you must link against the umbrella framework in which it resides.

Umbrella framework

This type of framework includes other umbrella frameworks and subframeworks. The exact composition of an umbrella's subframeworks is an implementation detail which is subject to change over time. The developer need not be concerned with such changes, since it is only necessary to link against the umbrella framework and include only the umbrella framework's header file. One advantage to this approach is that not only can definitions be moved from one header file of a framework to another, but in the case of umbrella frameworks, the definition of a function can even be moved to another framework if that framework is included in the umbrella framework.

To better understand the difference between simple and umbrella frameworks, compare the composition of the simple */System/Library/Frameworks/ AppKit.framework* with the umbrella framework */System/Library/ Frameworks/CoreServices.framework*. The umbrella framework contains several other frameworks, namely, *CarbonCore*, *CFNetwork*, *OSSerrvices*, *SearchKit*, and *WebServicesCore*. The simple framework does not contain subframeworks, nor is it a subframework contained within an umbrella framework.

Including a framework in your application

When including application-specific frameworks, you must let the preprocessor know where to search for framework header files. You can do this with the *–F* option, which is also accepted by the linker. For example:

```
-F directoryname
```

instructs the preprocessor to search the directory *directoryname* for framework header files. The search begins in *directoryname* and, if necessary, continues in the standard framework directories in the order listed earlier.

 The *–F* option is necessary only when building application-specific frameworks.

To include a framework object header, use #include in the following format:

```
#include <framework/filename.h>
```

Here, *framework* is the name of the framework without the extension, and *filename*.h is the source for the header file. If your code is in Objective-C, the #import preprocessor directive may be used in place of #include. The only difference beyond that is that #import makes sure the same file is not included more than once.

The *–F* option is accepted by the preprocessor and the linker, and is used in either case to specify directories in which to search for framework header files. (This is similar to the *–I* option, which specifies directories to search for *.h* files.) By default, the linker searches the standard directories, */Local/Library/Frameworks* and */System/Library/Frameworks*, for frameworks. The directory search order can be modified with *–F* options. For example:

```
cc -F dir1 -F dir2 -no-cpp-precomp myprog.c
```

results in *dir1* being searched first, followed by *dir2*, followed by the standard framework directories. While the *–F* flag is needed only when building application specific frameworks, the *–framework* is always needed to link against a framework. Specifically, inclusion of this flag results in a search for the specified framework named when linking. Example 8-1 shows "Hello, World" in Objective-C. Notice that it #includes the AppKit framework.

Example 8-1. Saying hello from Objective-C

```
#include <Appkit/AppKit.h>

int main(int argc, const char *argv[])
{
  NSLog(@"Hello, World\n");
  return 0;
}
```

Save Example 8-1 as *hello.m*. To compile it, use *-framework* to pass in the framework name:

```
cc -framework AppKit -o hello hello.m
```

The *-framework* flag is accepted only by the linker and is used to name a framework.

 If you are linking against a framework, such as GLUT and/ or OpenGL from C code, you will probably need to include -lobjc, since the frameworks will depend on the Objective-C runtime. For example, you can compile SGI's *prim.c* (OpenGL primitives example) with cc prim.c -framework GLUT -framework OpenGL -lobjc (be sure to include the GLUT framework with #include <GLUT/glut.h> rather than <GL/glut.h>).

Compiler flags of particular interest in Mac OS X are related to the peculiarities of building shared code; for example, the compiler flag *-dynamiclib*, which is used to build Mach-O *dylibs*. For more details, see Chapter 9.

Compiler Flags

An extensive list of compiler flags can be found at *http://developer.apple.com/ technotes/tn2002/tn2071.html* or by viewing the *gcc* man page. In particular, the *gcc* manpage describes many PowerPC-specific flags, as well as Darwin-specific flags. Table 8-3 describes a few common Mac OS X GCC compiler flags that are specific to Mac OS X. These flags should be used when porting Unix-based software to Mac OS X.

Table 8-3. Selected Mac OS X GCC compiler flags

Flag	Effect
-no-cpp-precomp	Turns off the Mac OS X preprocessor in favor of the GNU preprocessor.
-ObjC, -ObjC++	Specifies *objective-c* and *objective-c++*, respectively. Also passes the *-ObjC* flag to *ld*.
-faltivec	Enables AltiVec language extension.
-arch ppc970	Compiles for the PowerPC 970 (aka G5) processor, and assembles only 64-bit instructions.
-mcpu=970, -mcpu=G5	Enables the use of G5-specific instructions.
-mtune=970, -mtune=G5	Optimizes code for the G5.
-force_cpusubtype_ALL	Forces a runtime check to determine which CPU is present and will allow code to run on the G3, G4, or G5, regardless of which CPU was used to compile the code. Exercise caution if you use this and G5-specific features at the same time.
-mpowerpc64	Enables the G5's support for native 64-bit long long when used in combination with *-mcpu=970*, *-mtune=970*, and *-force_cpusubtype_ALL*.

Table 8-3. Selected Mac OS X GCC compiler flags (continued)

Flag	Effect
–mpowerpc-gpopt	Uses the hardware-based floating-point square function on the G5. (Use with –mcpu=970, -mtune=970, and –mpowerpc64.)
–fasm-blocks	Allows blocks and functions of assembly code in C or C+ source code.
–fconstant-cfstrings	Automatically creates CoreFoundation-type constantString. (see *gcc* manpage for details.)
–fpascal-strings	Allows the use of Pascal-style strings.
–fweak-coalesced	Linker ignores weakly coalesced definitions in favor of one ordinary definition.
–findirect-virtual-calls	Uses the vtable to call virtual functions, rather than making direct calls.
–fapple-kext	Makes kernel extensions loadable by Darwin kernels. Use in combination with –fno-exceptions and –static.
–fcoalesce-templates.	Coalesces instantiated templates.
–fobjc-exceptions	Supports structured exception handling in Objective-C. (See the *gcc* manpage for more details.)
–fzero-link.	Instructs *dyld* to load the object file at runtime
–Wpragma-once	Issues a warning about #pragma, use only once if necessary.
–Wextra-tokens	Issues a warning if preprocessor directives end with extra tokens.
–Wnewline-eof	Issues a warning if a file ends without a newline character.
–Wno-altivec-long-deprecated	Doesn't issue a warning about the keyword 'long' used in an AltiVec data type declaration.
–Wmost	Same effect as –Wall –Wno-parentheses.
–Wno-long-double	Doesn't issue a warning if the long-double type is used.
–fast	Optimizes for PPC7450 and G5. The –fast flag optimizes for G5, by default. This flag can be used to optimize for PPC7450 by adding the flag –mcpu=7450. To build shared libraries with –fast, include the –fPIC flag.
–static	Inhibits linking with shared libraries provided that all of your libraries have also been compiled with –static.
–shared	Not supported on Mac OS X.
–dynamiclibs	Used to build Mach-O dylibs (see Chapter 9).
–mdynamic-no-pic	Compiled code will itself not be relocatable, but will have external references that are relocatable.
–mlong-branch	Calls that use a 32-bit destination address are compiled.
–all_load	All members of static archive libraries will be loaded. (See the *ld* manpage for more information.)
–arch_errors_fatal	Files that have the wrong architecture will result in fatal errors.
–bind_at_load	Binds all undefined references when the file is loaded.
–bundle	Results in Mach-O bundle format. (See the *ld* manpage for more information.)
–bundle_loader executable	The executable that will load the output file being linked. (See the *ld* manpage for more information.)

Architectural Issues

There are a few architectural issues to be aware of when developing or porting software on Mac OS X. In particular, pointer size, endianness, and inline assembly code tend to be the most common issues developers run in to.

On a 32-bit system, such as Mac OS X running on the G3 or G4, C pointers are 32 bits (4 bytes). On a 64-bit system, they are 64 bits (8 bytes). As long as your code does not rely on any assumptions about pointer size, it should be 64-bit clean. For example, on a 32-bit system, the following program prints "4", and on a 64-bit system, it prints "8":

```
#include <stdio.h>
int main( )
{
  printf("%d\n", sizeof(void *));
  return 0;
}
```

Some 64-bit operating systems, such as Solaris 8 on Ultra hardware (sun4u), have a 64-bit kernel space, but support both 32- and 64-bit mode applications, depending on how they are compiled. On a G5 system, the pointer size is 64-bits. Other data types are mapped onto the 64-bit data type. For example, single precision floats, which are 32-bit, are converted to double precision floats when they are loaded into registers. In the registers, single precision instructions operate on these single precision floats stored as doubles performing the required operations on the data. The results, however, are rounded to single precision 32-bit. Quad precision floating point numbers, defined by the IEEE as 128-bit are not directly supported on current PowerPC hardware. Apple has provided at least two technical notes containing information and advice on optimizing code to take advantage of the G5 architecture:

- TN2086: Tuning for G5: A Practical Guide *http://developer.apple.com/ technotes/tn/tn2086.html*
- TN2087: PowerPC G5 Performance Primer *http://developer.apple.com/ technotes/tn/tn2087.html*

 Additional information can be found at *http://developer. apple.com/hardware/ve/g5.html*. These documents describe in detail the issues involved in tuning code for the G5. We note only a few issues here.

The architecture of the G5 allows for much greater performance relative to the G4. This performance potential is partly due to the fact that the G5 allows 200 instructions in core, compared to only 30 for the G4. Moreover, the G5 has 16 pipeline stages, 2 load/store units, and 2 floating points units, compared to 7 pipeline stages, 1 load/store unit, and 1 floating points unit on the G4. The L1 cacheline size is also 128 bytes on the G5, compared to 32 bytes on the G4. Additionally the processor and memory bandwidth is much greater on the G5, relative to the G4. The technical notes mentioned earlier in this section have additional information on hardware differences.

One important implication of the greater number of pipeline stages on the G5 relative to the G4 is that instruction latencies are greater on the G5. You can often gain significant improvements in performance by using performance tools to identify loops that account for a large percentage of computation time. Once identified, you can either manually unroll these loops, or use the *–funroll-loops* compiler flag. The compiler flag *–mtune-970* can also be useful in this situation, as it schedules code more efficiently for the G5. The *–fast* compiler flag sets these options (among others) automatically.

To better take advantage of the longer cacheline size in L1 cache on the G5, algorithms should be designed for greater data locality, and use contiguous memory accesses when possible. For example, arrays in C store entries row-wise. To ensure contiguous memory accesses, design your code so that it accesses array elements row-by-row. The G5 has four hardware prefetchers, which (if accesses to memory are contiguous) are triggered automatically to help reduce cache misses. Performance tools, such as the CHUD suite (see Chapter 9), can help you optimize code by profiling computation and memory usage; some of them even make suggestions on how to improve performance.

CPU architectures are designed to treat the bytes of words in memory as being arranged in big- or little-endian order. Big-endian ordering has the most significant byte in the lowest address, while little endian has the most significant byte at the highest byte address.

The PowerPC is *biendian*, meaning that the CPU is instructed at boot time to order memory as either big or little endian. In practice, biendian CPUs run exclusively as big or little endian. In general, Intel architectures are little endian, while most, but not all, Unix/RISC machines are big endian. Table 8-4 summarizes the endianness of various CPU architectures and operating systems. As shown in Table 8-4, Mac OS X is big endian.

Table 8-4. Endianness of some operating systems

CPU type	Operating system	Endianness
Dec Alpha	Digital Unix	little endian
Dec Alpha	VMS	little endian
Hewlett Packard PA-RISC	HP-UX	big endian
IBM RS/6000	AIX	big endian
Intel x86	Windows	little endian
Intel x86	Linux	little endian
Intel x86	Solaris x86	little endian
Motorola PowerPC	Mac OS X	big endian
Motorola PowerPC	Linux	big endian
SGI R4000 and up	IRIX	big endian
Sun SPARC	Solaris	big endian

As far as inline assembly code is concerned—if you have any—it will have to be rewritten. Heaven help you if you have to port a whole Just-In-Time (JIT) compiler! For information on the assembler and PowerPC machine language, see the Mac OS X Assembler Guide (*/Developer/Documentation/ DeveloperTools/Reference/Assembler/index.html*).

X11-Based Applications and Libraries

Fink (see Chapter 11) can be used to install many X11-based applications, such as the GNU Image Manipulation Program (GIMP), *xfig/transfig*, ImageMagick, *nedit*, and more. Since Fink understands dependencies, installing some of these applications causes Fink to first install several other packages. For example, since the text editor *nedit* depends on Motif libraries, Fink will first install *lesstif*. (This also gives you the Motif window manager, *mwm*.) Similarly, when you install the GIMP via Fink, you will also install the packages for GNOME, GTK+, and *glib*.

You can also use Fink to install libraries directly. For example:

```
$ fink install qt
```

will install the X11-based Qt libraries.

Building X11-Based Applications and Libraries

If you cannot find binaries for X11-based applications, or prefer to build the applications yourself, many tools are available to do so. When you install the Xcode Tools, make sure you install the optional *X11SDK*, which contains development tools and header files for building X11-based applications. If you didn't install *X11SDK* when you first installed Xcode, you can still install it from the Xcode CD.

The process of building software usually begins with generating one or more *makefiles* customized to your system. For X11 applications, there are two popular methods for generating makefiles:

- You can use a *configure* script, as described earlier in this chapter.
- The other popular method for generating makefiles involves using the *xmkmf* script, which is a frontend to the *imake* utility. *xmkmf* invokes *imake*, which creates the makefile for you. To do this, *imake* looks for a template file called *Imakefile*.

With *imake*-driven source releases, you'll find *Imakefile* in the top-level source directory after you download and unpack a source tarball. After reading the *README* or *INSTALL* files, examine the *Imakefile* to see if you need to change anything. The next step is usually to issue the command:

```
$ xmkmf -a
```

When invoked with the *-a* option, *xmkmf* reads *imake*-related files in */usr/X11R6/lib/X11/config* and performs the following tasks recursively, beginning in the top-level directory and then in the subdirectories, if there are any:

```
$ make Makefiles
$ make includes
$ make depend
```

The next steps are usually *make, make test* (or *make check*), and *make install*.

To illustrate this method of building software, consider the script in Example 8-2, which downloads and builds an X11-based game.

Example 8-2. Downloading and building an X11 game

```
# Download the source tarball
curl -O ftp://ftp.x.org/contrib/games/xtic1.12.tar.gz

# Unpack the tarball
gnutar xvfz xtic1.12.tar.gz

# Change to the top-level build directory
cd xtic1.12/

# Generate the Makefile
xmkmf -a

# Build everything (some X11 apps use 'make World')
make

# Have fun!
./src/xtic
```

AquaTerm

The X Window System is useful to Unix developers and users, since many Unix-based software packages depend on the X11 libraries. An interesting project that sometimes eliminates the need for X windows is the BSD-licensed AquaTerm application, developed by Per Persson (*http://aquaterm. sourceforge.net*). AquaTerm is a Cocoa application that can display vector graphics in an X11-like fashion. It does not replace X11, but it is useful for applications that generate plots and graphs.

The output graphics formats that AquaTerm supports are PDF and EPS. Applications communicate with AquaTerm through an adapter that acts as an intermediary between your old application's API and AquaTerm's API.

At the time of this writing, AquaTerm has adapters for *gnuplot* and *PGPLOT*, as well as example adapters in C, FORTRAN, and Objective-C. For example, assuming that you have installed both X11SDK and Aqua-Term, you can build *gnuplot* (*http://www.gnuplot.info*) so that graphics can be displayed either in X windows or in AquaTerm windows.

See AquaTerm's web site for extensive documentation, including the latest program developments, examples, mailing lists and other helpful resources.

## CHAPTER 9

Libraries, Headers, and Frameworks

This chapter discusses the linking phase of building Unix-based software under Mac OS X. In particular, header files and libraries are covered.

Header Files

There are two types of header files in Mac OS X:

Ordinary header files
> These header files are inserted into source code by a preprocessor prior to compilation. Ordinary header files have a *.h* extension.

Precompiled header files
> These header files have a *.p* extension.

Header files serve four functions:

- They contain C declarations.
- They contain macro definitions.
- They provide for conditional compilation.
- They provide line control when combining multiple source files into a single file that is subsequently compiled.

> The mechanism for enabling *POSIX.4* compliance is built into the system header files. The preprocessor variables _ANSI_SOURCE, __STRICT_ANSI__, and _POSIX_SOURCE are supported. Because Mac OS X itself is not *POSIX.4* compliant, you cannot achieve strict *POSIX.4* compliance. Using these mechanisms, however, is the best way to approximate *POSIX.4* compliance.

Unix developers will find the ordinary header files familiar, since they follow the BSD convention. The C preprocessor directive #include includes a header file in a C source file. There are essentially three forms of this syntax:

#include <headername.h>

> This form is used if the header file is located in the directory */usr/include*.

#include <directory/headername.h>

> This form is used if the header file is located in the directory */usr/ include/directory*, where *directory* is a subdirectory of */usr/include*.

#include "headername.h"

> This form is used if the header file is located in a user or nonstandard directory. The form should either be in the same directory as the source file you are compiling or in a directory specified by *cc*'s *–Idirectory* switch.

You can use #include, followed by a macro, which, when expanded, must be in one of the aforementioned forms.

As noted in the previous chapter, frameworks in Mac OS X are common when you step outside of the BSD portions of the operating system. To include a framework header file in Objective-C code, use the following format:

```
#import <frameworkname/headerfilename.h>
```

where *frameworkname* is the name of the framework without the extension and *headerfilename* is the name of the header file. For example, the included declaration for a Cocoa application would look like:

```
#import <Cocoa/Cocoa.h>
```

Note that you must use #include rather than #import when including a framework in Carbon code. When preprocessing header files or any preprocessor directives, the following three actions are always taken:

- Comments are replaced by a single space.
- Any backslash line continuation escape symbol is removed, and the line following it is joined with the current line. For example:

```
#def\
ine \
NMAX 2000
```

  is processed as:

```
#define NMAX 2000
```

- Any predefined macro name is replaced with its expression. In Mac OS X, there are both standard ANSI C predefined macros, as well as several predefined macros specific to Mac OS X. For example, _ _APPLE_CC_ _ is replaced by an integer that represents the compiler's version number.

Keep the following rules in mind:

- The preprocessor does not recognize comments or macros placed between the < and > symbols in an #include directive.

- Comments placed within string constants are regarded as part of the string constant and are not recognized as C comments.

- If ANSI trigraph preprocessing is enabled with *cc –trigraph*, you must not use a backslash continuation escape symbol within a trigraph sequence, or the trigraph will not be interpreted correctly. ANSI trigraphs are three-character sequences that represent characters that may not be available on older terminals. For example, ??< translates to {. ANSI trigraphs are a rare occurrence these days.

Precompiled Header Files

Mac OS X's Xcode Tools support and provide extensive documentation on building and using precompiled header files. This section highlights a few of the issues that may be of interest to Unix developers new to Mac OS X when it comes to working with precompiled headers.

Precompiled header files are binary files that have been generated from ordinary C header files, and then preprocessed and parsed using *cpp-precomp*. When such a precompiled header is created, both macros and declarations present in the corresponding ordinary header file are sorted, resulting in a faster compile time, a reduced symbol table size, and consequently, faster lookup. Precompiled header files are given a *.p* extension and are produced from ordinary header files that end with a *.h* extension. There is no risk that a precompiled header file will get out of sync with the *.h* file, because the compiler checks the timestamp of the actual header file.

When using precompiled header files, you should not refer to the *.p* version of the name, but rather to the *.h* version in the #include directive. If a precompiled version of the header file is available, it is used automatically; otherwise, the real header file (*.h*) is used. So, to include *foo.p*, specify *foo.h*. The fact that *cc* is using a precompiled header is totally hidden from you.

In addition to checking the timestamp, the preprocessor also checks whether the current context is the same as the context in which the precompilation was performed. For the precompiled header to be used, the timestamp needs to indicate that the modification time of the *.p* version is more recent than the *.h* version, and therefore, that the contexts are equivalent. The context is the amalgamation of all defines (#define) in place at the time you compile a program. If the defines are different the next time you include the *.h* file, *cpp-precomp* will regenerate the *.p* file based on the current set of defines.

Mac OS X system headers are precompiled. For example, *AppKit.p*, *Cocoa.p*, *mach.p*, and other precompiled header files are stored in */System/Library/ Frameworks*. You can create your own precompiled header files using the *cc –precomp* compile driver flag. For example, the following command illustrates this process in its simplest, context-independent form:

```
cc -precomp header.h -o header.p
```

If there is context dependence (for example, some conditional compilation), the *–Dsymbol* flag is used. In this case, the command to build a precompiled header file (with the *FOO* symbol defined) is:

```
cc -precomp -DFOO header.h -o header.p
```

For more details on building and using precompiled header files, as well as using the *cpp-precomp* preprocessor, read the documentation stored in the */Developer/Documentation/DeveloperTools/ Preprocessor/* directory.

 Although the *cpp-precomp* and the standard GNU *cpp* preprocessors are similar in function, there are several incompatibilities. For this reason, you will find it is often necessary to use the *–no-cpp-precomp* switch when porting Unix-based software to Mac OS X.

A complete list of precompiled headers can be found in the *phase1. precompList* and *phase2.precompList* files, located in */System/Library/ SystemResources/PrecompLists*. Table 9-1 lists the contents of the files.

Table 9-1. Precompiled header files, as listed in phase1.precompList and phase2.precompList

Precompiled headers	Filesystem location
phase1.precompList	
libc.p	*/usr/include*
unistd.p	*/usr/include*
mach.p	*/usr/include/mach*
phase2.precompList	
CoreServices.p	*/System/Library/Frameworks/CoreServices.framework/Versions/A/Headers*
CoreServices.pp	*/System/Library/Frameworks/CoreServices.framework/Versions/A/Headers*
ApplicationServices.p	*/System/Library/Frameworks/ApplicationServices.framework/Versions/A/Headers*
ApplicationServices.pp	*/System/Library/Frameworks/ApplicationServices.framework/Versions/A/Headers*
Carbon.p	*/System/Library/Frameworks/Carbon.framework/Versions/A/Headers*
Carbon.pp	*/System/Library/Frameworks/Carbon.framework/Versions/A/Headers*

Table 9-1. Precompiled header files, as listed in phase1.precompList and phase2.precompList (continued)

Precompiled headers	Filesystem location
Foundation.p	/System/Library/Frameworks/Foundation.framework/Versions/C/Headers
Foundation.pp	/System/Library/Frameworks/Foundation.framework/Versions/C/Headers
AppKit.p	/System/Library/Frameworks/AppKit.framework/Versions/C/Headers
AppKit.pp	/System/Library/Frameworks/AppKit.framework/Versions/C/Headers
Cocoa.p	/System/Library/Frameworks/Cocoa.framework/Versions/A/Headers
Cocoa.pp	/System/Library/Frameworks/Cocoa.framework/Versions/A/Headers

Although the filenames in *phase1.precompList* and *phase2.precompList* are listed as *filename.p* (for example, *libc.p*), the actual file used depends on the compiler version. For example, *gcc3* will use *libc-gcc3.p*.

 The *.pp* files referred to in *phase2.precompList* are not present on the system, but *gcc3* versions can be generated by running *sudo fixPrecomps -gcc3all*.

PFE precompilation

The *gcc3.3* compiler supports an alternative precompilation mechanism called Persistent Front End (PFE). This mechanism offers the same performance benefits as *cpp-precomp*, but supports C++ and Objective-C++. (*cpp-precomp* does not support either language.) To precompile a header file with PFE, compile the header, specifying the *--dump-pch* switch with the name of the output file. You'll also need to supply the language with the *−x* switch (see "Supported Languages" in Chapter 8):

```
gcc -x c --dump-pch header.pfe header.h
```

Then, you can compile *main.c* by using the *--load-pch* switch and supplying the name of the precompiled file:

```
gcc --load-pch header.pfe main.c -o main
```

Example 9-1 shows *header.h*.

Example 9-1. The header.h file
```
/* header.h: a trivial header file. */

#define x 100
```

Example 9-2 shows *main.c*.

Example 9-2. The main.c application

```
/* main.c: a simple program that includes header.h. */

#include <stdio.h>
#include "header.h"

int main( )
{
 printf("%d\n", x);
 return 0;
}
```

malloc.h

make may fail to compile some types of Unix software if it cannot find *malloc.h*. Software designed for older Unix systems may expect to find this header file in */usr/include*; however, *malloc.h* is not present in this directory. The set of malloc( ) function prototypes is actually found in *stdlib.h*. For portability, your programs should include *stdlib.h* instead of *malloc.h*. (This is the norm; systems that require *malloc.h* are the rare exception these days.) GNU *autoconf* will detect systems that require *malloc.h* and define the HAVE_MALLOC_H macro. If you do not use GNU *autoconf*, you will need to detect this case on your own and set the macro accordingly. You can handle such cases with this code:

```
#include <stdlib.h>
#ifdef HAVE_MALLOC_H
#include <malloc.h>
#endif
```

For a list of libraries that come with Mac OS X, see the "Interesting and Important Libraries" section, later in this chapter.

poll.h

One issue in porting software from a System V platform to a BSD platform (e.g., Mac OS X) is the lack of the poll( ) system call function, which provides a mechanism for I/O multiplexing. Panther provides this function through emulation, which makes use of its BSD analog select( ). The associated header file, */usr/include/poll.h*, is included with Panther.

wchar.h and iconv.h

Another issue in porting Unix software to previous versions of Mac OS X was the relatively weak support for wide (i.e., more than 8-bits) character datatypes (e.g., Unicode). Panther improves this situation by including the GNU *libiconv*, which provides the iconv( ) function to convert between various text encodings. Additionally, the *wchar_t* type is supported in Panther. The header files *iconv.h* and *wchar.h* are also included. Alternatively, you can use the APIs available in the CoreFoundation's String services, which are described in *CFString.h*.

dlfcn.h

This header file, along with its associated *dlcompat* library functions, is included in Panther. The *dlcompat* library functions such as dlopen( ) are actually included in *libSystem*.

alloc.h

Although this header file is not included with Mac OS X, its functionality is provided by *stdlib.h*. If your code makes a specific request to include *alloc.h*, you have several choices. One option is to remove the *#include <alloc.h>* statement in your source code. This may be cumbersome, however, if your include statement appears in many files. Another alternative is to create your own version of *alloc.h*. A sample *alloc.h* is suggested in The Apple Developer Connection's Technical Note TN2071 (*http://developer.apple.com/technotes/tn2002/tn2071.html*).

lcyrpt.h

Although *lcrypt.h* is not included in Mac OS X, its functionality is provided in *unistd.h*.

values.h

The *values.h* file, another header file found on many Unix systems, is not included in Mac OS X. Its functionality, however, is provided by *limits.h*.

The System Library: libSystem

In Darwin, much is built into the system library, */usr/lib/libSystem.dylib*. In particular, the following libraries are included in *libSystem*:

libc
> The standard C library. This library contains the functions used by C programmers on all platforms.

libinfo
> The NetInfo library.

libkvm
> The kernel virtual memory library.

libm
> The math library, which contains arithmetic functions.

libpthread
> The POSIX threads library, which allows multiple tasks to run concurrently within a single program.

libdlcompat
> This library provides functions, such as dlopen( ), that interface to the dynamic linker using the native dyld, NSModule, and NSObjectFileImage functions.

libdbm
> Database routines.

Symbolic links are provided as placeholders for these libraries. For example, *libm.dylib* is a symbolic link in */usr/lib* that points to *libSystem.dylib*. Thus, –*lm* or –*lpthread* do no harm, but are unnecessary. The –*lm* option links to the math library, while –*lpthread* links to the POSIX threads library. Since *libSystem* provides these functions, you don't need to use these options. However, you should use them to make sure your application is portable to other systems. (Since *libm. dylib* and *libpthread.dylib* are symbolic links to *libSystem.dylib*, the extra –*l* options refer to the same library.)

> In Mac OS X 10.1 and earlier versions, the *curses* screen library (a set of functions for controlling a terminal display) was part of *libSystem.dylib*. In Mac OS X 10.2 and 10.3, the *curses* library (*/usr/lib/libncurses.5.dylib*) is used in place of *curses*. You may still encounter source code releases that look for curses in *libSystem.dylib*, which will result in linking errors. You can work around this problem by adding –*lcurses* to the linker arguments. This is portable to earlier versions of Mac OS X as well, since */usr/lib/libcurses.dylib* is a symlink to *libncurses* in 10.3 and 10.2, and to *libSystem* in earlier versions.

Interestingly enough, there is no symbolic link for *libutil*, whose functionality is also provided by *libSystem*. (*libutil* is a library that provides functions related to login, logout, terminal assignment, and logging.) So, if a link fails because of *–lutil*, try taking it out to see if that solves the problem.

Shared Libraries Versus Loadable Modules

The Executable and Linking Format (ELF), developed by the Unix System Laboratories, is common in the Unix world. On ELF systems, there is no distinction between shared libraries and loadable modules; shared code can be used as a library for dynamic loading. ELF is the default binary format on Linux, Solaris 2.*x*, and SVR4. Since these systems cover a large share of the Unix base, most Unix developers have experience on ELF systems. Thus, it may come as a surprise to experienced Unix developers that shared libraries and loadable modules are not the same on Mac OS X. This is because the binary format used in Mac OS X is *Mach-O*, which is different from ELF.

Mach-O shared libraries have the file type MH_DYLIB and the *.dylib* (dynamic library) suffix and can be linked to with static linker flags. So, if you have a shared library named *libcool.dylib*, you can link to this library by specifying the *–lcool* flag. Although shared libraries cannot be loaded dynamically as modules, they can be loaded through the *dyld* API (see the manpage for *dyld*, the dynamic link editor). It is important to point out that shared libraries cannot be unloaded.

Loadable modules, called *bundles* in Mac OS X, have the file type MH_BUNDLE. Most Unix-based software ports usually produce bundles with a *.so* extension, to maintain consistency across platforms. Although Apple recommends giving bundles a *.bundle* extension, it isn't mandatory.

You must use special flags with *cc* when compiling a shared library or a bundle on Darwin. One difference between Darwin and many other Unix systems is that no *position-independent code* (PIC) flag is needed, since it is the default for Darwin. Next, since the linker does not allow common symbols, the compiler flag *–fno-common* is required for both shared libraries and bundles. (A common symbol is one that is defined multiple times. You should instead define a symbol once and use C's *extern* keyword to declare it in places where it is needed.)

To build a shared library, use *cc*'s *–dynamiclib* option. Use the *–bundle* option to build a loadable module or bundle.

Building a Shared Library

Suppose you want to create a shared library containing one or more C functions, such as the one shown in Example 9-3.

Example 9-3. A simple C program

```
/*
 * answer.c: The answer to life, the universe, and everything.
 */
int get_answer( )
{
  return 42;
}
```

If you compile the program containing the function into a shared library, you can test it with the program shown in Example 9-4.

Example 9-4. Compiling answer.c into a shared library

```
/*
 * deep_thought.c: Obtain the answer to life, the universe,
 * and everything, and act startled when you actually hear it.
 */
#include <stdio.h>
int main( )
{
  int the_answer;
  the_answer = get_answer( );
  printf("The answer is... %d\n", the_answer);

  fprintf(stderr, "%d??!!\n", the_answer);
  return 0;
}
```

The *makefile* shown in Example 9-5 compiles and links the library, and then compile, link, and execute the test program.

Example 9-5. Sample makefile for creating and testing a shared library

```
# Makefile: Create and test a shared library.
#
# Usage: make test
#
CC = cc
LD = cc
CFLAGS = -O -fno-common

all: deep_thought

# Create the shared library.
#
answer.o: answer.c
        $(CC) $(CFLAGS) -c answer.c

libanswer.dylib: answer.o
        $(LD) –dynamiclib  -install_name  libanswer.dylib \
        -o libanswer.dylib answer.o

# Test the shared library with the deep_thought program.
#
deep_thought.o: deep_thought.c
        $(CC) $(CFLAGS) -c deep_thought.c

deep_thought: deep_thought.o libanswer.dylib
        $(LD) -o deep_thought deep_thought.o -L. -lanswer
```

Example 9-5. Sample makefile for creating and testing a shared library (continued)

```
test: all
       ./deep_thought

clean:
       rm -f *.o core deep_thought libanswer.dylib
```

The preceding makefile made use of the *ld* flag *–install_name,* which is the Mach-O analog of *–soname,* used for building shared libraries on ELF systems. The *–install_name* flag is used to specify where the executable, linked against it, should look for the library. The *–install_name* in the makefile shown in Example 9-5 specifies that the *deep_thought* executable is to look for the library *libanswer.dylib* in the same directory as the executable itself. The command *otool* can be used to verify this:

```
$ otool -L deep_thought
deep_thought:
        libanswer.dylib (compatibility version 0.0.0, current version 0.0.0)
        /usr/lib/libSystem.B.dylib (compatibility version 1.0.0, current
        version 71.0.0)
```

The *–install_name* flag is often used with *@executable_path* to specify a relative pathname of the library. The pathname of the library is relative to the executable. For example, change the makefile in Example 9-5 by adding an install target:

```
install: libanswer.dylib
        cp libanswer.dylib ../lib/.
```

Then add *install* to the *all* target's dependency list and change the *libanswer* target to the following:

```
libanswer.dylib: answer.o
        $(LD) -dynamiclib -install_name \
        @executable_path/../lib/libanswer.dylib \
        -o libanswer.dylib answer.o
```

The *deep_thought* executable built using this makefile will then look for the *libanswer.dylib* in the *../lib* directory. Output from *otool* shows this change:

```
$ otool -L deep_thought
deep_thought:
        @executable_path/../lib/libanswer.dylib (compatibility version 0.0.0,
        current version 0.0.0)
        /usr/lib/libSystem.B.dylib (compatibility version 1.0.0, current
        version 71.0.0)
```

The *–install_name* flag is often used with *@executable_path* when building a private framework associated with an application, since private frameworks are located within the application's contents.

Dynamically Loading Libraries

You can turn *answer.o* into a bundle, which can be dynamically loaded using the commands shown in Example 9-6.

Example 9-6. Commands for converting answer.o into a bundle

```
cc -bundle -o libanswer.bundle answer.o
```

You do not need to specify the bundle at link time. Instead, use the *dyld* functions NSCreateObjectFileImageFromFile and NSLinkModule to load the library. Then, you can use NSLookupSymbolInModule and NSAddressOfSymbol to access the symbols that the library exports. Example 9-7 loads *libanswer.bundle* and invokes the *get_answer* function. Example 9-7 is similar to Example 9-4, but many lines (shown in bold) have been added.

Example 9-7. Dynamically loading a bundle and invoking a function

```
/*
 * deep_thought_dyld.c: Obtain the answer to life, the universe,
 * and everything, and act startled when you actually hear it.
 */
#include <stdio.h>
#import <mach-o/dyld.h>

int main( )
{
  int the_answer;
  int rc;                  // Success or failure result value
  NSObjectFileImage img;   // Represents the bundle's object file
  NSModule handle;         // Handle to the loaded bundle
  NSSymbol sym;            // Represents a symbol in the bundle

  int (*get_answer) (void);  // Function pointer for get_answer

  /* Get an object file for the bundle. */
  rc = NSCreateObjectFileImageFromFile("libanswer.bundle", &img);
  if (rc != NSObjectFileImageSuccess) {
    fprintf(stderr, "Could not load libanswer.bundle.\n");
    exit(-1);
  }

  /* Get a handle for the bundle. */
  handle = NSLinkModule(img, "libanswer.bundle", FALSE);

  /* Look up the get_answer function. */
  sym = NSLookupSymbolInModule(handle, "_get_answer");
  if (sym == NULL)
  {
    fprintf(stderr, "Could not find symbol: _get_answer.\n");
    exit(-2);
```

```
}

/* Get the address of the function. */
get_answer = NSAddressOfSymbol(sym);

/* Invoke the function and display the answer. */
the_answer = get_answer( );
printf("The answer is... %d\n", the_answer);

fprintf(stderr, "%d??!!\n", the_answer);
return 0;
}
```

For more information on these functions, see the NSObjectFileImage, NSModule, and NSSymbol manpages. To compile the code in Example 9-7, use the following command:

```
cc -O -fno-common -o deep_thought_dyld deep_thought_dyld.c
```

Two-Level Namespaces

In Mac OS X 10.0, the dynamic linker merged symbols into a single (flat) namespace. So, if you link against two different libraries that both define the same function, the dynamic linker complains because the same symbol was defined in both places. This approach prevented collisions that were known at compile time. However, a lack of conflict at compile time does not guarantee that a future version of the library won't introduce a conflict.

Suppose you linked your application against Version 1 of *libfoo* and Version 1 of *libbar*. At the time you compiled your application, *libfoo* defined a function called logerror( ), and *libbar* did not. But when Version 2 of *libbar* came out, it included a function called logerror( ). Since the conflict was not known at compile time, your application doesn't expect *libbar* to contain this function. If your application happens to load *libbar* before *libfoo*, it will call *libbar*'s logerror( ) method, which is not what you want.

So, Mac OS X 10.1 introduced two-level namespaces, which the compiler uses by default. (Neither Mac OS X 10.2 or 10.3 introduced any changes to two-level namespaces.) With this feature, you can link against Version 1 of *libfoo* and *libbar*. The linker creates an application that knows logerror( ) lives in *libfoo*. So, even if a future version of *libbar* includes a logerror( ) function, your application will know which logerror() it should use.

If you want to build an application using a flat namespace, use the *–flat_namespace* linker flag (see the *ld* manpage for more details).

Library Versions

Library version numbering is one area where Mac OS X differs from other Unix variants. In particular, the dynamic linker *dyld* checks both major and minor version numbers. Also, the manner in which library names carry the version numbers is different. On ELF systems, shared libraries are named with an extension similar to the following:

```
libname.so.major_version_no.minor_version_no
```

Typically, a symbolic link is created in the library named *libname.so*, which points to the most current version of the library. For example, on an ELF system like Solaris, *libMagick.so.5.0.44* is the name of an actual library. If this is the latest installed version of the library, you can find symbolic links that point to this library in the same directory. These symbolic links are typically created during the installation process.

In this example, both *libMagick.so* and *libMagick.so.5* are symbolic links that point to *libMagick.so.5.0.44*. Older versions of the library may also be present, such as *libMagick.so.5.0.42*. However, although older versions of the library may be present, whenever a newer version is installed, the symbolic links are updated to point to the latest version. This works because when you create a shared library, you need to specify the name of the library to be used when the library is called by a program at runtime.

> In general, you should keep older versions of libraries around, just in case an application depends on them. If you are certain there are no dependencies, you can safely remove an older version.

On Mac OS X, the *libMagick* library is named *libMagick.5.0.44.dylib*, and the symbolic links *libMagick.dylib* and *libMagick.5.dylib* point to it. Older versions, such as *libMagick.5.0.42.dylib*, may also be found in the same directory. One difference that is immediately apparent on Mac OS X systems is that the version numbers are placed between the library name and the *.dylib* extension rather than at the end of the filename, as on other Unix systems (e.g., *libMagick.so.5.0.42*).

Another difference on Darwin is that the absolute pathname is specified when the library is installed. Thus, *ldconfig* is not used in Darwin, since paths to linked dynamic shared libraries are included in the executables. On an ELF system, you typically use *ldconfig* or set the LD_LIBRARY_PATH variable. In Darwin, use DYLD_LIBRARY_PATH instead of LD_LIBRARY_PATH (see the *dyld* manpage for more details).

You can link against a particular version of a library by including the appropriate option for *cc*, such as *-lMagick.5.0.42*. Minor version checking is another way that the Mach-O format differs from ELF. To illustrate this, let's revisit Example 9-4, shown earlier in this chapter.

Suppose that the library shown in Example 9-4 is continually improved: minor bugs are fixed, minor expanded capabilities are added, and, in time, major new features are introduced. In each of these cases, you'll need to rename the library to reflect the latest version. Assume that the last version of the library is named *libanswer.1.2.5.dylib*. The major version number is *1*, the minor revision is *2*, and the bug-fix (i.e., fully compatible) revision number is *5*. Example 9-8 illustrates how to update this library to release *libanswer.1.2.6.dylib*, which is fully compatible with the release 1.2.5, but contains some bug fixes.

In the *makefile* shown earlier in Example 9-5, replace the following lines:

```
libanswer.dylib: answer.o
        $(LD) -dynamiclib -install_name libanswer.dylib \
        -o libanswer.dylib answer.o
```

with the code shown in Example 9-8.

Example 9-8. Versioning the answer library

```
libanswer.dylib: answer.o
    $(LD) -dynamiclib -install_name libanswer.1.dylib \
            -compatibility_version 1.2 -current_version 1.2.6 \
                -o libanswer.1.2.6.dylib $(OBJS)
    rm -f libanswer.1.dylib  libanswer.1.2.dylib libanswer.dylib
    ln -s libanswer.1.2.6.dylib libanswer.1.2.dylib
    ln -s libanswer.1.2.6.dylib libanswer.1.dylib
    ln -s libanswer.1.2.6.dylib libanswer.dylib'
```

Symbolic links are established to point to the actual library: one link reflects the major revision, one reflects the minor revision, and one simply reflects the name of the library.

The compatibility version number checks that the library used by an executable is compatible with the library that was linked in creating the executable. This is why the phrase *compatibility version* makes sense in this context.

Creating and Linking Static Libraries

The creation of static libraries in Mac OS X is the same as in many Unix variants: after installation in the destination directory, *ranlib* must be used to recatalog the newly installed archive libraries (i.e., the *lib*.a* files).

Another issue involving static libraries is the order in which things are listed when libraries are linked. The Darwin link editor loads object files and libraries in the exact order given in the *cc* command. For example, suppose we've created a static archive library named *libmtr.a*. Consider the following attempt to link to this library:

```
$ cc -L. -lmtr -o testlibmtr testlibmtr.o
/usr/bin/ld: Undefined symbols:
_cot
_csc
_sec
```

The rewrite of the command works as follows:

```
$ cc -o testlibmtr testlibmtr.o -L. -lmtr
```

In the first case, the library is placed first and no undefined symbols are encountered, so the library is ignored (there's nothing to be done with it). However, the second attempt is successful, because the object files are placed before the library. For the link editor to realize that it needs to look for undefined symbols (which are defined in the library), it must encounter the object files before the static library.

Creating Frameworks

A shared library can be packaged, along with its associated resources, as a framework. To create a framework, you must build and install a shared library in a framework directory. As an example, let's package the *libanswer. dylib* shared library as a versioned framework, using the name *ans*. That is, the framework will be a directory named *ans.framework*, which will contain the shared library file named *ans*. Three basic steps are required to build a versioned framework:

1. Create the framework directory hierarchy. If this is the first version of the framework on the system, the bottom level directory will be A. This is where the shared library will be installed. If you subsequently install a later version of the shared library it will be installed in a directory B at the same level of the directory hierarchy as A.

    ```
    mkdir -p ans.framework/Versions/A
    ```

2. Build the shared library in the framework Versions directory.

    ```
    cc -dynamiclib -o ans.framework/Versions/A/ans answer.o
    ```

3. Create symbolic links. For the first installation of the shared library (i.e., in *A*), *Current* points to *A*. When a later version of the library is subsequently installed in *B*, the *Current* symbolic link will be changed to point to *B*. The older version in *A* can stay on the system in case an application needs the older version. Since the symbolic link *ans.framework/ans* also points the most recent version of the shared library, it will also need to be updated when the framework is updated.

```
ln -s ans.framework/Versions/A  ans.framework/Versions/Current
ln -s ans.framework/Versions/A/ans  ans.framework/ans
```

Prebinding

Whenever you install an update to the Mac OS X operating system, there is a long phase at the end called *optimization*. What the splash screen calls "optimization" is a particular type of optimization, called *prebinding*, which applies only to Mach-O executables. We will only describe the essential idea behind prebinding. For more details and specific instructions on building libraries and executables with prebinding enabled, consult the document */Developer/ Documentation/ReleaseNotes/Prebinding.html.*

To understand what prebinding is and how it can speed up the launch of an application, let's consider what happens when you launch an application that was built without prebinding. When such an application (or dynamic library) is built, *ld* (the static linker) records the names of undefined symbols (i.e., the names of symbols that the application must link against). Later, when the application is launched, the dynamic linker (*dyld*) must bind the undefined references from the application to their definitions.

In contrast, if an executable or dynamic library is built with prebinding, the binding essentially occurs at build time. In particular, the library is predefined at a specified address range, a process that would otherwise have to occur when an application is launched. Rather than mark symbols as undefined, the dynamic linker can use address symbols in a prebound library. The library is then consulted when an application or some other dynamic library links against the dynamic library. Additionally, if the prebound library depends on other libraries (a common situation), then the static linker records the timestamps of the other libraries. Later, when the prebound library is used, the dynamic linker checks the timestamps of the dependent libraries and checks for the existence of overlapping executable addresses.

If the timestamps do not match those of the build timestamps, or if there are overlapping executable addresses, the prebinding is broken and normal binding is performed.

Performance and Debugging Tools

The developer tools that ship with Panther include an impressive array of debugging and tuning tools. Extensive documention, including examples and demonstrations of using these tools is available at *http://developer.apple.com/documentation/Performance/Conceptual/Performance/index.html*. The following short list is just to give you an idea of what is available:

gdb
> The GNU debugger.

MallocDebug
> Analyzes memory usage.

ObjectAlloc
> Analyzes both memory allocation and deallocation.

heap
> Analyzes memory usage.

leaks
> Lists the addresses and sizes of unreferenced malloc buffers.

malloc_history
> Lists the malloc allocation history of a given process.

vm_stat
> Lists virtual memory statistics.

vmmap
> Displays a virtual memory map in a process, including the attributes of memory regions such as starting addresses, sizes, and permissions.

OpenGL Profiler
> Profiles OpenGL-based applications.

QuartzDebug
> A debugging tool related to the Quartz graphics system.

Sampler
> Performs a statistical analysis of where an application spends its time by providing information such as how often allocation routines, system calls, or other functions are called.

Thread Viewer
> Profiles individual threads in multithreaded applications.

gprof

>   Profiles execution of programs by reporting information such as execution times and the number of calls for individual functions.

otool

>   The *otool* command-line utility is used to display information associated with object files or libraries. Earlier, we used it with the −L option, which displays the names and version numbers of the shared libraries used by the given object file. For more details see the *otool* manpage.

CHUD Tools

In addition to the tools listed in the previous section, a set of performance and optimization tools, bundled as the Computer Hardware Understanding Development Tools (CHUD), is available on the Xcode CD as an optional installation. You can also download the latest version from *ftp://ftp.apple. com/developer/Tool_Chest/Testing_ _Debugging/Performance_tools/*.

CHUD tools are used to configure and display the performance monitor counters provided on Apple systems. These performance monitors record events such as cache misses, page faults, and other performance issues. The list provides information on a few of the tools provided with the CHUD collection. For more details see *http://developer.apple.com/tools/performance/*.

Shark

>   Provides instruction-level profiling of execution time of a program, using statistical sampling. Advice on optimization is also provided. (A command-line version, */usr/bin/shark*, is also provided.)

Monster

>   Provides hardware-related performance measurements and displays the results in a spreadsheet format. (A command-line version, */usr/bin/ monster*, is also provided.)

Saturn

>   Provides exact (as opposed to statistical) profiling at the function level. For example, it reports how many times a given function is called. Results are represented in graphical format.

CacheBasher

>   Analyzes cache performance.

Reggie SE

>   Analyzes and modifies CPU and PCI configuration registers.

Skidmarks GT

>   Measures processor performance, specifically, integer, floating-point, and vector performance.

Amber

Command-line tool for instruction-level trace of execution threads.

acid

Command-line tool used to analyze traces provided by Amber.

SimG5

Command-line tool that simulates the G5 processor. You can use this cycle-accurate simulator to run through a trace file generated by Amber.

SimG4

Command-line tool that simulates the G4 processor. You can use this cycle-accurate simulator to run through a trace file generated by Amber.

A CHUD framework (*/System/Library/Frameworks/CHUD.framework*) that enables you to write your own performance tools (among other things) is also provided.

Interesting and Important Libraries

Table 9-2 lists some significant libraries included with Mac OS X, while Table 9-3 lists some significant libraries that *do not* come with Mac OS X (but are available through Fink).

Table 9-2. Important Mac OS X libraries

Library	Description	Headers
libalias	A packet aliasing library for masquerading and network address translation	Not included in Mac OS X; see the *network_cmds* module in the Darwin CVS archive
libl.a	The *lex* runtime library	Not applicable; lexical analyzers that you generate with *lex* have all the necessary definitions
libMallocDebug	A library for the *MallocDebug* utility (*/Developer/ Applications*)	Not applicable; you don't need to do anything special with your code to use this utility
libncurses (*libcurses* is available for backward compatibility)	The new *curses* screen library, a set of functions for controlling a terminal's display screen	*/usr/include/ncurses.h* (*curses.h* is available for backward compatibility)
libobjc	The library for the GNU Objective-C compiler	*/usr/include/objc/**
libpcap	Packet capture library	*/usr/include/pcap**
libssl and *libcrypto*	An open source toolkit implementing Secure Sockets Layer (SSL) Versions 2 and 3, Transport Layer Security (TLS) Version 1, and a full-strength, general-purpose cryptography library	*/usr/include/openssl/**
libtcl	The Tcl runtime library	*/usr/include/tcl.h*

Table 9-2. Important Mac OS X libraries (continued)

Library	Description	Headers
liby.a	The *yacc* runtime library	Not applicable; parsers that you generate with *yacc* have all the necessary definitions
libz	A general-purpose data-compression library (*Zlib*)	zlib.h
libbz2	Compression of files	bzlib.h
libpoll	System V *poll(2)* emulation library	poll.h
libiconv	Character set conversion library	iconv.h
libcharset	Character set determination library	libcharset.h
libcups	Common Unix Printing System (CUPS)	Not available
libcurl	Command-line tool for file transfer	/usr/include/curl/*
libgimpprint	Print plug-in, Ghostscript and CUPS driver	Not available
libncurses	Free software emulation of System V *curses*	*ncurses.h*, which is symbolic link to *curses.h*
libpam	Interface library for the Pluggable Authentication Module (PAM)	/usr/include/pam/*
libpanel	Panel stack extension for *curses*	panel.h
libxml2	XML parsing library, Version 2	/usr/include/libxml2/*
libruby	Interpreted object-oriented scripting language	/usr/lib/ruby/1.6/powerpc-darwin7.0 /*
libtcl	Tcl scripting language	tcl.h
libwrap	TCP wrappers; monitors and filters incoming requests for TCP-based services	tcpd.h
freetype2	TrueType font rendering library, Version 2	*/usr/X11R6/include/freetype2/**

Table 9-3. Libraries not included with Mac OS X

Fink package	Description	Home page
aalib	ASCII art library	*http://aa-project.sourceforge.net/aalib*
db3	Berkeley DB embedded database	*http://www.sleepycat.com/*
db4	Berkeley DB embedded database	*http://www.sleepycat.com/*
dtdparser	Java DTD Parser	*http://www.wutka.com/dtdparser.html*
expat	C library for parsing XML	*http://expat.sf.net*
fnlib	Font rendering library for X11	*http://www.enlightenment.org/*
freetype	TrueType font rendering library, Version 1	*http://www.freetype.org/*
gc	General-purpose garbage collection library	*http://www.hpl.hp.com/personal/Hans_Boehm/gc/*
gd	Graphics generation library	*http://www.boutell.com/gd/*

Table 9-3. Libraries not included with Mac OS X (continued)

Fink package	Description	Home page
gdal	Translator for raster geospatial data formats	*http://www.remotesensing.org/ gdal/*
gdbm	GNU dbm	*http://www.gnu.org*
giflib	GIF image format handling library, LZW- enabled version	*http://prtr-13.ucsc.edu/ ~badger/software/ libungif/*
glib	Low-level library that supports GTK+ and GNOME	*http://www.gtk.org/*
gmp	GNU multiple precision arithmetic library	*http://www.swox.com/gmp/*
gnomelibs	GNOME libraries	*http://www.gnome.org*
gnujaxp	Basic XML processing in Java	*http://www.gnu.org/software/ classpathx/jaxp*
gtk	GTK+, the GIMP widget toolkit used by GNOME	*http://www.gtk.org/*
imlib	General image handling library	*http://www.enlightenment.org/ pages/imlib2. html*
libdivxdecore	OpenDivX codec	*http://www.projectmayo.com/*
libdnet	Networking library	*http://libdnet.sourceforge.net/*
libdockapp	Library that eases the creation of WindowMaker Dock applets	*http://solfertje.student.utwente. nl/~dalroi/libdockapp/*
libdv	Software decoder for DV format video	*http://www.sourceforge.net/ projects/libdv/*
libfame	Fast assembly MPEG encoding library	*http://fame.sourceforge.net/*
libghttp	HTTP client library	*http://www.gnome.org/*
libiodbc	ODBC libraries	*http://www.mysql.com/*
libjconv	Japanese code conversion library	*http://www.kondara.org/ libjconv/index.html. en*
libjpeg	JPEG image format handling library	*http://www.ijg.org/*
libmpeg	GIMP MPEG library	*http://www.gimp.org*
libmusicbrainz	Client library for the MusicBrainz CD Index	*http://www.musicbrainz.org*
libnasl	Nessus Attack Scripting Language	*http://www.nessus.org/*
libnessus	Libraries package for Nessus without SSL support	*http://www.nessus.org/*
libole2	Library for the OLE2 compound file format	*http://www.gnome.org/*
libproplist	Routines for string list handling	*http://www.windowmaker.org/*
libshout	Library for streaming to icecast	*http://developer.icecast.org/ libshout/*
libsigc++	Callback system for widget libraries	*http://developer.icecast.org/ libshout/*
libstroke	Translates mouse strokes to program commands	*http://www.etla.net/libstroke/*
libtiff	TIFF image format library	*http://www.libtiff.org/*

Table 9-3. Libraries not included with Mac OS X (continued)

Fink package	Description	Home page
libungif	GIF image format handling library, LZW-free version	*http://www.gnu.org/directory/ libs/image/libungif.html*
libunicode	Low-level Unicode processing library	*http://www.sourceforge.net/ projects/ libunicode/*
libwww	General-purpose Web API written in C for Unix and Windows	*http://www.w3c.org/Library/ Distribution.html*
libxml	XML parsing library	*http://www.gnome.org/*
libxml++	C++ interface to the *libxml2* XML parsing library	*http://sourceforge.net/projects/ libxmlplusplus/*
libxpg4	Locale-enabling preload library	*http://fink.sourceforge.net/pdb/ package.php/libxpg4*
libxslt	XSLT library	*http://www.xmlsoft.org/XSLT/*
log4j	Library that helps the programmer output log statements to a variety of output targets	*http://jakarta.apache.org/log4j*
lzo	Real-time data compression library	*http://www.oberhumer.com/ opensource/lzo*
neon	HTTP/WebDAV client library with a C API	*http://www.webdav.org/neon/*
netpbm	Graphics manipulation programs and libraries	*http://netpbm.sourceforge.net*
pcre	Perl Compatible Regular Expressions library	*http://www.pcre.org*
pdflib	A library for generating PDFs	*http://www.pdflib.com/pdflib*
pil	The Python Imaging Library; adds image-processing capabilities to Python	*http://www.pythonware.com/ products/pil*
pilot-link	Palm libraries	*http://www.pilot-link.org/*
popt	Library for parsing command-line options	*http://www.gnu.org/directory/ popt.html*
pth	Portable library that provides scheduling	*http://www.gnu.org/software/ pth/pth.html*
readline	Terminal input library	*http://cnswww.cns.cwru.edu/ ~chet/readline/ rltop.html*
slang	Embeddable extension language and console I/O library	*http://space.mit.edu/~davis/ slang/*
stlport	ANSI C++ standard library implementation	*http://www.stlport.org/*
tk	Graphical companion to Tcl	*http://sourceforge.net/projects/ tcltkaqua/*

The list of available libraries is ever-growing, thanks to an influx of open source ports from FreeBSD and Linux. One of the best ways to keep on top of the latest ports is to install Fink (see Chapter 11), which lets you install precompiled versions of libraries and applications or install them from source.

Numerical Libraries

Panther ships with an impressive array of resources used for numerical computing. In addition to the optimized mathematical library, *libm*, many numerical libraries are packaged within the vecLib framework. This framework is located in */System/Library/Frameworks/vecLib.framework*, and its libraries have been optimized to take advantage of the G5 and the Velocity engine. The vecLib framework contains the following libraries:

BLAS
> Complete set (levels 1, 2, and 3) of the basic linear algebra subprograms. (See *http://www.netlib.org/blas/faq.html*.)

LAPACK
> Linear algebra package, written on top of the BLAS library. (See *http://www.netlib.org/lapack/index.html*.) Lapack is designed to run efficiently having most of the actual computations performed by optimized BLAS routines.

vDSP
> Digital signal processing.

vBasicOps
> A set of basic arithmetic operations. (See */System/Library/Frameworks/vecLib.framework/Versions/Current/Headers/vBasicOps.h*.)

vBigNum
> A set of basic arithmetic operations on large (128-bit) integers. (See */System/Library/Frameworks/vecLib.framework/Versions/Current/Headers/vBasicOps.h*.)

vMathLib
> A set of basic vectorized transcendental functions, optimized for the Velocity engine. (See *http://developer.apple.com/hardware/ve*.)

To compile code using the vecLib framework, you must include the header file with the following line of code:

```
#include <vecLib/vecLib.h>
```

You can compile a program named *prog.c*, which makes use of this framework, as follows:

```
$ gcc -faltivec -framework vecLib prog.c
```

CHAPTER 10

Perl

As far as Perl is concerned, Mac OS X is just another Unix. But there are some niceties and some quirks that make things a little different from the developer's perspective. Mac OS X's version of Apache also includes *mod_perl*, which allows you to embed Perl inside the Apache web server. This is described in the "Personal Web Sharing" section of Chapter 13.

Perl for Mac OS X Geeks

The following sections list a few of the extras that either come with Mac OS X or can be easily installed.

Mac::Carbon

This module comes by way of MacPerl (*http://www.macperl.org*), a distribution of Perl for Mac OS 9 and earlier. Mac::Carbon (available from the Download link on the MacPerl web site) gives Perl programmers access to the Carbon APIs. Its test suite is great; make sure you have your speaker volume turned up when you run it. One of the many modules included with Mac::Carbon is MacPerl; here's an example that pops up a dialog box and asks a question:

```
#!/usr/bin/perl -w

use MacPerl qw(:all);

$answer = MacPerl::Ask("Tell me how good you thought my poem was.");
if ($answer =~
    /counterpoint the surrealism of the underlying metaphor/i) {
  $die_in_the_vacuum_of_space = 1;
}
```

You can install Mac::Carbon with the CPAN shell, described later in this chapter. After it's installed, you can read the documentation with *perldoc Mac::Carbon*.

PerlObjCBridge.pm

This module ships along with Mac OS X, and it gives you a way to call into the Objective-C runtime on Mac OS X. Given an Objective-C call of the form:

```
Type x = [Class method1:arg1 method2:arg2];
```

you can use the equivalent Perl code:

```
$x = Class->method1_method2_($arg1, $arg2);
```

You could also create an NSString and display it with the following script:

```
#!/usr/bin/perl -w

use strict;
use Foundation; # import Foundation objects

my $string = NSString->stringWithCString_("Hello, World");
print $string, "\n";     # prints NSCFString=SCALAR(0x858398)
print $string->cString(); # prints Hello, World
```

You can read the documentation for this module with *perldoc PerlObjCBridge*.

Mac::Glue

This module lets you invoke Apple Events from Perl. To use it with an application, you'll need to create a layer of glue between this module with the *gluemac* utility, which is installed along with Mac::Glue. For example, to create the glue for the Terminal application, do the following:

```
$ sudo gluemac  /Applications/Utilities/Terminal.app/
Password: ********
What is the glue name? [Terminal]:
Created and installed App glue for Terminal.app, v1.4.1 (Terminal)
```

This also creates documentation for the module. To read it, use *perldoc Mac::Glue::glues::appname*, as in *perldoc Mac::Glue::glues::Terminal*.

Here's a short example that uses the Terminal glue to open a telnet session to the Weather Underground:

```
#!/usr/bin/perl -w

use strict;
use Mac::Glue;
my $terminal = new Mac::Glue 'Terminal';
$terminal->geturl("telnet://rainmaker.wunderground.com");
```

You can install Mac::Glue with the CPAN shell (described later).

There are many complicated dependencies; we found that Mac::Glue failed the first time through on one of the dependencies, and again the second time we tried to install it. We quit the CPAN shell, restarted it, and tried the install a third time—that was the charm. When you install Mac::Glue, pay close attention to the list of *glues* it creates, so you don't end up recreating them unnecessarily. When we installed Mac::Glue, this was its output:

```
Created and installed Dialect glue for AppleScript.rsrc
  (AppleScript)
Created and installed Addition glue for Digital Hub Scripting.osax
  (Digital_Hub_Scripting)
Created and installed Addition glue for StandardAdditions.osax
  (StandardAdditions)
Created and installed App glue for Image Capture Scripting.app
  (Image_Capture_Scripting)
Created and installed App glue for Finder.app, v10.3
  (Finder)
Created and installed App glue for Keychain Scripting.app
  (Keychain_Scripting)
Created and installed App glue for System Events.app, v1.2.1
  (System_Events)
Created and installed App glue for ColorSyncScripting.app
  (ColorSyncScripting)
Created and installed App glue for URL Access Scripting.app
  (URL_Access_Scripting)
Created and installed App glue for FontSyncScripting.app, v2.0d1
  (FontSyncScripting)
```

Installing CPAN Modules

We suggest limiting your customization of the Perl that came with Mac OS X, since it's fair game for modification during an upgrade or patch. You could either end up modifying something that the system depends on, or you could end up with a partially broken Perl installation the next time Software Update performs a big Mac OS X update.

It's fine to install whatever Perl modules you want, but if you choose to install a customized or newer version of Perl, install it in */usr/local* so it doesn't interfere with the one in */usr*. You should use */usr/bin/cpan* (a shell interface to the *CPAN.pm* module) to install modules, but don't stray too far from your desk when you're doing this—you might come back to find that your module selection led to a dependency that tried to do you a favor by upgrading Perl to the latest version.

Jaguar users won't have */usr/bin/cpan*. Use the *perl –MCPAN –e shell* command instead.

The first time you use the CPAN shell, it asks many questions about how you'd like to set it up (you can enter the initial CPAN configuration any time by issuing the command *o conf init* within the CPAN shell):

```
$ sudo cpan
Password: ********

/System/Library/Perl/5.8.1/CPAN/Config.pm initialized.

CPAN is the world-wide archive of perl resources. It consists of about
100 sites that all replicate the same contents all around the globe.
Many countries have at least one CPAN site already. The resources
found on CPAN are easily accessible with the CPAN.pm module. If you
want to use CPAN.pm, you have to configure it properly.

If you do not want to enter a dialog now, you can answer 'no' to this
question and I'll try to autoconfigure. (Note: you can revisit this
dialog anytime later by typing 'o conf init' at the cpan prompt.)

Are you ready for manual configuration? [yes]
```

From here on in, all of the default options are safe. When it comes time to select your preferred CPAN mirrors, follow the prompts and choose your geographic location. When you're finished, CPAN lists the mirrors you've selected and prompts you for your next action:

```
New set of picks:
  ftp://archive.progeny.com/CPAN/
  ftp://carroll.cac.psu.edu/pub/CPAN/
  ftp://cpan-du.viaverio.com/pub/CPAN/
  ftp://cpan-sj.viaverio.com/pub/CPAN/
  ftp://cpan.calvin.edu/pub/CPAN

commit: wrote /System/Library/Perl/5.8.1/CPAN/Config.pm
Terminal does not support AddHistory.

cpan shell -- CPAN exploration and modules installation (v1.76)
ReadLine support available (try 'install Bundle::CPAN')

cpan>
```

The string cpan> is the CPAN module's shell prompt. Your first order of business should be to run the command *install Bundle::CPAN*. This installs a bunch of modules that make your CPAN experience a bit nicer, including modules that support command-line history with the up and down arrows and command-line editing. Before doing this, Jaguar users should refer to the following section; Panther and Jaguar users should see the section, "CPAN and Dependency Problems," later in this chapter, for notes on some potential problems installing this bundle.

Jaguar and CPAN

Jaguar users should immediately upgrade to the latest version of the CPAN module, since the version of the module that shipped with Jaguar will try to upgrade all of Perl under many circumstances. This could make things very messy. The most recent versions of the CPAN module, including the one that ships with Panther, don't have this problem.

Jaguar users should not use the CPAN shell for the initial upgrade of the CPAN module. Instead, follow these steps:

1. Download the latest tarball from *http://search.cpan.org/dist/CPAN/*
2. Extract it and *cd* to its top-level directory
3. Run *perl Makefile.PL* to configure the source
4. Run *make test* to compile it and run the tests
5. If all goes well, run *sudo make install* to install it
6. Start a new instance of the CPAN shell with *perl –MCPAN –e shell*

If you see that CPAN has decided to install Perl, press Control-C a couple of times; it usually recovers just fine. Here's what it looked like on Jaguar when we tried to issue the command *install Bundle::CPAN* on a fresh install of Jaguar:

```
Running make for N/NW/NWCLARK/perl-5.8.2.tar.gz
Issuing "/usr/bin/ftp -n"
Connected to archive.progeny.com.
220 archive.progeny.com FTP server ready.
[... output abbreviated ...]
local: perl-5.8.2.tar.gz remote: perl-5.8.2.tar.gz
229 Entering Extended Passive Mode (|||50600|)
150 Opening BINARY mode data connection for 'perl-5.8.2.tar.gz'
(11896287 bytes).
 15% |*******                           |  1767 KB  196.36 KB/s^C
```

CPAN and Dependency Problems

You may run into dependency problems with some of the CPAN modules; and sometimes the answers to these problems won't be immediately obvious. For example, after setting up a fresh install of Panther, we ran *cpan* for the first time. After going through the initial configuration, we installed

Bundle::CPAN. Although it installed most of the required modules, it complained on *libnet* (Perl modules for network programming):

```
CPAN is up to date.
Bundle summary: The following items in bundle Bundle::CPAN had
Installation problems:
  Bundle::libnet and the following items had problems during recursive
  bundle calls: Data::Dumper

CPAN: Term::ReadLine::Perl loaded ok
...................
20 subroutines in Term::ReadLine redefined

cpan shell -- CPAN exploration and modules installation (v1.76)
ReadLine support enabled

cpan>
```

So we scrolled back to see what had happened with Data::Dumper. Oddly enough, everything looked fine:

```
Running make install
Installing /Library/Perl/5.8.1/
darwin-thread-multi-2level/auto/Data/Dumper/Dumper.bs
Installing /Library/Perl/5.8.1/
darwin-thread-multi-2level/auto/Data/Dumper/Dumper.bundle
Files found in blib/arch: installing files in blib/lib into
architecture dependent library tree
Installing /Library/Perl/5.8.1/darwin-thread-multi-2level/Data/Dumper.pm
Writing ///Library/Perl/5.8.1/
darwin-thread-multi-2level/auto/Data/Dumper/.packlist
Appending installation info to ///System/Library/Perl/
5.8.1/darwin-thread-multi-2level/perllocal.pod
  /usr/bin/make install  -- OK
```

Just to be sure we had only the latest Data::Dumper on our Mac, we configured *cpan* to uninstall existing versions of modules (by setting make_install_arg as shown in the following listing), and for extra measure, force-installed Data::Dumper, and finally reset make_install_arg back to its original setting:

```
cpan> o conf make_install_arg UNINST=1
    make_install_arg    UNINST=1

cpan> force install Data::Dumper
Running install for module Data::Dumper
Running make for I/IL/ILYAM/Data-Dumper-2.121.tar.gz
[... output abbreviated ...]
Appending installation info to ///System/Library/Perl/5.8.1/darwin-thread-
multi-2level/perllocal.pod
  /usr/bin/make install UNINST=1 -- OK
cpan> o conf make_install_arg ""
    make_install_arg
```

Next, we exited *cpan* with quit, and ran it again. Just to make sure it didn't get hung up about some of the failed installs that had gone before, we tried to install the Bundle::CPAN again. This time, it completed successfully:

```
$ sudo cpan

cpan shell -- CPAN exploration and modules installation (v1.76)
ReadLine support enabled

cpan> install Bundle::CPAN
CPAN: Storable loaded ok
Going to read /Users/bjepson/.cpan/Metadata
  Database was generated on Tue, 25 Nov 2003 08:46:32 GMT
File::Spec is up to date.
Digest::MD5 is up to date.
Compress::Zlib is up to date.
Archive::Tar is up to date.
Data::Dumper is up to date.
Net::Telnet is up to date.
Running install for module Net::Cmd
Running make for G/GB/GBARR/libnet-1.17.tar.gz
[... output abbreviated ...]
Appending installation info to
///System/Library/Perl/5.8.1/darwin-thread-multi-2level/perllocal.pod
  /usr/bin/make install  -- OK
Term::ReadKey is up to date.
Term::ReadLine::Perl is up to date.
CPAN is up to date.
```

Compiling Your Own Perl

If you want to go all-out and install the latest version of Perl along with all your favorite modules, you can compile and install a separate build in */usr/ local* and not worry about interfering with the one that came with Mac OS X:

```
rm -f config.sh Policy.sh
sh Configure -de
make
make test
make install
```

By default, Perl installs itself under */usr/local* with a directory layout that matches other Unix systems. If you specify a prefix of */usr* to Configure (sh Configure -de -Dprefix=/usr), it switches to the Mac OS X-style directory layout, putting modules in */System/Library/Perl* and */Library/Perl* (you can look at the output of perl -V for complete configuration details).

Using a prefix of */usr* on a production system is not recommended, since it will probably interfere with the operating system's idea of where Perl should be and how it should behave.

PART III

Working with Packages

There are a good number of packaging options for software that you com-pile, as well as software you obtain from third parties. This part of the book covers software packaging on Mac OS X.

- Chapter 11, *Fink*
- Chapter 12, *Creating and Installing Packages*

Fink

Fink is essentially a port of the Debian Advanced Package Tool (APT), with some frontends and its own centralized collection site, which stores packaged binaries, source code, and patches needed to build software on Mac OS X. The Fink package manager allows you to install a package, choosing whether to install it from source or a binary package. Consistent with Debian, binary package files are in the *dpkg* format with a *.deb* extension and are managed with the ported Debian tools *dpkg* and *apt-get*.

Fink also provides tools that create a *.deb* package from source. It maintains a database of installed software that identifies packages by the combination of name, version, and revision. Moreover, Fink understands dependencies, uses *rsync* to propagate software updates, supports uninstallation, and makes it easy to see available packages and installed packages. Fink can be used to install over a thousand Unix packages that are freely available and will run on Mac OS X. Fink recognizes and supports Apple's X11 implementation for running X windows applications, but you can also use Fink to install XFree86 if you prefer.

Fink installs itself and all of its packages, with the exception of XFree86, in a directory named */sw*, thus completely separating it from the main */usr* system directory. If problems occur with Fink-installed packages, you can simply delete the entire */sw* directory tree without affecting your system.

Installing Fink

You can install Fink from binary, from a source tarball, or from source in CVS.

Installing Fink from a Disk Image

The binary installation involves the following steps:

1. Download the binary installer disk image (a *.dmg* file) from *http://fink. sourceforge.net/download*.

2. The disk image should mount automatically and show up in the Finder's Sidebar. If the disk image does not mount after it has downloaded, locate and double-click the *.dmg* file to mount the disk image.

3. Open the mounted disk image and double-click the Fink Installer package inside. At the time of this writing, the name of the package was *Fink 0.6.2 Installer.pkg*.

4. Follow the instructions on the screen.

5. As Fink installs, it will launch the Terminal application and check to see whether you have a *.profile* file in your Home directory. If you don't, Fink will ask you if you want it to create one and add the . */sw/bin/init.sh* line to it. At the prompt, type in a Y and hit Return to create this file. After *.profile* is created, Fink automatically logs you out of the Terminal session; you will need to close the Terminal window with ⌘-W.

After Fink has completed its installation, unmount the disk image and drag the *.dmg* file to the Trash.

> The disk image also includes FinkCommander, a graphical frontend to using Fink. For more information, see the "Fink-Commander" section, later in this chapter.

Installing Fink from Source

To install the latest release of Fink from source, perform the following steps:

1. Open *http://fink.sourceforge.net/download/srcdist.php* in your web browser. After you select the link for the tarball, you must choose a mirror site from which to download the tarball. If your web browser downloads this file to your Desktop, move it to a working directory, such as */tmp*:

   ```
   $ mv ~/Desktop/fink-0.6.2-full.tar.gz /tmp/
   ```

> Some versions of StuffIt Expander may corrupt tar files (StuffIt Expander 7.0 and later should be fine); if you have an older version, unpack the tarball from the command line. If your browser automatically turned StuffIt Expander loose on it, you may be left with a tar file and a directory. If this is the case, you will have to *mv* the *fink-0.6.2-full.tar* instead of the *.gz* file.

2. Extract the archive:

```
$ gnutar -xzf fink-0.6.2-full.tar.gz
```

3. Change into the top-level directory and run the *bootstrap* script:

```
$ cd fink-0.6.2-full
$ ./bootstrap.sh
```

4. Follow the instructions on the screen.

Installing Fink from CVS

You can also install the latest version source of Fink via CVS:

1. Change to a temporary directory (not containing a subdirectory named *fink*). Log into the Fink CVS server. When prompted for a password press, press Return to enter an empty password:

```
$ cd /tmp
$ cvs -d :pserver:anonymous@cvs.sourceforge.net:/cvsroot/fink login
```

2. Download the package descriptions:

```
$ cvs -d :pserver:anonymous@cvs.sourceforge.net:/cvsroot/fink \ co fink
```

3. Change to the *fink* subdirectory and run the bootstrap script to install and configure Fink:

```
$ cd fink
$ ./bootstrap.sh
```

4. Follow the instructions on the screen.

Post-Installation Setup

When you install Fink, it should configure your shell initialization files to call either */sw/bin/init.sh* (*sh*, *bash*, and similar shells) or */sw/bin/init.csh* (*csh* or *tcsh*). If not, or if you need to configure Fink for another user, open a Terminal window and run the command */sw/bin/pathsetup.command*. When that's finished, you should close the Terminal window and open a new one to begin using Fink.

Fink can later be updated by entering the commands:

```
fink selfupdate
fink update-all
```

The first command updates Fink itself, including the list and descriptions of available packages, while the second command updates any installed packages. The first time you run *selfupdate*, Fink will prompt you to choose whether to use *rsync* (faster, less bandwidth), CVS, or to "Stick to point releases":

```
$ fink selfupdate
sudo /sw/bin/fink  selfupdate
```

```
Password: ********
fink needs you to choose a SelfUpdateMethod.

(1)     rsync
(2)     cvs
(3)     Stick to point releases

Choose an update method [1] 1
I will now run the rsync command to retrieve the latest package
descriptions.
```

The last option means that you'll stay away from the bleeding edge: Fink
will be more stable, but you may not get the latest and greatest versions of
applications. You can change the *selfupdate* method to CVS by using the
command *fink selfupdate-cvs*. You can switch back to using *rsync* with *fink
selfupdate-rsync*.

Using Fink

Once Fink has been installed, you can see what packages are available by
entering the command *fink list*. You can install a package from source with
the command *fink install package*.

The *fink* command is used from the command line to maintain, install, and
uninstall packages from source. Table 11-1 lists some examples of its usage.

Table 11-1. Various fink commands

Command	Description
fink apropos foo	Lists packages matching the search keyword, *foo*.
fink build foo	Downloads and builds package *foo*. No installation is performed.
fink checksums	Verifies the integrity of source tarballs.
fink configure	Rerun the configuration process.
fink describe foo	Describes package *foo*.
fink fetch foo	Downloads package foo, but doesn't install it.
fink fetch-all	Downloads source files for all available packages.
fink fetch-missing	Like *fetch-all*, but fetches only source code that's not already present.
fink index	Forces a rebuild of the package cache.
fink install foo	Downloads source, then builds and installs package *foo*.
fink list	Lists available packages. "i" is placed next to installed packages. Takes many options. For example, *fink list –i* lists only installed packages. Execute *fink list –help* for a complete set of options.
fink purge foo	Same as *remove* but also removes all configuration files. Use *apt-get remove* instead.

Table 11-1. Various fink commands (continued)

Command	Description
fink rebuild foo	Downloads and rebuilds package *foo*. Installation is performed.
fink reinstall foo	Reinstalls *foo* using *dpkg*.
fink remove foo	Deletes package *foo*, ignoring dependencies. Use *apt-get remove* instead.
fink selfupdate	Updates Fink along with package list. Uses latest officially released Fink source. Do this first unless you're updating via CVS.
fink selfupdate-cvs	Updates Fink along with the package list using CVS.
fink selfupdate-rsync	Updates Fink, along with the package list, using *rsync*.
fink update foo	Updates package *foo*.
fink update-all	Updates all installed packages.

FinkCommander

The FinkCommander application provides a graphical user interface for Fink's commands. FinkCommmander is distributed with Fink on the Fink installer disk image, but you can also download it directly from the Fink-Commander site (*http://finkcommander.sourceforge.net*).

To install FinkCommander, simply drag and drop the application from the disk image into your */Applications* folder (or */Applications/Utilities*, depending on what your preferences are).

You can use FinkCommander's search field, located in the upper-right of the main window, to find packages you are interested in. By default, the menu to the left of the search field is set to search package names. However, you can set it to something else (Description, Category, Maintainer, or Status) before you search. You can also select Binary, Stable, or Unstable to search only binary packages, only packages in the stable branch, or only packages in the unstable branch. Figure 11-1 shows the main window of FinkCommander with a search in progress for packages whose description includes "game".

To install a package with FinkCommander, select it in the main window and select Binary → Install to install a binary package, or Source → Install to install that package from source. You can remove a package by selecting it in the list and clicking Source → Remove or Binary → Remove.

FinkCommander also lets you run its commands in a Terminal window so you can interact directly with it. Use Source → Run in Terminal → *Command* or Binary → Run in Terminal → *Command* to run the selected command in a new Terminal window, as shown in Figure 11-2.

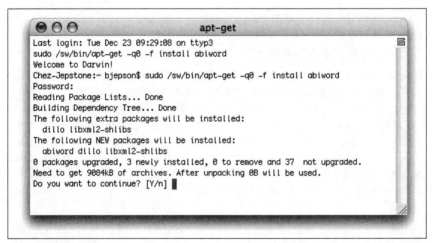

Figure 11-1. Searching FinkCommander

```
                        apt-get
Last login: Tue Dec 23 09:29:08 on ttyp3
sudo /sw/bin/apt-get -q0 -f install abiword
Welcome to Darwin!
Chez-Jepstone:~ bjepson$ sudo /sw/bin/apt-get -q0 -f install abiword
Password:
Reading Package Lists... Done
Building Dependency Tree... Done
The following extra packages will be installed:
  dillo libxml2-shlibs
The following NEW packages will be installed:
  abiword dillo libxml2-shlibs
0 packages upgraded, 3 newly installed, 0 to remove and 37  not upgraded.
Need to get 9084kB of archives. After unpacking 0B will be used.
Do you want to continue? [Y/n] █
```

Figure 11-2. Running the Install command in a Terminal Window

Installing Binaries

You can download and install binaries via *dselect* (shown in Figure 11-3), a
console-based frontend to *dpkg*. To use *dselect*, you must have superuser (or
administrator) privileges, so you'll need to run *sudo dselect* in the Terminal.
Once *dselect* has started, you can use the the options shown to maintain,
install, and uninstall packages.

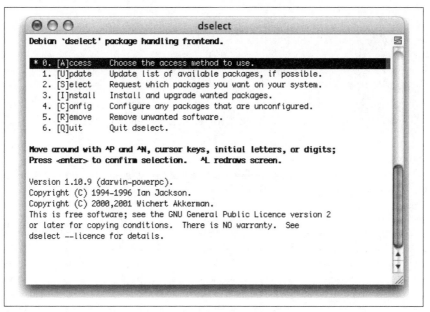

```
  ● ○ ○                        dselect
 Debian `dselect' package handling frontend.                              ▨

  * 0. [A]ccess     Choose the access method to use.
    1. [U]pdate     Update list of available packages, if possible.
    2. [S]elect     Request which packages you want on your system.
    3. [I]nstall    Install and upgrade wanted packages.
    4. [C]onfig     Configure any packages that are unconfigured.
    5. [R]emove     Remove unwanted software.
    6. [Q]uit       Quit dselect.


 Move around with ^P and ^N, cursor keys, initial letters, or digits;
 Press <enter> to confirm selection.   ^L redraws screen.

 Version 1.10.9 (darwin-powerpc).
 Copyright (C) 1994-1996 Ian Jackson.
 Copyright (C) 2000,2001 Wichert Akkerman.
 This is free software; see the GNU General Public Licence version 2
 or later for copying conditions.  There is NO warranty.  See
 dselect --licence for details.
```

Figure 11-3. The dselect program's main menu

[A]ccess

Chooses the access method to use. Configures the network access method to use.

[U]pdate

Downloads the list of available packages from the Fink site. This option is equivalent to running *apt-get update*. Table 11-2 lists the *apt-get* and *dpkg* command-line options.

Table 11-2. Some apt-get and dpkg commands

Command	Description
apt-get update	Updates list of available packages. Do this first.
apt-get install foo	Downloads and installs package *foo*.
apt-get remove foo	Deletes package *foo*.
dpkg --list	Lists all installed packages.
dpkg --listfiles foo	Lists all the files from package *foo*.
dpkg --install foo	Installs package *foo*.
dpkg --remove foo	Deletes package *foo*. Leaves configuration files.
dpkg --purge foo	Deletes *foo* and configuration files.
dpkg -S /path/to/file	Tells you which package owns a file.

You must run *[U]pdate* at least once after installing Fink.

[S]elect

Requests the packages you want on your system. Displays the actual package listing, which is used to select and deselect the packages you want on your system.

[I]nstall

Installs, upgrades, and configures selected packages. Also removes deselected packages.

[C]onfig

Configures any packages that are unconfigured. Not actually needed, since *[I]nstall* does this after you've installed a package.

[R]emove

Removes unwanted software. Not actually needed, since *[I]nstall* will do this.

[Q]uit

Quits *deselect*.

Mixing Binary and Source Installations

Using Fink, you can mix binary and source installations. That is, you can install some packages from their precompiled *.deb* files and install others from source. If you do this, you must first use *apt-get* to update the available binaries and then use *fink selfupdate*, followed by *fink update-all*, to update packages installed from source.

## CHAPTER 12

Creating and Installing Packages

In Chapter 11 we discussed installing packages with Fink; this chapter shows you how to create packages using tools provided with Mac OS X Panther, as well as with Fink.

The following packaging options are supported on Mac OS X by default:

PackageMaker

Found in */Developer/Applications/Utilities*, PackageMaker can be used to create packages (*.pkg*), which are bundles consisting of all the items that the Mac OS X Installer (*/Applications/Utilities*) needs to perform an installation. PackageMaker can also create metapackages (*.mpkg*), which can be used to install multiple packages at the same time.

When a package is installed, a "receipt" is placed in the */Library/Receipts* folder. These receipts are named with a *.pkg* extension and appear in the Finder as packages, even though they are not. You cannot use these files to install or update software. Instead, they are used to maintain a record of which packages have been installed on your system. This is how, for example, System Update knows not to install a package (or to update a package) that you've already installed. Disk Utility's Repair Permissions feature also uses the receipt to restore the permissions on installed files to their original state.

gnutar and gzip

The Unix tape archive tool *gnutar* is used to bundle the directories and resources for distribution. (The *tar* command is provided as a hard link to *gnutar*.) GNU Zip (*gzip*) is used to compress the tar archives to make file sizes as small as possible. Using these tools is generally the simplest way to copy a collection of files from one machine to another.

 Mac OS X Panther supports archiving files and directories in the *.zip* format directly from the Finder by Control-clicking on a file or directory and selecting "Create Archive of…" from the contextual menu.

Disk Utility

One of the easiest ways to distribute an application is to use the Disk Utility (*/Applications/Utilities*) to create a disk image. You can use the Disk Utility to create a double-clickable archive, which mounts as a disk image on the user's computer. From there, the user can choose to mount the disk image each time the application is run, copy the application to the hard drive (usually to */Applications*), or burn the image to a CD. Disk Utility has a command-line counterpart, *hdiutil*, which we'll cover in the later section, "Creating a Disk Image from the Command Line."

Each of these tools is discussed separately in the following sections.

Using PackageMaker

Apple's native format for packaging and distributing software is Package-Maker. Packages created with PackageMaker have a *.pkg* extension. When a user double-clicks on a package, the Installer application (*/Applications/Utilities*) is invoked and the installation process begins. These packages are bundles that contain all of the items the Installer needs.

You can also use PackageMaker to create *metapackages* for installing multiple packages. Metapackages contain meta-information, files, and libraries associated with a given application. Packages can also contain multiple versions of an application; typically, both Mac OS X and Classic versions.

PackageMaker documentation is available in the Help Viewer accessible from PackageMaker's Help option in the menu bar.

The basic components of a package are:

- A bill of materials (*.bom*) binary file describing the contents of the package. You can view the contents of a bill of materials with the *lsbom* command. After a package is installed, you can find a copy of this file in */Library/Receipts/packagename/Contents/Archive.bom*.

- An information file (*.info*) containing the information entered in the GUI application PackageMaker when the package was created.

- An archive file (*.pax*) containing the complete set of files to be installed by the package (similar to a *tar* archive). The file may be compressed, and have a *.gz* extension.

- A size calculation file (*.sizes*) listing the sizes of the compressed and uncompressed software.

- Resources that the installer uses during the installation, such as *README* files, license agreements, and pre- and post-install scripts. These resources are typically not installed; instead, they are used only during the installation process.

Setting up the Directory

To demonstrate how to create a package, we'll create a short C program and its associated manpage. Example 12-1 shows *hellow.c*, and Example 12-2 shows its manpage, *hellow.1*.

Example 12-1. The Hello, World sample program

```
/*
 * hellow.c - Prints a friendly greeting.
 */

#include <stdio.h>

int main( )
{
  printf("Hello, world!\n");
  return 0;
}
```

Example 12-2. The manpage for hellow.c

```
.\" Copyright (c) 2002, O'Reilly & Associates, Inc.
.\"
.Dd April 15, 2002
.Dt HELLOW 1
.Os Mac OS X
.Sh NAME
.Nm hellow
.Nd Greeting generator
.Sh DESCRIPTION
This command prints a friendly greeting.
```

PackageMaker expects you to set up the files using a directory structure that mirrors your intended installation. So, if you plan to install *hellow* into */usr/bin*, and *hellow.1* into */usr/share/man/man1*, you must create the appropriate subdirectories under your working directory. However, you can use a makefile to create and populate those subdirectories, so to begin with, your hellow directory looks like this:

```
$ find hellow
hellow
hellow/hellow.1
hellow/hellow.c
hellow/Makefile
```

Suppose that your *hellow* project resides in *~/src/hellow*. To keep things organized, you can create a subdirectory called *stage* that contains the installation directory. In that case, you'd place the *hellow* binary in *~/src/hellow/ stage/bin* and the *hellow.1* manpage in *~/src/hellow/stage/share/man/man1*.

The makefile shown in Example 12-3 compiles *hellow.c*, creates the *stage* directory and its subdirectories, and copies the distribution files into those directories when you run the command *make prep*.

Example 12-3. Makefile for hellow

```
hellow:
        cc -o hellow hellow.c

prep: hellow
        mkdir -p -m 755 stage/bin
        mkdir -p -m 755 stage/share/man/man1
        cp hellow stage/bin/
        cp hellow.1 stage/share/man/man1/
```

To get started, you need only *hellow.c*, *hellow.1*, and *makefile*. When you run the command *make prep*, it compiles the program and copies the files to their locations in the *stage* directory. After running *make prep*, the *hellow* directory will look like this:

```
$ find hellow
hellow
hellow/hellow
hellow/hellow.1
hellow/hellow.c
hellow/Makefile
hellow/stage
hellow/stage/bin
hellow/stage/bin/hellow
hellow/stage/share
hellow/stage/share/man
hellow/stage/share/man/man1
hellow/stage/share/man/man1/hellow.1
```

Now you're ready to launch PackageMaker and bundle up the application.

Creating the Package

Run PackageMaker and set the options as appropriate for your package. Figures 12-1 through 12-5 show the settings for the *hellow* sample. The options are as follows:

Description tab
    Contains items that describe the package so the person installing the package can find its name and version.

Title
    The title, or name, of the package.

Version
    The version number of the package.

Description

A description of the package.

Delete Warning

A custom warning message to display when a user removes the package. Mac OS X does not have a utility to uninstall a package, though.

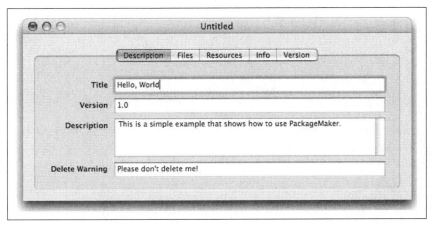

Figure 12-1. PackageMaker's Description tab

Files tab

Contains information related to file locations and compression.

Root

This option indicates where PackageMaker can find the top-level staging directory.

Compress Archive

You should leave this option enabled, since it makes the package smaller.

Figure 12-2. PackageMaker's Files tab

Resources tab

Specifies the location of extra resources.

Resources

The Resources directory contains files, such as *README* files, that are used by the installer but aren't installed on the disk. See PackageMaker's help for details.

Figure 12-3. PackageMaker's Resources tab

Info tab

Specifies miscellaneous package options.

Default Location

Indicates the default target location for the package.

Restart Action

If set to Required Restart, the system must be rebooted when the installation is finished. Other options include No Restart Required, Recommended Restart, and Shutdown Required.

Authorization Action

If set to Root Authorization, the user must supply authentication to install the package. (This escalates the user's privileges to *root* temporarily.) Other options include No Authorization Required and Admin Authorization (if the user needs only to *be* an Admin user, but does not need to escalate privileges). If the package will be installed into a protected directory (such as */usr*), you should use Root Authorization.

Allows Back Rev.

Allows the user to install an older version of the package over a newer one.

Install Fat

Supports multiple architecture binaries.

Relocatable
> Allows the user to choose an alternate location for the installed files.

Required
> Implies that certain packages (when installed as part of a larger install) are required.

Root Volume Only
> Requires the user to install the package on the current root volume (the volume from which they booted Mac OS X).

Update Installed Languages Only
> Updates only the currently installed localization projects.

Overwrite Permissions
> Causes the installer to change the permissions to match what Pack-ageMaker finds in the staging area if the installer overwrites an existing file or directory.

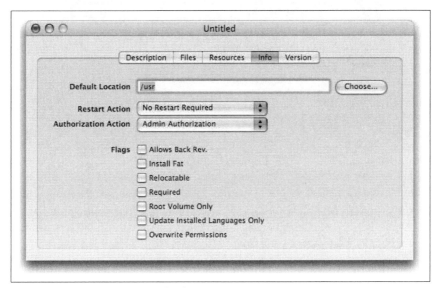

Figure 12-4. PackageMaker's Info tab

Version tab
> Specifies detailed version information.

> *Display name*
>> The name of the package to use when reporting its version.

> *Identifier*
>> A unique package name.

Get-Info string
> The version number to use when inspecting the package in the Finder with Get Info.

Short version
> An abbreviated version number.

Version: Major
> A major version number (the *1* in 1.0).

Version: Minor
> A minor version number (the *0* in 1.0).

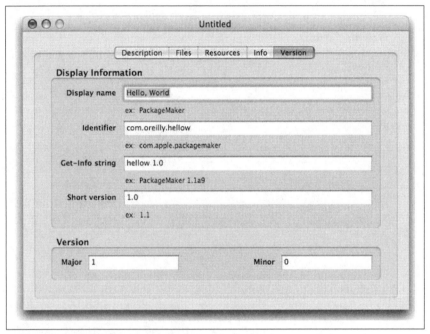

Figure 12-5. PackageMaker's Version tab

After filling in the package settings, select File → Create Package to create the *.pkg* file. To install it, double-click on the file and install as you would any other Mac OS X package. When you quit PackageMaker, you'll be prompted to save the PackageMaker session with its currently filled in values as a *.pmsp* document. If you subsequently double-click your *.pmsp* document, PackageMaker will open with the values that were saved in the *.pmsp* file.

Using GNU tar

For Unix software that does not involve resource forks or creator types, *gnutar* and *gzip* can be used to create a *.tar.gz* or *.tgz* tarball. This type of tarball preserves paths, permissions, symbolic links, as well as authentication and compression. Tools to uncompress the tarball are available for many platforms.

The automated creation of such a tarball can be worked into the same *makefile* that is used to build the software. Preservation of resource forks is tricky, but possible, in this method. For example, the following command preserves Macintosh resource forks (where *foo/* is a directory):

```
$ tar -pczf foo.tgz foo/
```

Every good tarball has a single top-level directory that contains everything else. You should not create tarballs that dump their contents into the current directory. To install software packaged this way, use the following command:

```
$ tar -pxzf foo.tgz
```

This simply unpacks the tarball into the file and directory structure that existed prior to packaging. Basically, it reverses the packing step. This method can be used to write files to the appropriate places on the system, such as */usr/local/bin*, */usr/local/lib*, */usr/local/man*, */usr/local/include*, and so on.

> When creating packages, you should keep your package contents out of directories such as */etc*, */usr/bin*, */usr/lib*, */usr/include*, or any top-level directory reserved for the operating system, since you have no way of knowing what a future software update or Mac OS X upgrade will include. For example, the Fink project stays out of Mac OS X's way by keeping most of its files in */sw*. We suggest using */usr/local* for the packages that you compile.

This packaging method can also be arranged so that the unpacking is done first in a temporary directory. The user can then run an install script that relocates the package contents to their final destination. This approach is usually preferred, since the *install* script could be designed to do some basic checking of dependencies, the existence of destination directories, the recataloging of libraries, etc. You could also include an *uninstall* script with your distribution.

The disadvantages of the tarball method of distributing software are:

- There is no built-in mechanism for keeping track of which files go where.
- There is no built-in method for uninstalling the software.
- It is difficult to list what software is installed and how the installed files depend on each other or on other libraries.
- There is no checking of dependencies and prerequisite software prior to the installation.

These tasks could be built into *install* and *uninstall* scripts, but there is no inherently uniform, consistent, and coherent method for accomplishing these tasks when multiple software packages are installed in this manner. Fortunately, more sophisticated methods of packaging, distributing, and maintaining software on Unix systems have been devised, such as Red Hat's RPM, Debian's *dpkg*, and Apple's PackageMaker.

Disk Images

Many applications in Mac OS X do not require a special installer. Often, they can be installed by simply dragging the application's folder or icon to a convenient location in the directory structure, usually the */Applications* folder. Applications that are distributed this way are typically packaged as a *disk image*. A disk image is a file that, when double-clicked, creates a virtual volume that is mounted as shown in Figure 12-6.

Inside Applications

Actually, an application *is* a folder with the extension *.app*, which is typically hidden from the user. This folder contains all of the application's resources. To view the contents of an application bundle, Control-click on the application icon and select Show Package Contents from the pop-up menu. This will open the application's *Contents* folder in the Finder.

 You can turn a Java application into a *.app* with *Jar Bundler* (*/Developer/Applications/Java Tools*). Since Mac OS X comes with Java, you can place your Java application on a disk image, secure in the knowledge that any Mac OS X user can double-click on the application to launch it.

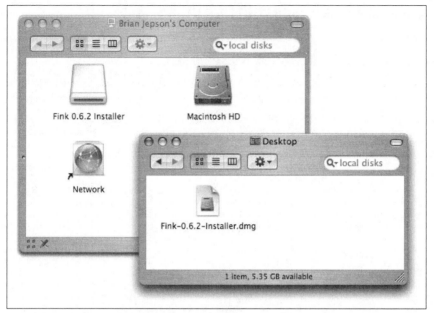

Figure 12-6. A disk image and its mounted volume

Disk images can be created by using Disk Utility (*/Applications/Utilities*) or via the command line (described later). There are two types of disk images. One is a *dual fork* disk image with an *.img* extension, and the other is a *single fork* disk image with a *.dmg* extension. A dual fork disk image requires additional (MacBinary) encoding in order for it to be transferred across networks. The single fork version is preferred for distributing software in Mac OS X, as it requires no additional encoding and, as we shall see later, can be "Internet-enabled."

The Unix command *df* reveals a disk image as a mounted volume that will appear in the */Volumes* directory. When you are done with the mounted volume, unmount it by clicking on the volume (in Figure 12-6, the mounted volume is named Fink 0.6.2 Installer) to select it and choose File → Eject (⌘-E). You could also Control-click and select Eject Disk from the contextual menu, or drag the mounted volume to the Trash.

 If you've used earlier versions of the Mac OS, you're probably familiar with the Put Away command (⌘-Y); however, that command no longer exists for Mac OS X. Instead, you must use Eject to unmount a disk image.

Creating a Disk Image with Disk Utility

To create a disk image using Disk Utility, perform the following steps:

1. Launch Disk Utility (*/Applications/Utilities*).

2. Either select Images → New → Blank Image or click the New Image icon from the toolbar. Either way, Disk Utility prompts you for a name, location, size (the maximum size is limited by available disk space), encryption options, and format, as shown in Figure 12-7. If you choose to enable encryption, Disk Utility will prompt you for a passphrase.

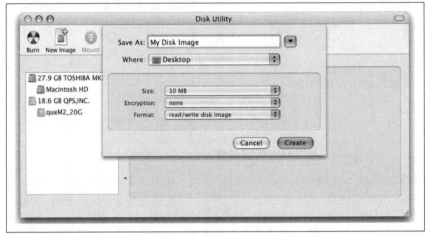

Figure 12-7. Creating a new blank image with Disk Utility

3. Name the new image "My Disk Image" and choose the Desktop as the location. The new image will be created as *My Disk Image.dmg* and mounted as *My Disk Image*. You can change this Volume name to, say, "SampleVol," in the Finder.

4. Double-click on the disk icon to open the empty volume in a Finder window, as shown in Figure 12-8.

5. Select File → New Finder Window (or ⌘-N) to open a new Finder window, where you can select the files you want to place in the disk image, as shown in Figure 12-9.

6. To copy the files to the mounted volume, select and then drag the items into the empty SampleVol window.

Figure 12-8. A blank Disk Image, ready to be loaded up with files

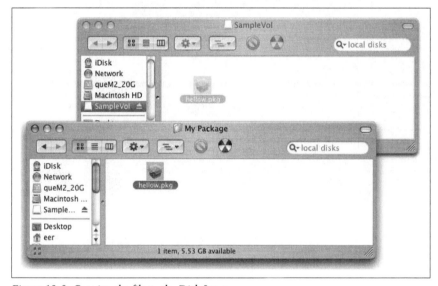

Figure 12-9. Copying the file to the Disk Image

7. Once you've placed the files into the disk image, eject this disk (⌘-E, click the eject icon next to the SampleVol in the left column of the Finder, or drag SampleVol to the Trash).

8. Return to the Disk Utility application, highlight *My Disk Image.dmg* in the left column of Disk Utility, and select Images → Convert as shown in Figure 12-10.

9. In the Convert Image window, enter either a new name or the same name in the Save As field, and then select read-only from the Image Format pull-down menu, as shown in Figure 12-11. (You can also compress the disk image from this menu.)

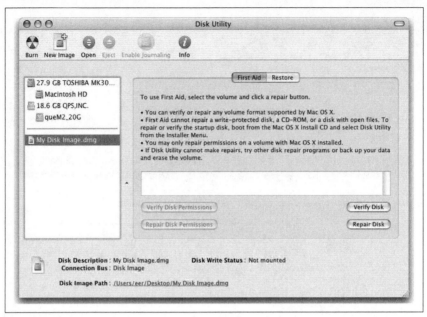

Figure 12-10. Choosing the image to convert in Disk Utility

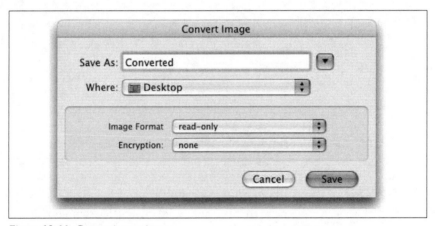

Figure 12-11. Converting an image

10. Click the Save button. If you've given the disk image the same filename as the original image you created, an alert window will appear, asking you to confirm whether you want to replace the older file with the new one. Click Replace to finish the process. Quit Disk Utility.

Creating a Disk Image from the Command Line

The following example illustrates how to create a disk image at the command line:

1. Change (*cd*) to the directory where you want to create the disk image:

   ```
   $ cd ~/Documents
   ```

2. Create the disk image of a given size (10 MB in this example) using *hdiutil*:

   ```
   $ hdiutil create -megabytes 10 -fs HFS+ -volname SampleVol Sample.dmg
   ```

3. Mount the image as a volume. Since you named it *SampleVol* when you issued the *hdiutil create* command, it will be mounted as *SampleVol* and will be available in */Volumes/SampleVol*:

   ```
   $ hdiutil mount Sample.dmg
   ```

4. Use the Finder or command-line tools to write to the volume *SampleVol*.

5. When you are done writing to the volume, you can eject it with *hdiutil unmount*:

   ```
   $ hdiutil unmount /Volumes/SampleVol/
   ```

6. Copy the disk image to a compressed, read-only image named *Ready4Dist.dmg*:

   ```
   $ hdiutil convert Sample.dmg -o Ready4Dist.dmg
   ```

Whenever you want to mount this volume again, double-click the file *Ready4Dist.dmg* in the finder. Note that the writable disk image *Sample.dmg* is not destroyed in this process.

Distributing Your Image

Once you've created a disk image, you can share it with the world. Put the image up on a web server or FTP server for others to enjoy, share it on your iDisk, or burn it to a CD using Disk Utility (select File → Burn Image).

Internet-enabled disk images

An Internet-enabled disk image is a read-only disk image that cleans up after itself, leaving only the software and no by-products of the download. If you distribute your software as an Internet-enabled disk image, the user just needs to perform these steps:

1. Download the *.dmg* file to the Desktop (i.e., *~/Desktop*) using a web browser.

2. When the download completes, the following sequence of events happens automatically:

    a. The *.dmg* file is mounted.

    b. Its contents are copied to the user's default download folder (e.g., *~/Desktop*).

    c. The disk image is unmounted.

    d. The Internet-enabled flag of the *.dmg* file is set to No.

    e. The *.dmg* file is moved to the Trash.

3. Locate the software and move it to its appropriate location.

The disk image is mounted in a hidden location until its contents are copied to the user's default download folder, which is typically the Desktop folder. If the disk image contains a single file, only this file is copied. On the other hand, if the disk image contains more than one file, a new folder is created in the download folder bearing the root name of the *.dmg* file. Files contained in the disk image are then copied to this folder. For example, if the Internet-enabled disk image containing multiple files is named *Sample.dmg*, a folder named *Sample* will be created in the download folder and the files contained in the disk image will be copied to the *Sample* folder.

In this scheme, the user does not deal directly with the *.dmg* file (other than initiating the download). This is in contrast to the situation before Internet-enabled disk images were supported, in which the user had to manually unmount the disk image and drag it to the Trash.

To create an Internet-enabled disk image, first create a read-only *.dmg* formatted disk image as described earlier (neither read-write disk images nor older *.img/.smi* formats can be Internet-enabled), then set the Internet-enabled flag with the *hdiutil* command:

```
$ hdiutil internet-enable -yes Ready4Dist.dmg
```

If you want to disable the Internet-enabled flag, enter this command:

```
$ hdiutil internet-enable -no Ready4Dist.dmg
```

If you are not sure how a disk image has its Internet-enabled flag set, the following command reveals this information:

```
$ hdiutil internet-enable -query Ready4Dist.dmg
```

As noted earlier, Internet-enabled disk images are moved to the Trash after they are downloaded and acted upon by Mac OS X. Although their Internet-enabled flags are set to No during the process, you can still rescue *.dmg* files from the Trash in case you want to reinstall the software later.

Creating Fink Packages

You can create your own Fink packages by identifying a source archive and creating a *.info* file in your */sw/fink/dists/local/main/finkinfo* directory.

Creating and Publishing the Tarball

The Fink package system needs a tarball that can be downloaded with the *curl* utility. To illustrate how to create a Fink package, let's use the *hellow-1.0* program (see "Using PackageMaker" earlier in this chapter). Before you proceed, you should create a tarball named *hellow-1.0.tar.gz* with the following contents, and move it to the */Users/Shared/hellow/src* directory:

```
hellow-1.0/
hellow-1.0/hellow.1
hellow-1.0/hellow.c
hellow-1.0/Makefile
```

The *curl* utility can download this file with the following URL: *http://www.jepstone.net/downloads/hellow-1.0.tar.gz*. (You could also host your own files on a public web server, FTP server, or a local filesystem by using *file:* URL.)

Creating the .info File

Next, create a *.info* file to tell Fink where to download the package from and how to install it. Fink uses this information to download, extract, and compile the source code, and then to generate and install a Debian package (*.deb* file). This file must be in */sw/fink/dists/local/main/finkinfo*, so you'll need superuser privileges to create it (use the *sudo* utility to temporarily gain these privileges). Example 12-4 shows */sw/fink/dists/local/main/finkinfo/hellow-1.0.info*.

Example 12-4. -The hellow-1.0 info file

```
Package: hellow
Version: 1.0
Revision: 1
Source: http://www.jepstone.net/downloads/%n-%v.tar.gz
Source-MD5: 4ca04528f976641d458f65591da7985c
CompileScript: make
InstallScript: mkdir -p %i/bin
 cp %n %i/bin
 mkdir -p %i/share/man/man1
 cp %n.1 %i/share/man/man1/%n.1
Description: Hello, World program
DescDetail: <<
Prints a friendly greeting to you and your friends.
<<
License: Public Domain
Maintainer: Brian Jepson <bjepson@oreilly.com>
```

The *hellow-1.0.info* file includes several entries, described in the following list. See the Fink Packaging Manual at *http://fink.sourceforge.net/doc/packaging/* for more details.

Package
> The name of the package.

Version
> The package version.

Revision
> The package revision number.

Source
> The URL of the source distribution. You can use percent expansion in the name. (In this example, %n is the name of the package and %v is the package version.) See the Fink Packaging Manual for more percent expansions.

Source-MD5
> The MD5 sum for the file, as calculated by the md5sum binary (*/sw/bin/md5sum*) that comes with Fink. You may need to replace the MD5 sum in the *hellow-1.0.info* file if it's different than what's shown in Example 12-4.

CompileScript
> The command (or commands) needed to compile the source package. The command(s) may span multiple lines, but must begin after the colon.

InstallScript
> The command (or commands) that install the compiled package. The command(s) may span multiple lines, but must begin after the colon.

Description
> A short description of the package.

DescDetail
> A longer description of the package, enclosed with << >>.

License
> The license used by the package. See the Fink Packaging Manual for information on available licenses.

Maintainer
> The name and email address of the maintainer.

Installing the Package

To install *hellow*, use the command *fink install hellow*. This command downloads the source to a working directory, and then extracts, compiles, and packages it, generating the file */sw/fink/dists/local/main/binary-darwin-powerpc/hellow_1.0-1_darwin-powerpc.deb*.

If */sw/etc/fink.conf* has the entry MirrorOrder: MasterFirst (the default), it will try to find the *.tar.gz* file on the server designated as Mirror-master. Since it is unlikely that *hellow-1.0.tar.gz* will be hosted on that server, it will fail, and you'll be presented with several options, including "Retry using original source URL," which will download the file from the location specified in *hellow-1.0.info*. You could avoid this by changing the MirrorOrder to MasterLast, but we do not recommend changing the default behavior of Fink, since it could have unpredictable results down the road.

After Fink creates this file, it installs it using *dpkg*. After you've installed *hellow*, you can view its manpage and run the *hellow* command:

```
$ man hellow

HELLOW(1)          System General Commands Manual          HELLOW(1)

NAME
     hellow - Greeting generator

DESCRIPTION
     This command prints a friendly greeting.

Mac OS                      April 15, 2002                      Mac OS
$ hellow
Hello, world!
```

This example shows only a portion of Fink's capabilities. For example, Fink can be used to download and apply patches to a source distribution. For more information, see the Fink Packaging Manual (*http://fink.sourceforge.net/doc/packaging/index.php*), which contains detailed instructions on how to build and contribute a *.deb* package to the Fink distribution.

## PART IV

Serving and System Management

This part of the book talks about using Mac OS X as a server, as well as system administration.

- Chapter 13, *Using Mac OS X as a Server*
- Chapter 14, *MySQL and PostgreSQL*
- Chapter 15, *System Management Tools*

Using Mac OS X as a Server

While most people think of Mac OS X as a client system only, you can also run Mac OS X as a server. If you need Apple's advanced administration tools, you could purchase and use Mac OS X Server (*http://www.apple.com/ server/macosx*), but if you're comfortable with the command line, the client version can be coerced a bit to run as a server.

The services that power the Sharing preference panel are based on the same servers that power much of the Internet:

- OpenSSH for remote login
- Samba for Windows file sharing
- Apache for web publishing

However, the System Preferences are limited in what they will let you do. To unleash the full power of Mac OS X as a server, you'll need to install your own administrative tools or edit the configuration files by hand.

Getting Connected

If you're using a Mac as a production server, then you are probably either co-locating it at your hosting provider's facility or bringing a dedicated line into your home or office.

If you're running a Mac as a server for personal use, you can probably get away with plugging into a residential broadband connection and opening a hole in your firewall. You can do many fun things with a personal server:

Secure mail server

If your email provider isn't reliable, or doesn't support the way you want to access your email, you can forward all your email to your per-sonal server and retrieve it from there—whether you're in your home office or on the road.

SSH server

When you're on the road, there might be some things you want to access back at the home office. Or perhaps you want to help a family member troubleshoot a computer problem while you're on the road.

VNC/remote desktop/X11

One step up from a VPN or SSH connection is a remote connection that lets you completely take over the desktop of a computer in your home (see Chapter 5). This takes remote access and troubleshooting to the next level. For more information, see Chapter 5.

Life Behind a Firewall

If you have a Small Office/Home Office (SOHO) router between your Internet connection and your Mac, the router probably has a built-in firewall that protects your Mac from the outside world. Since most access points and routers have a firewall that blocks incoming network traffic, you'll need to open a hole in that firewall for each service you want to use. Here are our recommendations for exposing a server to the outside world on a SOHO network:

Use a wired connection

If you have a wireless access point, such as an AirPort Base Station, that's doing double-duty as your wired Ethernet router, we suggest plugging your Mac server into one of the LAN ports on your access point or one of the LAN ports on a switch that's plugged into your access point's LAN port.

Although Wi-Fi speeds typically exceed broadband by quite a lot, actual speeds are often half that of the quoted speed of Wi-Fi networks, and bandwidth is shared among all computers on a given network. So, an 802.11b Wi-Fi network with a raw speed of 11 Mbps is more likely to share 5 to 6 Mbps among machines, and an 802.11g Wi-Fi (AirPort Extreme) network is more likely to have 20 to 25 Mbps available than the 54 Mbps raw speed of the network. This is because Wi-Fi networks have a significant amount of overhead, are susceptible to interference from consumer electronics, and can experience a sharp drop-off in speeds as the distance between the computer and Base Station increases.

Be aware of your ISP's Terms of Service

If your ISP does not permit you to run servers on your network, consider asking them whether they have another tier of service that does permit this. As an added bonus, those tiers of service often include one or more static IP addresses. On the downside, they tend to cost quite a bit more than their consumer offerings.

Consider non-standard ports

If your ISP's Terms of Service do not explicitly prohibit running services, chances are good that they are blocking access to common ports such as 80 (HTTP) in an attempt to reduce paths by which worms can attack Microsoft systems. Although we can't prove that Mac OS X is inherently more secure than Microsoft systems, there are fewer exploits that affect it. If you are diligent about applying security updates and understand the risks and consequences of opening a service (such as a web or IMAP server) to the outside world, you could choose to run these services on an alternate port that's not blocked. You can do this by either reconfiguring the server, or using your router to handle the redirection.

Open your ports

One thing a firewall is really good at is keeping traffic out. However, if you want to run a server on your network, you need to selectively let traffic in.

To configure an AirPort Base Station to send traffic to a Mac that's acting as a server, open the AirPort Admin Utility (in */Applications/ Utilities*), select your Base Station, and choose Show All Settings → Port Mapping. Figure 13-1 shows an AirPort Base Station configured to forward traffic coming in from the outside world on port 8008 to a machine inside the network with the private address 192.168.254.201 on port 80. Non-Apple wireless access points may have similar functionality. Look in your access point's documentation for information on port mapping (sometimes referred to as *forwarding*).

This means that people can type *http://YOUR_IP_ADDRESS:8008* into their web browser and be directed to the web browser listening on port 80 (the standard HTTP port) inside the firewall. You can find the value for *YOUR_IP_ADDRESS* by clicking Show Summary from within the AirPort Admin Utility and looking at the Public (WAN) IP Address, as shown in Figure 13-2.

LDAP

Mac OS X includes OpenLDAP (*http://www.openldap.org*), an open source implementation of LDAPv3. By default, it's disabled on Mac OS X. To enable the OpenLDAP server, add the following line to */etc/hostconfig* (for more information on *hostconfig*, see Chapter 2):

```
LDAPSERVER=-YES-
```

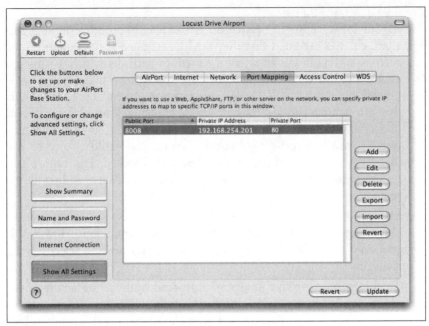

Figure 13-1. Setting up a port mapping with the AirPort Admin Utility

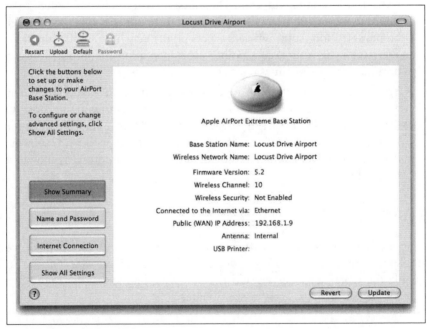

Figure 13-2. Looking up the public IP address of an AirPort Base Station

By default, OpenLDAP is configured to consult the network domain. If your Mac is running the default (standalone) Directory Services configuration, you'll only have the local domain. So, you'll need to edit */etc/openldap/slapd. conf* and set the datasource entry to:

```
datasource /var/db/netinfo/local.nidb
```

If your Mac's Directory Services configuration has been altered to participate in a larger network, you should be careful about changing your LDAP configuration. Consult your system administrator for more information. (And if you are the system administrator, have at it!)

When you reboot your computer, LDAP automatically starts up. To start LDAP without rebooting, run the command *sudo SystemStarter start LDAP*. This LDAP server shares the same database as NetInfo (see Chapter 3).

Postfix

As of Mac OS X Panther, setting up a local mail server just got a lot easier. Apple has given up on the aging and clunky sendmail, and is instead using Postfix, which is easy to configure. (However, Postfix includes a sendmail-compatibility wrapper in */usr/sbin/sendmail*.) The following sections describe how to configure Postfix in various scenarios.

 After you make any changes to Postfix's configuration files, you should reload its configuration by running the command *sudo postfix reload*.

Configuring Postfix to Send Email

By default, Mac OS X runs a program called *postfix-watch*, which corresponds to the MAILSERVER=-AUTOMATIC- in */etc/hostconfig* (a setting of -YES-starts the *postfix* server). The *postfix-watch* daemon monitors the outgoing mail queue, and runs Postfix on the queue as needed.

If you want to use Postfix on a standalone server, you must configure two settings in */etc/postfix/main.cf*. The first is the hostname (myhostname). This should be a real hostname, something that can be found in a reverse DNS lookup against your IP address. The second is your origin (myorigin), which is the domain name from which email appears to originate. This can be the same as your hostname (this will probably be the case for small sites). However, if it is not, be sure to specify the correct hostname. For example, here are the settings for a computer named *ip192-168-0-1.ri.ri.cox.net* with all email originating from that machine appearing to come from *username@cox.net*:

```
myhostname = ip192-168-0-1.ri.ri.cox.net
myorigin = cox.net
```

Configuring Postfix to Receive Email

To enable Postfix to act as a legitimate email destination (that is, mail for *username@yourhost* will go directly to your Macintosh), you must set MAILSERVER to -YES- in */etc/hostconfig* and uncomment the following line in */etc/postfix/master.cf*:

```
#smtp     inet  n       -       n       -       -       smtpd
```

After that change, it should now read:

```
smtp      inet  n       -       n       -       -       smtpd
```

To receive email at your host, you will need a Mail Exchange (MX) record pointing to your machine. The MX record is an entry in DNS that identifies the mail server for a particular domain. If your ISP provides you with a static IP address and supports the use of hostnames (this is a given if your Mac is co-located), contact them about setting up the appropriate MX record. If you have residential (or low-end business) broadband, it's very likely that your ISP does not support this, and what's more, they probably block access to port 25 within their network as a security precaution.

If your system can support the use of port 25, you must change the setting for inet_interfaces in */etc/postfix/main.cf*. By default, it listens only on 127. 0.0.1 (localhost), so you must add the IP address you want it to listen on. For example, we've set up a server behind a firewall, but configured the firewall to relay port 25 to the server (see "Life Behind a Firewall," earlier in this chapter). The private network address of the server is 192.168.254.104, and because traffic on port 25 is going from the outside world to the private network, we must configure inet_interfaces to listen on the 192.168.254.104 interface as well as localhost:

```
inet_interfaces = localhost 192.168.254.104
```

After you make this change, stop and restart Postfix with *postfix stop* and *postfix start* (it may not be enough to use the command *postfix reload*).

Configuring Postfix with a Relay Host

If you don't have a permanent domain name for your Mac OS X machine, we suggest configuring Postfix to use a relay host (most likely your ISP's SMTP server). To configure Postfix to use a relay, add an entry for relayhost in */etc/postfix/main.cf*. For example, we use the following setting:

```
relayhost = smtp-server.ora.com
```

Along the same lines, you should configure Postfix to masquerade as the appropriate host using the myorigin setting in */etc/postfix/main.cf*. In the case of the previous example, the origin is *oreilly.com* (as in *bjepson@oreilly.com*):

```
myorigin = oreilly.com
```

Built-in Services: The Sharing Panel

Mac OS X includes many built-in services that are based on common open source servers such as Samba, Apache, and OpenSSH. Although you can enable and disable these using the Sharing preference panel (System Preferences → Sharing), there's not much configuration you can do there. This section describes each of these services and what you can do to customize them to your liking.

Personal File Sharing

This option controls the AppleTalk Filing Profile (AFP) service, and corresponds to the AFPSERVER entry in */etc/hostconfig* (see Chapter 2 for more information on *hostconfig*). When you enable Personal File Sharing, your Mac shares your Home directory and any mounted volumes (including external drives) with the connected machine.

Windows File Sharing

This option turns on the Samba service, and toggles the `disable` entry in */etc/xinetd.d/nmbd* (NetBIOS name server for resolving Windows server names) and */etc/xinetd.d/smbd* (the server that handles Windows file sharing).

On Mac OS X, Samba hooks into Open Directory for user authentication. Because of this, you don't need to use *smbpasswd* to set the password for someone logging into your Mac from a Windows machine; users can authenticate themselves by using their login username and password.

You can add a new share by editing */etc/smb.conf*, and adding an entry. For example, you could share your Applications directory with this entry:

```
[Applications]
path = /Applications
read only = yes
```

Next, use the command *sudo killall –HUP smbd nmbd* to restart Samba networking with the new configuration file, and without closing any existing connections. Stopping and restarting Windows File Sharing terminates any existing connections. Although Windows clients will usually reconnect to shared resources without complaining, they will get an error if a file transfer is in progress when you interrupt the connection.

Personal Web Sharing

The Apache server is activated when you enable Personal Web Sharing in the Sharing preferences panel (it is disabled by default). This corresponds to the WEBSERVER entry in */etc/hostconfig*. Apache's main configuration file is */etc/httpd/httpd.conf*. Individual users' sites are configured with the files that you can find in */etc/httpd/users*. Apache keeps its log files in */var/log/httpd*.

The Apache server that comes with Mac OS X Panther is based on Apache 1.3.28, and includes several optional modules, which you can enable or disable by uncommenting/commenting the corresponding LoadModule and AddModule directives in */etc/httpd/httpd.conf*. These modules are described in the following sections.

After you've made any changes to these modules, you should test the changes to the configuration with the command *sudo apachectl configtest*, and then have Apache reload its configuration files with *sudo apachectl graceful*.

You can browse the source code to Apple's version of Apache, as well as the optional modules, by visiting *http://www.opensource.apple.com/darwinsource/*.

dav_module (mod_dav)

This is the WebDAV (Web-based Distributed Authoring and Versioning) module, which lets you export a web site as a filesystem (this is how Apple's iDisk is exported, for example).

If you enable this module, you can turn on WebDAV sharing by including the directive DAV on within a <Directory> or <Location> element in *httpd.conf* or one of the user configuration files in */etc/httpd/users*. You will also need to specify the lockfile that *mod_dav* will use. For example, you can enable WebDAV for your web server root by changing *httpd.conf* as shown in **bold**:

```
DAVLockDB /tmp/DAVLock

<Directory />
    Options FollowSymLinks
    DAV on
    AllowOverride None
</Directory>
```

After you make this change and restart Apache, you'll be able to mount your web site with the following command:

```
mount_webdav http://127.0.0.1/ /mnt
```

See *http://www.webdav.org/mod_dav/install.html* for complete information on configuring this module.

perl_module (mod_perl)

This module embeds the Perl interpreter in each Apache process, letting you run Perl web applications without the overhead of launching a CGI script. *mod_perl* also lets you develop Perl applications that can hook into Apache's responses at various stages. Panther ships with *mod_perl* 1.26.

After you've enabled *mod_perl* on your server, you can get up and running quickly by using the Apache::Registry module, which runs most well-behaved Perl CGI scripts under *mod_perl*. You can set up a virtual directory for Perl scripts by adding the following to *httpd.conf* and restarting Apache:

```
Alias /perl/ /Library/WebServer/Perl/
PerlModule Apache::Registry
<Location /perl>
  SetHandler perl-script
  PerlHandler Apache::Registry
  Options ExecCGI
</Location>
```

Next, create the directory */Library/WebServer/Perl*, save the following program into that directory in a file called *HelloWorld*, and set that file as executable with *chmod*:

```
#!/usr/bin/perl -w

use strict;

# workaround for a bug in Mac OS X 10.3
tie *STDOUT, 'Apache';

# run 'perldoc CGI' for more information
use CGI qw(:standard);
print STDOUT header();
print STDOUT start_html("Sample Script");
print "hello, world";
print end_html();
```

If you point your browser at *http://localhost/perl/HelloWorld*, you should see a friendly greeting. If not, check */var/log/httpd/error_log* for error messages. You can find complete documentation for *mod_perl* at *http://perl.apache.org/docs/1.0/index.html*.

ssl_module (mod_ssl)

This module allows you to serve documents securely using the HTTPS (TLS/SSL) protocol. To configure this properly, you should obtain a server certificate signed by a Certifying Authority (CA). However, you can whip something up pretty quickly for testing using the following steps, after you've enabled *mod_ssl* in *httpd.conf*:

1. Create and change to a working directory for creating and signing your certificates:

```
$ mkdir ~/tmp
$ cd ~/tmp
```

2. Create a new CA. This will be an untrusted CA. You'll be able to sign things, but browsers will not implicitly trust you:

```
$ /System/Library/OpenSSL/misc/CA.sh -newca
CA certificate filename (or enter to create)

Making CA certificate ...
Generating a 1024 bit RSA private key
.......................................++++++
..++++++
writing new private key to './demoCA/private/./cakey.pem'
Enter PEM pass phrase: ********
Verifying - Enter PEM pass phrase: ********
-----
You are about to be asked to enter information that will be incorporated
into your certificate request.
What you are about to enter is what is called a Distinguished Name or a
DN.
There are quite a few fields but you can leave some blank
For some fields there will be a default value,
If you enter '.', the field will be left blank.
-----
Country Name (2 letter code) [AU]:US
State or Province Name (full name) [Some-State]:Rhode Island
Locality Name (eg, city) []:Providence
Organization Name (eg, company) [Internet Widgits Pty Ltd]:Gold and
Appel Transfers
Organizational Unit Name (eg, section) []:
Common Name (eg, YOUR name) []:Hagbard Celine
Email Address []:hagbard@jepstone.net
Next, create a certificate request; this will generate an unsigned
certificate that you'll have to sign as the CA you just created:
$ /System/Library/OpenSSL/misc/CA.sh -newreq
Generating a 1024 bit RSA private key
................++++++
.............................................................++++++
writing new private key to 'newreq.pem'
Enter PEM pass phrase: ********
Verifying - Enter PEM pass phrase: ********
-----
You are about to be asked to enter information that will be incorporated
into your certificate request.
What you are about to enter is what is called a Distinguished Name or a
DN.
```

```
There are quite a few fields but you can leave some blank
For some fields there will be a default value,
If you enter '.', the field will be left blank.
-----
Country Name (2 letter code) [AU]:US
State or Province Name (full name) [Some-State]:Rhode Island
Locality Name (eg, city) []:Kingston
Organization Name (eg, company) [Internet Widgits Pty Ltd]:Jepstone
Organizational Unit Name (eg, section) []:
Common Name (eg, YOUR name) []:Brian Jepson
Email Address []:bjepson@jepstone.net

Please enter the following 'extra' attributes
to be sent with your certificate request
A challenge password []:
An optional company name []:
Request (and private key) is in newreq.pem
```

3. Now, you must sign the key. The passphrase you must enter in this step should be the passphrase you used when you created the CA:

```
$ /System/Library/OpenSSL/misc/CA.sh -sign
Using configuration from /System/Library/OpenSSL/openssl.cnf
Enter pass phrase for ./demoCA/private/cakey.pem:   ********
Check that the request matches the signature
Signature ok
Certificate Details:
        Serial Number: 1 (0x1)
        Validity
            Not Before: Nov 11 19:34:22 2003 GMT
            Not After : Nov 10 19:34:22 2004 GMT
        Subject:
            countryName             = US
            stateOrProvinceName     = Rhode Island
            localityName            = Kingston
            organizationName        = Jepstone
            commonName              = Brian Jepson
            emailAddress            = bjepson@jepstone.net
        X509v3 extensions:
            X509v3 Basic Constraints:
            CA:FALSE
            Netscape Comment:
            OpenSSL Generated Certificate
            X509v3 Subject Key Identifier:
            1C:AA:2E:32:15:28:83:4B:F4:54:F1:97:87:12:11:45:7C:33:47:96
            X509v3 Authority Key Identifier:
            keyid:DC:C0:D7:A5:69:CA:EE:2B:1C:FA:1C:7A:8A:B2:90:F1:EE:
            1E:49:0C
            DirName:/C=US/ST=Rhode Island/L=Providence/O=Gold and Appel
            Transfers/CN=Hagbard Celine/emailAddress=hagbard@jepstone.net
            serial:00
```

```
Certificate is to be certified until Nov 10 19:34:22 2004 GMT (365 days)
Sign the certificate? [y/n]:y

1 out of 1 certificate requests certified, commit? [y/n]y
[... output truncated ...]
Signed certificate is in newcert.pem
```

At this point, you have two files for use: the signed certificate (~/tmp/
newcert.pem) and the request file, which also contains the server's private
key (~/tmp/newreq.pem). The private key is protected by the passphrase you
supplied when you generated the request. To configure your server for
HTTPS support:

1. Convert the server key so that it doesn't need a passphrase to unlock it
   (you'll need to supply the passphrase you used when you generated the
   request). This removes the protection of the passphrase, but is fine for
   testing. If you don't do this, you'll need to supply a passphrase each
   time Apache starts up (this means you'd need to start your computer in
   verbose mode each time you boot up, or start Apache manually after
   you boot):

   ```
   $ sudo openssl rsa -in newreq.pem -out serverkey.pem
   Enter pass phrase for newreq.pem: ********
   writing RSA key********
   ```

2. Copy these files to a location on your filesystem that's outside of the
   web server's document tree:

   ```
   $ mkdir /Library/WebServer/SSL
   $ cp ~/tmp/serverkey.pem /Library/WebServer/SSL/
   $ cp ~/tmp/newcert.pem /Library/WebServer/SSL/
   ```

3. Add the following lines to *httpd.conf*:

   ```
   <IfModule mod_ssl.c>
     SSLCertificateFile    /Library/WebServer/SSL/newcert.pem
     SSLCertificateKeyFile /Library/WebServer/SSL/serverkey.pem
     SSLEngine on
     Listen 443
   </IfModule>
   ```

4. Stop and restart the web server (it is not enough to use *apachectl
   graceful* when you install a new certificate):

   ```
   $ sudo apachectl stop
   /usr/sbin/apachectl stop: httpd stopped
   $ sudo apachectl start
   Processing config directory: /private/etc/httpd/users/*.conf
    Processing config file: /private/etc/httpd/users/bjepson.conf
   /usr/sbin/apachectl start: httpd started
   ```

Now, try visiting *https://localhost* in a web browser. You should get a warning that an unknown authority signed the server certificate. It's OK to continue past this point.

For more information about configuring *mod_ssl* for Mac OS X, see *Using mod_ssl* at *http://developer.apple.com/internet/macosx/modssl.html*. The *mod_ssl* FAQ includes information on getting a server certificate that's been signed by a trusted CA: *http://www.modssl.org/docs/2.8/ssl_faq.html#cert-real*.

php4_module (mod_php4)

Enable this module to start serving PHP 4 documents from your Macintosh. After you turn on this module and restart Apache, you can install PHP scripts ending with *.php* into your document directories. For example, save the following script as *hello.php* in */Library/WebServer/Documents*:

```
<html>
<head><title>PHP Demo</title></head>
<body>
<?
  foreach (array("#FF0000", "#00FF00", "#0000FF") as $color) {
    echo "<font color=\"$color\">Hello, World<br /></font>";
  }
?>
</body>
</html>
```

Next, open *http://localhost/hello.php* in a web browser; the phrase "Hello, World" should appear in three different colors. If it does not, consult */var/log/httpd/error_log* for messages that might help diagnose what went wrong.

For information on using PHP with MySQL, see Chapter 14.

hfs_apple_module (mod_hfs_apple)

This module is enabled by default, and provides compatibility with the HFS+ filesystem's case insensitivity. For more information, see *http://docs.info.apple.com/article.html?artnum=107310*.

rendezvous_apple_module (mod_rendezvous_apple)

This module is enabled by default. In Jaguar, it advertised the document root (files contained in */Library/WebServer/Documents*) and individual user sites (files contained in *~/Sites*) over Rendezvous (*http://developer.apple.com/macosx/rendezvous/*). As of Mac OS X Panther, *mod_rendezvous* does not automatically advertise these files. Instead, it only advertises user sites whose *index.html* has been modified.

If you are using PHP as the index document (*~/Sites/index.php*), Apache may not register your site as changed, and thus will not advertise it over Rendezvous. For *mod_rendezvous* to notice that a file has changed, you must restart Apache (*sudo apachectl restart*) after a page is modified for the first time.

If you want to override the default *mod_rendezvous* settings and advertise all user sites on your server, change the relevant section of *httpd.conf*. Here is the default configuration for the *mod_rendezvous* section:

```
<IfModule mod_rendezvous_apple.c>
    # Only the pages of users who have edited their
    # default home pages will be advertised on Rendezvous.
    RegisterUserSite customized-users
    #RegisterUserSite all-users

    # Rendezvous advertising for the primary site is off by default.
    #RegisterDefaultSite
</IfModule>
```

To advertise all user sites, comment out the existing `RegisterUserSite` directive, and uncomment the one that specifies the `all-users` options, as shown here:

```
<IfModule mod_rendezvous_apple.c>
    # Only the pages of users who have edited their
    # default home pages will be advertised on Rendezvous.
    #RegisterUserSite customized-users
    RegisterUserSite all-users

    # Rendezvous advertising for the primary site is off by default.
    #RegisterDefaultSite
</IfModule>
```

You can also enable Rendezvous advertising of the primary site by specifying the `RegisterDefaultSite` directive. Sites that are advertised on Rendezvous will appear automatically in Safari's Rendezvous bookmarks (Safari → Preferences → Bookmarks → Include Rendezvous).

Remote Login

When you turn on Remote Login, the OpenSSH server is enabled. This option toggles the `disable` entry in */etc/xinetd.d/ssh*. You can configure the OpenSSH server by editing */etc/sshd_config*. For example, you can configure OpenSSH to allow remote users to request X11 forwarding by uncommenting the line:

```
#X11Forwarding yes
```

to:

```
X11Forwarding yes
```

After you make a change to *sshd_config*, restart *xinetd* with *sudo killall –HUP xinetd*.

FTP Access

When you turn on FTP Access in the Sharing preferences panel, the disable entry in */etc/xinetd.d/ftpd* is toggled on to enable the FTP server. Although Mac OS X comes with an FTP server, its capabilities are limited. We suggest bypassing the FTP server that's included with Mac OS X, and installing ProFTPd via Fink (see Chapter 11).

To install ProFTP, issue the command *fink install proftpd*. You will be prompted to choose which *proftpd* to use; we suggest selecting the default (*proftpd-pam*), since it integrates with Linux-PAM (see Chapter 3):

```
$ fink install proftpd
sudo /sw/bin/fink  install proftpd
Password: ********
Information about 1593 packages read in 2 seconds.

fink needs help picking an alternative to satisfy a virtual dependency. The
candidates:

(1)     proftpd-pam: Incredibly configurable and secure FTP daemon
(Default)
(2)     proftpd-tls: Incredibly configurable and secure FTP daemon (TLS)
(3)     proftpd-ldap: Incredibly configurable and secure FTP daemon (LDAP)
(4)     proftpd-mysql: Incredibly configurable and secure FTP daemon
(MySQL)
(5)     proftpd-pgsql: Incredibly configurable and secure FTP daemon
(PostgreSQL)

Pick one: [1]1
The following package will be installed or updated:
 proftpd
The following 5 additional packages will be installed:
 anacron daemonic ftpfiles libxml2 proftpd-pam
Do you want to continue? [Y/n]Y
```

If you haven't already installed it, you will be asked if you want to enable *anacron*. We suggest doing so, since it will take care of running *cron* jobs that your system misses. However, *anacron* will run only *cron* jobs defined in Fink's */sw/etc* directory, not the Mac OS X *cron* jobs described in the "Scheduling Tasks" section of Chapter 2.

```
Setting up anacron (2.3-4) ...

This script allows you to decide whether you would like for anacron to
run at startup, then to periodically check for system tasks that need
to be run. Alternatively you could run anacron by hand once a day
(by typing `anacron -s' ), though this sort of defeats the purpose of
installing a command scheduler in the first place...
```

```
If you wish to make changes to your anacron settings in the
future, you can run this script again with the command:
update-anacron

Anacron is not currently set up to be run periodically by cron.
Would you like for anacron to be run automatically?
In most cases, you probably want to say yes to this option. [Y/n] Y

Added anacron to task schedule, and will run at startup
```

To switch Mac OS X over to ProFTPd, follow these steps:

1. Backup your existing */etc/xinetd.d/ftp* file (be sure to set the disable option to yes if you decide to back it up to a file in the */etc/xinetd.d* directory; otherwise, *xinetd* will activate both FTP servers) and replace its contents with the following:

   ```
   service ftp
   {
           disable = no
           socket_type     = stream
           instances       = 50
           wait            = no
           user            = root
           server          = /sw/sbin/proftpd
           server_args     = -d9
           groups          = yes
           flags           = REUSE IPv6

   }
   ```

2. The default configuration for Fink's ProFTPd assumes a standalone server. Edit the file */sw/etc/proftpd.conf* and change the line ServerType standalone to ServerType inetd.

3. Next, you must use NetInfo to create an *ftp* user and group. Follow the instructions in Chapter 3 to add a group named *ftp*, and a user named *ftp* that is a member of that group. Do not create a password for this user and be sure to use a gid and uid that are not already in use. For example:

   ```
   $ sudo dscl . create /groups/ftp gid 599
   $ sudo dscl . create /groups/ftp passwd '*'

   $ sudo dscl . create /users/ftp uid 599
   $ sudo dscl . create /users/ftp gid 599
   $ sudo dscl . create /users/ftp shell /usr/bin/false
   $ sudo dscl . create /users/ftp home /Users/ftp
   $ sudo dscl . create /users/ftp realname "Anonymous FTP"
   $ sudo dscl . create /users/ftp passwd \*
   ```

4. Create a home directory for the ftp user (*sudo mkdir /Users/ftp*), and set its owner and group to ftp:ftp (*sudo chown ftp:ftp /Users/ftp*).

5. Finally, restart *xinetd* with *sudo killall –HUP xinetd*. You can also use System Preferences → Sharing to stop and restart it.

To configure ProFTPd as an anonymous-only server, add the following line to */sw/etc/proftpd.conf* at the top-level (that is, not nested in the <Directory> or <Anonymous> elements):

```
<Limit LOGIN>
  DenyAll
</Limit>
```

and finally, add the following to the <Anonymous> element:

```
<Limit LOGIN>
  AllowAll
</Limit>
```

This configuration won't prevent uninformed users from trying to log in and typing their username and password, though, and both will go across the network in plain text. As a security precaution, you should inform users that only anonymous login is allowed (ideally, an anonymous FTP server would have no remote users aside from its administrators, and they'd log in using SSH).

Printer Sharing

When you turn on Printer Sharing, the *cups-lpd* server is enabled. This option toggles the disable entry in */etc/xinetd.d/printer*. For more information, see "Printer Sharing" in Chapter 4.

Internet Sharing and the Firewall

On Mac OS X, the default packet filter rules allow all traffic from any location to come into your computer, using the following *ipfw* rule (65535 is the priority level of the rule, the lowest priority possible):

```
65535 allow ip from any to any
```

When you turn on Internet Sharing (System Preferences → Sharing → Internet), Mac OS X starts the Network Address Translation daemon (*natd*). Mac OS X also adds an additional rule, which has a high priority (00010), and diverts any traffic coming in via the interface *en1* (wired Ethernet) to port 8668, which *natd* listens on:

```
00010 divert 8668 ip from any to any via en1
```

When you enable the firewall (System Preferences → Sharing → Firewall), Mac OS X sets up the following rules to keep traffic from getting into your computer:

```
02000 allow ip from any to any via lo*
02010 deny ip from 127.0.0.0/8 to any in
02020 deny ip from any to 127.0.0.0/8 in
02030 deny ip from 224.0.0.0/3 to any in
```

```
02040 deny tcp from any to 224.0.0.0/3 in
02050 allow tcp from any to any out
02060 allow tcp from any to any established
12190 deny tcp from any to any
```

In addition, the firewall sets up rules for any services you have enabled in the Sharing tab, such as this one, which allows SSH connections:

```
02070 allow tcp from any to any 22 in
```

You can add your own packet filter rules by clicking the New button on the Firewall tab. You can also add your own firewall rules using the *ipfw* utility, but the Firewall tab will remain disabled until you reboot or clear the rules with *sudo ipfw flush*. You may also need to quit and restart the System Preferences application before it notices that you've reset the firewall to the default rules. For more information on the packet filter mechanism that Mac OS X uses, see the *ipfw* manpage.

## CHAPTER 14

MySQL and PostgreSQL

Although there are some great binary distributions for MySQL and PostgreSQL, both build out of the box on Mac OS X. This chapter describes how to install them from source and get them set up so you can start playing with them. Fink is a good first stop for MySQL or PostgreSQL, since you can use it to install a binary build or compile from source.

You can also get MySQL as a binary package from MySQL AB (*http://www.mysql.com*), as well as Server Logistics (*http://www.serverlogistics.com/*). Server Logistics offers a selection of open source packages, one of which is Complete MySQL (*http://www.serverlogistics.com/mysql.php*), which includes the MySQL server, a System Preferences pane for MySQL, ODBC/JDBC drivers, and documentation.

MySQL

To get the source distribution of MySQL, download the latest tarball from *http://www.mysql.com/downloads/*. At the time of this writing, the latest production release was the 4.0.*x* series; we downloaded *mysql-4.0.16.tar.gz*.

Compiling MySQL

To compile MySQL from source:

1. Extract the tarball:

   ```
   $ cd ~/src
   $ tar xvfz ~/Desktop/mysql-4.0.16.tar.gz
   ```

2. Change to the top-level directory that *tar* created and run the configure script. We suggest specifying a prefix of */usr/local/mysql* so it stays out the way of any other binaries you have in */usr/local*.

   ```
   $ cd mysql-4.0.16
   $ ./configure --prefix=/usr/local/mysql
   ```

3. Next, type *make* to compile MySQL. Go get a few cups of coffee (compiling could take 30 minutes or more).

Installing MySQL

If the compilation succeeded, you're ready to install MySQL. If not, you should first search the MySQL mailing list archives (*http://lists.mysql.com*) to see if anyone has reported the same problem you experienced, and whether a fix is available (otherwise, you should submit a bug report). If you're having a lot of trouble here, you may want to install one of the binary packages. If everything went OK, you can now install MySQL:

1. Run *make install* as root:

   ```
   $ sudo make install
   ```

2. Install the default databases:

   ```
   $ sudo ./scripts/mysql_install_db
   ```

3. Set permissions on the MySQL directories:

   ```
   $ sudo chown -R root  /usr/local/mysql
   $ sudo chown -R mysql /usr/local/mysql/var
   $ sudo chgrp -R mysql /usr/local/mysql
   ```

4. Install a configuration file (*my-small.cnf*, *my-medium.cnf*, *my-large.cnf*, or *my-huge.cnf*):

   ```
   $ sudo cp support-files/my-medium.cnf /etc/my.cnf
   ```

5. Now you're ready to install a startup script for MySQL. See "Startup Items" in Chapter 2 for a sample MySQL startup script. (For now, leave out the --password=*password* from the startup script. You can add it back in, with the appropriate password, after you set the MySQL root password.) After you've created the startup script, start MySQL:

   ```
   $ sudo SystemStarter start MySQL
   ```

Configuring MySQL

Next, you need to configure MySQL. At a minimum, set the root user's password and create a user and a working database for that user. Before using MySQL, add the following line to your *.bash_profile* and start a new Terminal window to pick up the settings:

```
export PATH=$PATH:/usr/local/mysql/bin
```

To set the root password and create a new user:

1. Use *mysqladmin* to set a password for the root user (qualified as *root@localhost* and just plain old *root*). When you enter the second line,

there will be a root password in place, so you need to use –p, and you'll be prompted for the password you created on the first line:

```
$ mysqladmin -u root password 'password'
$ mysqladmin -u root -p -h localhost password 'password'
Enter password: ********
```

2. Create a database for your user (you'll be prompted for the *mysql* root user's password):

```
$ mysqladmin  -u root -p create dbname
Enter password: ********
```

3. Log into the *mysql* shell as root, and grant full control over that database to your user, qualified as *user@localhost* and just the username alone (the -> prompt indicates that you pressed return without completing the command, and the *mysql* shell is waiting for more input):

```
$ mysql -u root -p
Enter password: ********
Welcome to the MySQL monitor.  Commands end with ; or \g.
Your MySQL connection id is 12 to server version: 4.0.16-log

Type 'help;' or '\h' for help. Type '\c' to clear the buffer.

mysql> GRANT ALL PRIVILEGES ON dbname.* TO username@localhost
    -> IDENTIFIED BY 'password';
Query OK, 0 rows affected (0.08 sec)

mysql> GRANT ALL PRIVILEGES ON dbname.* TO username
    -> IDENTIFIED BY 'password';
Query OK, 0 rows affected (0.00 sec)

mysql> quit
Bye
```

Playing with MySQL

You should be able to log in to MySQL as the user defined in the previous section, and do whatever you want within your database:

```
$ mysql -u username -p dbname
Enter password: ********
Welcome to the MySQL monitor.  Commands end with ; or \g.
Your MySQL connection id is 16 to server version: 4.0.16-log

Type 'help;' or '\h' for help. Type '\c' to clear the buffer.

mysql> CREATE TABLE foo (bar CHAR(10));
Query OK, 0 rows affected (0.06 sec)

mysql> INSERT INTO foo VALUES('Hello');
Query OK, 1 row affected (0.00 sec)
```

```
mysql> INSERT INTO foo VALUES('World');
Query OK, 1 row affected (0.01 sec)

mysql> SELECT * FROM foo;
+-------+
| bar   |
+-------+
| Hello |
| World |
+-------+
2 rows in set (0.00 sec)

mysql> quit
Bye
```

PostgreSQL

To get the source distribution of PostgreSQL, download the latest tarball from one of the mirrors at *http://www.postgresql.org/mirrors-ftp.html*. At the time of this writing, the latest release was 7.4, so we downloaded *postgresql-7.4.tar.bz2*.

Compiling PostgreSQL

Before installing PostgreSQL, you must install readline (*http://www.gnu.org/directory/readline.html*). This program enables support for command-line editing and history in the PostgreSQL shell (*psql*). Use *fink install readline* to install it, if you have Fink installed. You also need the most recent version of *bison* (*http://www.gnu.org/software/bison/bison.html*), which you can obtain with *fink install bison* (double check to ensure that */sw/bin* appears first in your $PATH; this is the default after you've installed Fink).

To compile PostgreSQL from source:

1. Extract the tarball:

   ```
   $ cd ~/src
   $ tar xvfj ~/Desktop/postgresql-7.4.tar.bz2
   ```

2. Change to the top-level directory of the tar and run the *configure* script. We suggest specifying a prefix of */usr/local/pgsql* so it stays out the way of any other binaries you have in */usr/local*.

   ```
   $ cd postgresql-7.4
   $ ./configure --prefix=/usr/local/pgsql \
   >   --with-includes=/sw/include --with-libs=/sw/lib
   ```

3. Next, type *make* to compile PostgreSQL. Go take a walk around the block while you wait (compiling could take 30 minutes or more).

Installing PostgreSQL

If everything went OK, you're ready to install. If it didn't go OK, check the PostgreSQL mail list archives (*http://www.postgresql.org/lists.html*) to see if anyone has reported the same problem you experienced and whether a fix is available (otherwise, you should submit a bug report).

1. Run *make install* as root:

   ```
   $ sudo make install
   ```

2. Create the *postgres* group and user (this is the PostgreSQL superuser). Be sure to choose an unused group ID and user ID:

   ```
   $ sudo niload group . <<EOF
   > postgres:*:1001:
   > EOF
   $ sudo niload passwd . <<EOF
   > postgres:*:1001:1001::0:0:PostgreSQL:/usr/local/pgsql:/bin/bash
   > EOF
   ```

3. Create the data subdirectory and make sure that the *postgres* user is the owner of that directory:

   ```
   $ sudo mkdir /usr/local/pgsql/data
   $ sudo chown postgres /usr/local/pgsql/data
   ```

4. Use *sudo* to get a shell as the *postgres* user (supply your own password at this prompt):

   ```
   $ sudo -u postgres -s
   Password: ********
   postgres$
   ```

5. Run the following commands to initialize the PostgreSQL installation:

   ```
   $ /usr/local/pgsql/bin/initdb -D /usr/local/pgsql/data
   ```

6. You can now log out of the *postgres* user's shell.

Adding the Startup Item

Now you're ready to create a startup script for PostgreSQL (see "Adding Startup Items" in Chapter 2). First, create the script shown in Example 14-1, save it as */Library/StartupItems/PostgreSQL/PostgreSQL*, and mark it as an executable.

Example 14-1. Startup script for PostgreSQL

```
#!/bin/sh

# Source common setup, including hostconfig.
#
. /etc/rc.common
```

Example 14-1. Startup script for PostgreSQL (continued)

```
StartService( )
{
    # Don't start unless PostgreSQL is enabled in /etc/hostconfig
    if [ "${PGSQL:=-NO-}" = "-YES-" ]; then
        ConsoleMessage "Starting PostgreSQL"
        sudo -u postgres /usr/local/pgsql/bin/pg_ctl  \
          -D /usr/local/pgsql/data \
          -l /usr/local/pgsql/data/logfile start
    fi
}

StopService( )
{
    ConsoleMessage "Stopping PostgreSQL"
    /usr/local/pgsql/bin/pg_ctl -D /usr/local/pgsql/data stop
}

RestartService( )
{
    # Don't restart unless PostgreSQL is enabled in /etc/hostconfig
    if [ "${PGSQL:=-NO-}" = "-YES-" ]; then
        ConsoleMessage "Restarting PostgreSQL"
        StopService
        StartService
    else
        StopService
    fi
}

RunService "$1"
```

Next, create the following file as */Library/StartupItems/PostgreSQL/ StartupParameters.plist*:

```
{
  Description      = "PostgreSQL";
  Provides         = ("PostgreSQL");
  Requires         = ("Network");
  OrderPreference = "Late";
}
```

Then, add the following line to */etc/hostconfig*:

```
PGSQL=-YES-
```

Now PostgreSQL will start automatically when you reboot the system. If you want, you can start PostgreSQL right away with:

```
$ sudo SystemStarter start PostgreSQL
```

Configuring PostgreSQL

Before you proceed, you should add the following line to the *.bash_profile* and start a new Terminal window to pick up the settings (you should also add this to the *postgres* user's *.bash_profile*):

```
export PATH=$PATH:/usr/local/pgsql/bin
```

By default, PostgreSQL comes with weak permissions; any local user can connect to the database without authentication. Before changing anything, you must start a shell as the *postgres* user with *sudo* and stay in this shell until the end of this section:

```
$ sudo -u postgres -s
Password: ********
postgres$
```

To start locking things down and to set up a non-privileged user:

1. Create the *postgres* user's home database

   ```
   $ createdb
   ```

2. Set a password for the PostgreSQL superuser:

   ```
   postgres$ psql -U postgres -c \
   >    "alter user postgres with password 'password';"
   ```

3. Under the default permissions, any local user can impersonate another user. So, even though you've set a password, it's not doing any good! You should edit */usr/local/pgsql/data/pg_hba.conf* to require MD5 passwords, give the *postgres* user control over all databases, and change the configuration so users have total control over databases that have the same name as their username. To do this, change *pg_hba.conf* to read:

   ```
   # TYPE DATABASE USER      IP-ADDR    IP-MASK                                 METHOD
   local  all      postgres                                                     md5
   local  sameuser all                                                          md5
   host   all      postgres 127.0.0.1 255.255.255.255                           md5
   host   sameuser all       127.0.0.1 255.255.255.255                          md5
   host   all      postgres ::1 ffff:ffff:ffff:ffff:ffff:ffff:ffff:ffff md5
   host   sameuser all       ::1 ffff:ffff:ffff:ffff:ffff:ffff:ffff:ffff md5
   ```

4. Once you've made this change, reload the configuration with *pg_ctl* (from here on in, you'll be prompted for a password when you run *psql* as the *postgres* user):

   ```
   postgres$ pg_ctl -D /usr/local/pgsql/data reload
   ```

5. Now you're ready to add a normal user. Use the *psql* command to create the user and a database. Because the username and database name are the same, that user will be granted access to the database:

   ```
   postgres$ psql -U postgres -c "create database username;"
   Password: ********
   CREATE DATABASE
   ```

```
postgres$ psql -U postgres -c \
>    "create user username with password 'password';"
Password: ********
CREATE USER
```

To give more than one user access to a database, create a group with the
same name as the database (for example, *create group databasename*), and
create users with the *create user* command as shown in step 5. Finally, add
each user to the group with this command:

```
alter group databasename add user username
```

Playing with PostgreSQL

After configuring PostgreSQL's security and setting up an unprivileged user,
you can log in as that user and play around with the database:

```
$ psql -U username
Password: ********
Welcome to psql 7.4, the PostgreSQL interactive terminal.

Type:  \copyright for distribution terms
       \h for help with SQL commands
       \? for help on internal slash commands
       \g or terminate with semicolon to execute query
       \q to quit

username=> CREATE TABLE foo (bar CHAR(10));
CREATE TABLE
username=> INSERT INTO foo VALUES('Hello');
INSERT 17148 1
username=> INSERT INTO foo VALUES('World');
INSERT 17149 1
username=> SELECT * FROM foo;
    bar
------------
 Hello
 World
(2 rows)

username-> \q
```

For more information on building and using PostgreSQL, see *Practical
PostgreSQL* by John C. Worsley and Joshua D. Drake (O'Reilly). *Practical
PostgreSQL* covers installing, using, administrating, and programming
PostgreSQL.

PHP and Perl

On Mac OS X Panther, MySQL support is built in to PHP. If you want Post-greSQL support, you must reinstall PHP from source.

You can install general database support in Perl by installing the DBI module with the *cpan* utility (see Chapter 10). After that, you can install the DBD::mysql module for MySQL-specific support, and DBD::Pg for Postgr-eSQL-specific support. Because there are some steps to these installations that the *cpan* utility can't handle, you should download the latest builds of these modules from *http://www.cpan.org/modules/by-module/DBD/* and install them manually. Be sure to check the *README* files, since some aspects of the configuration may have changed.

The DBD:mysql module requires a database in which to perform its tests. You can use the database and username/password that you set up earlier in *Configuring MySQL*. To install DBD::mysql, you must first generate the *Makefile*, compile the code, test it, and then install the module if the test run is successful. For example:

```
$ perl Makefile.PL --testdb=dbname --testuser=username \
>  --testpassword=password
$ make
$ make test
$ sudo make install
```

> At the time of this writing, DBD::mysql failed to compile on Panther. The short description of the fix is to replace all occurrences of *MACOSX* with *env MACOSX* in the *Makefile* (after generating it with *perl Makefile.PL*).
>
> For a complete description, see the *Forwarding Address: OS X* weblog entry at *http://www.saladwithsteve.com/osx/2003_11_01_archive.html#106802251200041735*.

As with DBD::mysql, the DBD::Pg module needs a directory to perform its tests. If you'd like, you can use the database, username, and password that you set up earlier when configuring PostgreSQL.

You must first generate the *Makefile*, compile the code, set up environment variables that specify the database, username, and password, and then run the tests. If the tests run successfully, you can install DBD::Pg:

```
$ perl Makefile.PL
$ make
$ export DBI_DSN=dbi:Pg:dbname=username
$ export DBI_USER=username
$ export DBI_PASS=password
$ make test
$ sudo make install
```

CHAPTER 15

System Management Tools

Mac OS X comes with many tools for tweaking and spying on various aspects of your system, including memory, kernel modules, and kernel state variables. Some of these tools come directly from BSD, while others are unique to Mac OS X. Most of the BSD-derived utilities have been filtered through Mach and NeXTSTEP on their way to Mac OS X.

For more details on any of these utilities, see their respective manpages.

Diagnostic Utilities

Mac OS X includes many diagnostic utilities that you can use to monitor your system and investigate problems.

top

The *top* utility displays memory statistics and a list of running processes. It is divided into two regions: the top region contains memory statistics, and the bottom region contains details on each process.

You can specify the number of processes to show by supplying a numeric argument. By default, *top* refreshes its display every second and sorts the list of processes by process ID (PID) in descending order. You can set *top* to sort by CPU utilization with *-u*, and you can specify the refresh delay with the *-s* option. Figure 15-1 shows the output of *top -u 10* (if you wanted to refresh the output every 3 seconds, you could run *top -s3 -u 10*).

Table 15-1 describes the values shown in the top region, and Table 15-2 describes the columns in the bottom region (process information).

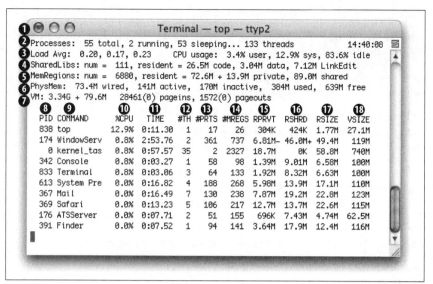

Figure 15-1. Sample output from top

Table 15-1. Memory information displayed by top

Item number	Item	Description
1	Processes	Number of processes and threads. A running process is currently using CPU time, while a sleeping process is not.
2	Load Avg.	Average system load (the number of jobs vying for the CPU's attention) over the last 1, 5, and 15 minutes.
3	CPU usage	Breakdown of CPU usage, listing time spent in user mode, kernel (sys) mode, and idle time.
4	SharedLibs	Number of shared libraries in use, along with their memory utilization.
5	MemRegions	Number of Mach virtual memory regions in use, along with memory utilization details.
6	PhysMem	Physical memory utilization. Memory that is wired cannot be swapped to disk. active memory is memory that's currently being used, inactive memory is memory that Mac OS X is keeping "on deck" for processes that need it, and free memory is memory that's not being used at all.
7	VM	Virtual memory statistics, including the total amount of virtual memory allocated (the sum of the VSIZE in the process list), as well as paging activity (data paged in and out of physical memory).

Table 15-2. Process information displayed by top

Item number	Item	Description
8	PID	Process ID
9	COMMAND	Program's name
10	%CPU	Percentage of the CPU that the process is using
11	TIME	Total amount of CPU time this process has used
12	#TH	Number of threads in this process
13	#PRTS	Number of Mach ports
14	#MREGS	Number of memory registers
15	RPRVT	Resident private memory
16	RSHRD	Resident shared memory
17	RSIZE	Resident memory
18	VSIZE	Process's total address space, including shared memory

fs_usage

The *fs_usage* utility shows a continuous display of filesystem-related system calls and page faults. You must run *fs_usage* as *root*. By default, it ignores anything originating from *fs_usage*, *Terminal*, *telnetd*, *sshd*, *rlogind*, *tcsh*, *csh*, or *sh*.

Figure 15-2 shows the output of *fs_usage*, which displays the following columns:

- Timestamp
- System call
- Filename
- Elapsed time
- Name of the process

latency

latency measures the number of context switches and interrupts, and reports on the resulting delays, updating the display once per second. This utility must be run as *root*. Example 15-1 shows a portion of its output.

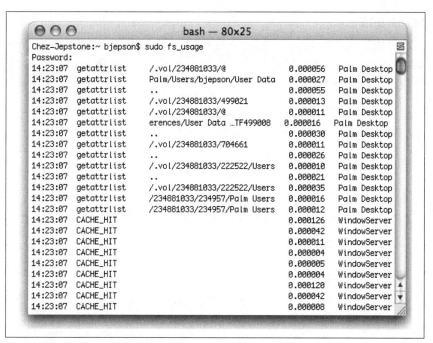

Figure 15-2. Monitoring filesystem operations with fs_usage

Example 15-1. Partial output from latency

Tue Dec 30 14:33:41			0:07:00
	SCHEDULER	INTERRUPTS	
total_samples	339307	548794	
delays < 10 usecs	296044	547403	
delays < 20 usecs	17033	1199	
delays < 30 usecs	5376	158	
delays < 40 usecs	3020	29	
delays < 50 usecs	1147	5	
delays < 60 usecs	812	0	
delays < 70 usecs	497	0	
delays < 80 usecs	358	0	
delays < 90 usecs	354	0	
delays < 100 usecs	308	0	
total < 100 usecs	324949	548794	

The SCHEDULER column lists the number of context switches and the INTER-RUPTS column lists the number of interrupts.

sc_usage

The *sc_usage* utility samples system calls and page faults, then displays them onscreen. *sc_usage* must be run by *root* or by someone with superuser privileges. The display is updated once per second. You must specify a PID, a command name, or a program to execute with the *-E* switch. For example, to monitor the Finder, use *sudo sc_usage Finder*. Figure 15-3 shows the output of running *sc_usage* on the Finder. Table 15-3 explains *sc_usage*'s output.

```
 ● ● ●                    sc_usage — 80x25
Finder              0 preemptions    4 context switches   2 threads    15:22:29
                    0 faults         8 system calls                    0:42:09
 ❶                              ❷           ❸           ❹
TYPE                          NUMBER     CPU_TIME   WAIT_TIME
--------------------------------------------------------------------------------
System     Idle                                    36:24.410( 0:00.943)
System     Busy                                     5:39.674( 0:00.059)
Finder     Usermode                      0:02.748

zero_fill                       1271     0:00.020   0:00.003
pagein                            36     0:00.004   0:00.489
cache_hit                       2440     0:00.028   0:00.046

mach_msg_trap                12720(4)    0:00.146  73:28.758( 0:01.002) W
semaphore_timedwait_sig          205     0:00.003   4:08.970( 0:01.003) W
pread_extended                   235     0:00.042   0:00.669
semaphore_wait_signal_t          868     0:00.004   0:00.431
pwrite_extended                  237     0:00.056   0:00.411
clock_sleep_trap                 986     0:00.011   0:00.379
mach_wait_until                   19     0:00.000   0:00.220
 ❺                        ❻                         ❼        ❽  ❾
CURRENT_TYPE          LAST_PATHNAME_WAITED_FOR   CUR_WAIT_TIME THRD# PRI
--------------------------------------------------------------------------------
mach_msg_trap         /.vol/234881033/9148          0:00.112    0   46
semaphore_timedwait_sig                             0:09.001    1   47
```

Figure 15-3. sc_usage monitoring the Finder

Table 15-3. Information displayed by sc_usage

Item number	Row	Description
1	TYPE	System call type
2	NUMBER	System call count
3	CPU_TIME	Processor time used by the system call
4	WAIT_TIME	Absolute time that the process spent waiting
5	CURRENT_TYPE	Current system call type
6	LAST_PATHNAME_WAITED_FOR	Last file or directory that resulted in a blocked I/O operation during a system call
7	CUR_WAIT_TIME	Cumulative time spent blocked
8	THRD#	Thread ID
9	PRI	Scheduling priority

vm_stat

The *vm_stat* utility displays virtual memory statistics. Unlike implementations of *vm_stat* in other Unix systems, it does not default to continuous display. Instead, it displays accumulated statistics.

To obtain a continuous display, specify an interval argument (in seconds), as in *vm_stat 1*. Figure 15-4 shows the output of *vm_stat* with no arguments.

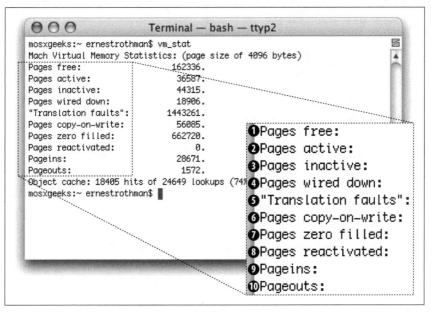

Figure 15-4. vm_stat displaying accumulated statistics

Figure 15-5 shows the output of *vm_stat 1*. Table 15-4 describes the information that *vm_stat* displays (the item numbers correspond to the callouts in both figures).

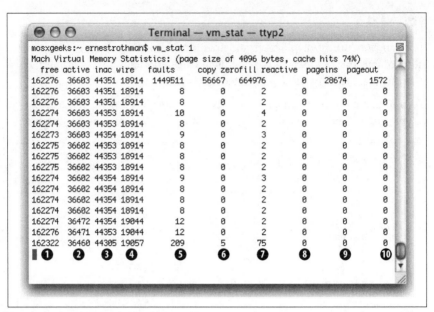

Figure 15-5. vm_stat's continuous output

Table 15-4. Information displayed by vm_stat

Item number	Accumulated mode	Continuous mode	Description
1	Pages free	free	Total free pages
2	Pages active	active	Total pages in use that can be paged out
3	Pages inactive	inac	Total inactive pages
4	Pages wired down	wire	Total pages wired into memory (cannot be paged out)
5	Translation Faults	faults	Number of times *vm_fault* has been called
6	Pages copy-on-write	copy	Number of faults that resulted in a page being copied
7	Pages zero filled	zerofill	Number of pages that have been zero-filled
8	Pages Reactivated	reactive	Number of pages reclassified from inactive to active
9	Pageins	pagein	Number of pages moved into physical memory
10	Pageouts	pageout	Number of pages moved out of physical memory

Kernel Utilities

Mac OS X includes various utilities that interact with the kernel. With these utilities, you can debug a running kernel, load and unload kernel modules or extensions, or set kernel variables.

ddb

The *ddb* utility can debug a running kernel. It is not included with the current version of Mac OS X. If you want to use *ddb*, you can find its source code in the *xnu* (Darwin kernel) source code (*http://www.opensource.apple.com/darwinsource/*).

ktrace

Use *ktrace* to perform kernel tracing (tracing system calls and other operations) on a process. To launch a program and generate a kernel trace (*ktrace.out*, which is not human-readable), use *ktrace command*, as in *ktrace emacs*. Kernel tracing ends when you exit the process or disable tracing with *ktrace -cp* pid. You can get human readable output from a *ktrace* file with *kdump*.

Kernel Module Utilities

The following list describes utilities for manipulating kernel modules. For more information, see the kernel extension tutorials available at *http://www.opensource.apple.com/projects/documentation/howto*. These utilities must be run with superuser privileges:

kextload
> Loads an extension bundle.

kextunload
> Unloads an extension bundle.

kextstat
> Displays the status of currently loaded kernel extensions. Table 15-5 describes this utility's output. Figure 15-6 shows sample output.

Table 15-5. -Information displayed by kextstat

Item number	Column	Description
1	Index	Index number of the loaded extension. Extensions are loaded in sequence; gaps in this sequence signify extensions that have been unloaded.
2	Refs	Number of references to this extension from other extensions.
3	Address	Kernel space address of the extension.
4	Size	Amount of kernel memory (in bytes) used by the extension.
5	Wired	Amount of *wired* kernel memory (in bytes) used by the extension.
6	Name (Version)	Name and version of the extension.
7	<Linked Against>	Index of kernel extensions to which this extension refers.

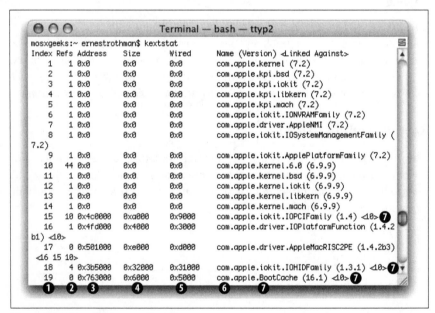

Figure 15-6. Partial output of kextstat

sysctl

sysctl is a standard BSD facility for configuring kernel state variables. Use *sysctl name* to display a variable name, as in *sysctl kern.ostype*. Use *sysctl -a* to display all variables. If you have superuser privileges, you can set a variable with *sysctl -w name=value*.

Table 15-6 lists the *sysctl* variables on Mac OS X. See the *sysctl(3)* manpage for a description of the *sysctl* system call and more detailed information on the kernel state variables.

Table 15-6. sysctl's kernel state variables

Name	Type	Writable	Description
hw.activecpu	int	no	The number of CPUs currently active and available (may be affected by power management settings).
hw.busfrequency	int	no	Bus frequency in hertz. Divide by one million for a megahertz figure.
hw.busfrequency_max	int	no	Maximum bus frequency in hertz.
hw.busfrequency_min	int	no	Minimum bus frequency in hertz.
hw.byteorder	int	no	Variable that returns 4321, showing the ordering of four bytes on the PowerPC platform.
hw.cachelinesize	int	no	The cache line size in bytes.
hw.cpufrequency	int	no	CPU frequency in hertz. Divide by one million for a megahertz figure.
hw.cpufrequency_max	int	no	Maximum CPU frequency in hertz.
hw.cpufrequency_min	int	no	Minimum CPU frequency in hertz.
hw.cpusubtype	int	no	The mach-o subtype of the CPU (see */System/ Library/Frameworks/Kernel.framework/ Versions/A/Headers/mach/machine.h*).
hw.cputype	int	no	The mach-o type of the CPU.
hw.epoch	int	no	Variable that indicates whether your hardware is "New World" or "Old World." Old World Macintoshes (pre-G3) have a value of 0.
hw.l1dcachesize	int	no	Level 1 data cache size in bytes.
hw.l1icachesize	int	no	Level 1 instruction cache size in bytes.
hw.l2cachesize	int	no	Level 2 cache size in bytes.
hw.l2settings	int	no	Level 2 cache settings.
hw.l3cachesize	int	no	Level 3 cache size in bytes.
hw.l3settings	int	no	Level 3 cache settings.
hw.machine	string	no	Machine class (*Power Macintosh* on most systems).
hw.model	string	no	Machine model.
hw.ncpu	int	no	Number of CPUs.
hw.optional.altivec	int	no	Indicates whether AltiVec is enabled.
hw.optional.datastreams	int	no	Indicates whether PowerPC data stream instructions are supported by the CPU.

Table 15-6. sysctl's kernel state variables (continued)

Name	Type	Writable	Description
hw.optional.dcba	int	no	Indicates whether the PowerPC DCBA instruction is supported by the CPU.
hw.optional.floatingpoint	int	no	Indicates whether floating point operations are supported by the CPU.
hw.optional.graphicsops	int	no	Indicates whether graphics operations are supported by the CPU.
hw.optional.stfiwx	int	no	Indicates whether the PowerPC STFIWX instruction is supported by the CPU.
hw.pagesize	int	no	Software page size in bytes.
hw.physmem	int	no	Physical memory in bytes.
hw.tbfrequency	int	no	The base frequency used by Mac OS X for its timing services.
hw.usermem	int	no	Non-kernel memory.
hw.vectorunit	int	no	Variable that indicates whether you are running on an AltiVec-enabled CPU.
kern.aiomax	int	no	Maximum AIO requests.
kern.aioprocmax	int	no	Maximum AIO requests per process.
kern.aiothreads	int	no	Maximum number of AIO worker threads.
kern.argmax	int	no	Maximum number of arguments supported by exec( ).
kern.boottime	struct timeval	no	The time when the system was booted.
kern.clockrate	struct clockinfo	no	System clock timings.
kern.dummy	n/a	n/a	Unused.
kern.hostid	int	yes	Host identifier.
kern.hostname	string	yes	Hostname.
kern.ipc.*	various	n/a	Various IPC settings.
kern.job_control	int	no	Variable that indicates whether job control is available.
kern.maxfiles	int	yes	Maximum number of open files.
kern.maxfilesperproc	int	yes	Maximum number of open files per process .
kern.maxproc	int	yes	Maximum number of simultaneous processes.
kern.maxprocperuid	int	yes	Maximum number of simultaneous processes per user.
kern.maxvnodes	int	yes	Maximum number of vnodes.
kern.netboot	int	no	Variable that indicates whether the system booted via NetBoot.
kern.ngroups	int	no	Maximum number of supplemental groups.

Table 15-6. sysctl's kernel state variables (continued)

Name	Type	Writable	Description
kern.nisdomainname	string	yes	NIS domain name.
kern.osrelease	string	no	Operating system release version.
kern.osrevision	int	no	Operating system revision.
kern.ostype	string	no	Operating system name.
kern.posix1version	int	no	The version of POSIX 1003.1 with which the system attempts to comply.
kern.saved_ids	int	no	This is set to 1 if saved set-group and set-user IDs are available.
kern.securelevel	int	increment only	The system security level.
kern.symfile	string	no	The kernel symbol file.
kern.sysv.*	various	n/a	System V semaphore settings. See */System/ Library/Frameworks/Kernel.framework/ Versions/A/Headers/sys/sysctl.h*.
kern.sysv.shmall	int	yes	The maximum size of a shared memory segment.
kern.sysv.shmmax	int	yes	The maximum number of shared memory pages.
kern.sysv.shmmin	int	yes	The maximum number of shared memory segments per process.
kern.sysv.shmmni	int	yes	The maximum number of shared memory segments.
kern.sysv.shmseg	int	yes	The minimum size of a shared memory segment.
kern.version	string	no	The kernel version string.
net.appletalk.routermix			Description unavailable at time of printing. Please see the errata at *http://www.oreilly. com/catalog/mpantherunix/*.
net.inet.*	various	n/a	IPv4 settings.
net.inet6.*	various	n/a	IPv6 settings.
net.key.*	various	n/a	IPSec key management settings.
net.link.ether.inet.*	various	n/a	Ethernet settings.
net.local.*	various	n/a	Description unavailable at time of printing. Please see the errata at *http://www.oreilly. com/catalog/mpantherunix/*.
user.bc_base_max	int	no	Maximum ibase/obase available in the *bc* calculator.
user.bc_dim_max	int	no	Maximum array size available in the *bc* calculator.

Table 15-6. sysctl's kernel state variables (continued)

Name	Type	Writable	Description
user.bc_scale_max	int	no	Maximum scale value available in the *bc* calculator.
user.bc_string_max	int	no	Maximum string length available in the *bc* calculator.
user.coll_weights_max	int	no	Maximum number of weights that can be used with LC_COLLATE in the locale definition file.
user.cs_path	string	no	Value for PATH that can find all the standard utilities.
user.expr_nest_max	int	no	Maximum number of expressions you can nest within parentheses using *expr*.
user.line_max	int	no	Maximum length in bytes of an input line used with a text-processing utility.
user.posix2_c_bind	int	no	Variable that returns 1 if the C development environment supports the POSIX C Language Bindings Option; otherwise, the result will be 0.
user.posix2_c_dev	int	no	Variable that returns 1 if the C development environment supports the POSIX C Language Development Utilities Option; otherwise, the result will be 0.
user.posix2_char_term	int	no	Variable that returns 1 if the systems supports at least one terminal type specified in POSIX 1003.2; otherwise, the result will be 0.
user.posix2_fort_dev	int	no	Variable that returns 1 if the system supports the POSIX FORTRAN Development Utilities Option; otherwise, the result will be 0.
user.posix2_fort_run	int	no	Variable that returns 1 if the system supports the POSIX FORTRAN Runtime Utilities Option; otherwise, the result will be 0.
user.posix2_localedef	int	no	Variable that returns 1 if the system allows you to create locale; otherwise, the result will be 0.
user.posix2_sw_dev	int	no	Variable that returns 1 if the system supports the POSIX Software Development Utilities Option; otherwise, the result will be 0.
user.posix2_upe	int	no	Variable that returns 1 if the system supports the POSIX User Portable Utilities Option; otherwise, the result will be 0.
user.posix2_version	int	no	Variable that returns the POSIX 1003.2 version with which the system attempts to comply.
user.re_dup_max	int	no	Maximum repeated occurrences of a regular expression when using interval notation.

Table 15-6. sysctl's kernel state variables (continued)

Name	Type	Writable	Description
user.stream_max	int	no	Maximum number of streams a process may have open.
user.tzname_max	int	no	Maximum number of types supported for a time zone name.
vfs.*	various	n/a	Various VFS settings.
vm.loadavg	string	no	Current load average.

System Configuration

Although you can perform most system configuration through the System Preferences program, the *scutil* and *defaults* commands let you poke around under the hood. You can get even further under the hood with the *nvram* command (perhaps further than most people would need or want to get).

scutil

Mac OS X stores network configuration in a database called the dynamic store. You can get at this database using *scutil*, the system configuration utility. Before you can do anything, you must connect to the configuration daemon (*configd*) with the *open* command (*close* the session with the close command, and exit scutil with *quit*):

```
Chez-Jepstone:~ bjepson$ sudo scutil
Password: ********
> open
```

List the contents (a collection of keys) of the configuration database with the *list* command. The following shows abbreviated output from this command:

```
> list
  subKey [0] = DirectoryService:PID
  subKey [1] = Plugin:IPConfiguration
  subKey [2] = Setup:
  subKey [3] = Setup:/
  subKey [4] = Setup:/Network/Global/IPv4
  subKey [5] = Setup:/Network/HostNames
  subKey [6] = Setup:/Network/Service/0
  subKey [7] = Setup:/Network/Service/0/Ethernet
  subKey [8] = Setup:/Network/Service/0/IPv4
  subKey [9] = Setup:/Network/Service/0/IPv6
  subKey [10] = Setup:/Network/Service/0/Interface
  subKey [11] = Setup:/Network/Service/0/Proxies
```

You can show the contents of a key with the show command. The contents of a key are stored as a dictionary (key/value pairs). For example, here are the default proxy settings for built-in Ethernet on Mac OS X (use *show Setup:/Network/Service/0/Interface* to verify that Service 0 shows a *UserDefinedName* of *Built-in Ethernet*):

```
> show Setup:/Network/Service/0/Proxies
<dictionary> {
  RTSPEnable : 0
  HTTPSEnable : 0
  SOCKSEnable : 0
  FTPPassive : 1
  GopherEnable : 0
}
```

Here are the proxy settings for a Mac OS X machine that's been configured to use a proxy server:

```
> show Setup:/Network/Service/0/Proxies
<dictionary> {
  RTSPEnable : 0
  HTTPSEnable : 0
  SOCKSEnable : 0
  FTPPassive : 1
  GopherEnable : 0
  HTTPPort : 8080
  HTTPProxy : 192.168.254.1
  HTTPEnable : 1
}
```

To change an entry, lock the database, initialize an empty dictionary entry with *d.init*, and get the current values of the key you want to change:

```
> lock
> d.init
> get Setup:/Network/Service/0/Proxies
```

Make your changes to the dictionary, then check them with *d.show*:

```
> d.add HTTPPort 8888
> d.add HTTPProxy proxy.nowhere.oreilly.com
> d.add HTTPEnable 1
> d.show
<dictionary> {
  FTPPassive : 1
  HTTPPort : 8888
  HTTPEnable : 1
  RTSPEnable : 0
  HTTPProxy : proxy.nowhere.oreilly.com
  GopherEnable : 0
  HTTPSEnable : 0
  SOCKSEnable : 0
}
```

If you are happy with the dictionary values, set the key (this copies the dictionary into the specified key), unlock the database, and examine the key:

```
> set Setup:/Network/Service/0/Proxies
> unlock
> show Setup:/Network/Service/0/Proxies
<dictionary> {
  RTSPEnable : 0
  HTTPSEnable : 0
  SOCKSEnable : 0
  FTPPassive : 1
  GopherEnable : 0
  HTTPPort : 8888
  HTTPProxy : proxy.nowhere.oreilly.com
  HTTPEnable : 1
}
```

Be careful while the database is locked. If you try to do something seemingly innocuous, such as switching network location, you could cause the system to behave erratically. It's best to get in and out of the database as quickly as possible.

defaults

When you customize your Mac using the System Preferences, most of those changes and settings are stored in what's known as the defaults system. Nearly everything that you've done to make your Mac your own is stored as XML data in the form of a *property list* (or *plist*). This property list is, in turn, stored in *~/Library/Preferences*.

Every time you change one of those settings, that particular property list is updated. For the initiated, there are two other ways to alter the property lists. The first is by using the Property List Editor application (*/Developer/ Applications/Utilities*) and the other is by using the *defaults* command in the Terminal. Whether you use System Preferences, Property List Editor, or the *defaults* command, any changes you make affect the current user.

Using the *defaults* command is not for the foolhardy. If you manage to mangle your settings, the easiest way to correct the problem is to go back to that application's Preferences pane and reset your preferences. In some cases, you can use *defaults delete*, which will be reset to the same defaults when you next log in. Since the *defaults* command affects only the current user, you could also create a user just for testing random *defaults* tips you pick up on the Internet.

Here are some examples of what you can do with the *defaults* command. For more information, see the manpage:

View all of the user defaults on your system
```
$ defaults domains
```
This command prints a listing of all of the *domains* in the user's defaults system. The list you'll see is run together with spaces in between—not quite the prettiest way to view the information.

View the settings for your Terminal
```
$ defaults read com.apple.Terminal
```
This command reads the settings from the *com.apple.Terminal.plist* file, found in *~/Library/Preferences*. This listing is rather long, so you might want to pipe the output to *less* or *more* to view the contents one screen at a time:
```
$ defaults read com.apple.Terminal | more
```
Change your Dock's default location to the top of the screen
```
$ defaults write com.apple.Dock orientation top
```
This command moves the Dock to the top of the screen underneath the menu bar. After changing this setting, you'll need to logout from the system and then log back in to see the Dock under the menu bar.

nvram

The *nvram* utility modifies Open Firmware variables, which control the boot-time behavior of your Macintosh. To list all Open Firmware variables, use *nvram -p*. The Apple Open Firmware page is *http://bananajr6000.apple.com/*.

To change a variable, you must run *nvram* as *root* or as the superuser. To set a variable, use *variable=value*. For example, to configure Mac OS X to boot verbosely, use *nvram boot-args=-v*. (Booting into Mac OS 9 or earlier will reset this variable.) Table 15-7 lists Open Firmware variables. Some variables use the Open Firmware Device Tree notation (see the technotes available at the Apple Open Firmware page).

Be careful changing the *nvram* utility, since incorrect settings can turn a G4 iMac into a $2000 doorstop. If you render your computer unbootable, you can reset Open Firmware by zapping the PRAM. To zap the PRAM, hold down Option-c-P-R as you start the computer, and then release the keys when you hear a second startup chime. (If your two hands are busy holding down the other buttons and you have trouble reaching the power button, remember that you can press it with your nose.)

Table 15-7. nvram variables

Variable	Description
auto-boot?	The automatic boot settings. If `true` (the default), Open Firmware will automatically boot an operating system. If `false`, the process will stop at the Open Firmware prompt. Be careful using this with Old World (unsupported) machines and third-party graphics adapters, since the display and keyboard may not be initialized until the operating system starts (in which case, you will not have access to Open Firmware).
boot-args	The arguments that are passed to the boot loader.
boot-command	The command that starts the boot process. The default is *mac-boot*, an Open Firmware command that examines the `boot-device` for a Mac OS startup.
boot-device	The device to boot from. The syntax is `device:[partition],path:filename`, and a common default is `hd:,\\:tbxi`. In the path, `\\` is an abbreviation for */System/Library/CoreServices*, and `tbxi` is the file type of the *BootX* boot loader. (Run */Developer/Tools/GetFileInfo* on *BootX* to see its type.)
boot-file	The name of the boot loader. (This is often blank, since `boot-command` and `boot-device` are usually all that are needed.)
boot-screen	The image to display on the boot screen.
boot-script	A variable that can contain an Open Firmware boot script.
boot-volume	Description unavailable at time of printing. Please see the errata at *http://www.oreilly.com/catalog/mpantherunix/*.
console-screen	A variable that specifies the console output device, using an Open Firmware Device Tree name.
default-client- ip	An IP address for diskless booting.
default-gateway- ip	A gateway address for diskless booting.
default-mac- address?	Description unavailable at time of printing. Please see the errata at *http://www.oreilly.com/catalog/mpantherunix/*.
default-router- ip	A router address for diskless booting.
default-server- ip	An IP address for diskless booting.
default-subnet- mask	A default subnet mask for diskless booting.
diag-device	A private variable; not usable for security reasons.
diag-file	A private variable; not usable for security reasons.
diag-switch?	A private variable; not usable for security reasons.
fcode-debug?	A variable that determines whether the Open Firmware Forth interpreter will display extra debugging information.
input-device	The input device to use for the Open Firmware console.
input-device-1	A secondary input device (so you can have a screen and serial console at the same time). Use *scca* for the first serial port.
little-endian?	The CPU endianness. If `true`, initializes the PowerPC chip as little endian. The default is `false`.
load-base	A private variable; not usable for security reasons.
mouse-device	The mouse device using an Open Firmware Device Tree name.

Table 15-7. nvram variables (continued)

Variable	Description
nvramrc	A sequence of commands to execute at boot time (if *use-nvramc?* is set to `true`).
oem-banner	A custom banner to display at boot time.
oem-banner?	The oem banner settings. Set to `true` to enable the oem banner. The default is `false`.
oem-logo	A 64-by-64 bit array containing a custom black-and-white logo to display at boot time. This should be specified in hex.
oem-logo?	The oem logo settings. Set to `true` to enable the oem logo. The default is `false`.
output-device	The device to use as the system console. The default is `screen`.
output-device-1	A secondary output device (so you can have everything go to both the screen and a serial console). Use *scca* for the first serial port.
pci-probe-mask	A private variable; not usable for security reasons.
ram-size	The amount of RAM currently installed. For example, 256 MB is shown as 0x10000000.
real-base	The starting physical address that is available to Open Firmware.
real-mode?	The address translation settings. If `true`, Open Firmware will use real-mode address translation. Otherwise, it uses virtual-mode address translation.
real-size	The size of the physical address space available to Open Firmware.
screen-#columns	The number of columns for the system console.
screen-#rows	The number of rows for the system console.
scroll-lock	Set by page checking output words to prevent Open Firmware text from scrolling off the top of the screen.
selftest-#megs	The number of MB of RAM to test at boot time. The default is 0.
use-generic?	The device node naming settings. Specifies whether to use generic device node names such as 'screen', as opposed to Apple hardware code names.
use-nvramrc?	The command settings. If this is `true`, Open Firmware uses the commands in *nvramrc* at boot time.
virt-base	The starting virtual address that is available to Open Firmware.
virt-size	The size of the virtual address space available to Open Firmware.

Third-Party Applications

Although you can perform system administration through the utilities supplied with Mac OS X, several third-party applications provide convenient frontends to these utilities:

Cocktail

Kristofer Szymanski's Cocktail (*http://www.macosxcocktail.com/*) is a shareware application that provides a GUI frontend to a wide range of system administrative tasks and interface configurations.

GeekTool

Tynsoe.org offers the free GeekTool (*http://projects.tynsoe.org/en/ geektool/*), which can redirect the output of system logs, Unix commands, and dynamically generated images to the desktop.

MacJanitor

Brian Hill's MacJanitor (*http://personalpages.tds.net/~brian_hill/ macjanitor.html*) is a freeware application that does one thing and does it well: it runs the *cron* jobs that are scheduled to run in the wee hours of the night by default (see "Default cron Jobs" in Chapter 2).

TinkerTool System

Marcel Bresink's TinkerTool System (*http://www.bresink.com/osx/ TinkerToolSys.html*) is a shareware application that can do many things, including run the periodic *cron* jobs mentioned earlier, manage log files, and tune the network configuration.

## PART V

Appendixes

These Appendixes include miscellaneous reference information.

- Appendix A, *The Mac OS X Filesystem*
- Appendix B, *Command-Line Tools: The Missing Manpages*
- Appendix C, *Mac OS X's Unix Development Tools*

The Mac OS X Filesystem

If you do an *ls -a /* on your Mac OS X box, you will see some familiar things, such as */etc* and */var*, but you will also notice some unfamiliar things, such as */TheVolumeSettingsFolder*, */Library*, and */Documents*. The Mac OS X filesystem contains traces of Unix, NeXTSTEP, and Mac OS 9. This appendix describes the contents of important directories. The tables in this chapter list directory entries (directories are denoted with a trailing slash) and provide a description of each file or directory.

Files and Directories

Table A-1 describes the files and directories you may find in your *root* directory. The remaining tables in this chapter describe significant subdirectories.

Table A-1. Mac OS X's root directory

File or directory	Description
.DS_Store	Contains Finder settings, such as icon location and window size. The file will appear in any directory that you've viewed with the Finder.
.hidden	Contains a list of files that should be invisible to the Finder.
.hotfiles.btree	Used by Panther's Hot File Adaptive Clustering, which automatically defragments frequently accessed files that are under 20 MB in size.
.Trashes/	Contains files that have been dragged to the Trash. On a boot volume, such files are stored in ~/.Trash. On a non-boot volume, these files are in /.Trashes/uid/.
.vol/	Maps HFS+ file IDs to files. If you know a file's ID, you can open it using /.vol/id.
Applications/	Holds all your Mac OS X applications. Its *Utilities* subdirectory includes lots of useful things, such as the Terminal, Console, and the Activity Monitor.
Applications (Mac OS 9)/	Contains all your OS 9 applications, if you've got Mac OS X and Mac OS 9 installed.
automount/	Handles static NFS mounts for the *automount* daemon.
bin/	Contains essential system binaries.

Table A-1. Mac OS X's root directory (continued)

File or directory	Description
Desktop DB	Along with *Desktop DF*, contains the desktop database that is rebuilt when you click Rebuild Desktop in System Preferences → Classic.
botlib.log	Quake III players have this.
cores/	A symbolic link (or *symlink*) to */private/cores*. If core dumps are enabled (with *tcsh*'s *limit* and *bash/sh*'s *ulimit* commands—see the *tcsh* and *bash* manpages for more details), they will be created in this directory as *core.pid*.
Desktop DF	See Desktop DB.
Desktop Folder/	The Mac OS 9 desktop folder.
dev/	Contains files that represent various devices. See Table A-6.
Developer/	Contains Apple's Xcode Tools and documentation. Available only if you have installed the Xcode Tools.
Documents/	The Mac OS 9 documents folder.
etc/	Contains system configuration files. See Table A-2. The directory is a symbolic link to */private/etc*.
Installer Log File	May be left by some third-party application installers.
Library/	Contains support files for locally installed applications, among other things. See Table A-4.
lost+found	Stores orphaned files discovered by *fsck*.
mach	A symbolic link to the */mach.sym* file.
mach.sym	Contains kernel symbols. It is generated during each boot by */etc/rc*.
mach_kernel	The Darwin kernel.
Network/	Contains network-mounted *Application*, *Library*, and *Users* directories, as well as a *Servers* directory, which contains directories mounted by the *automount* daemon.
private/	Contains the *tmp*, *var*, *etc*, and *cores* directories.
sbin/	Contains executables for system administration and configuration.
sw/	Contains the Fink installation (see Chapter 11).
Shared Items/	Gives OS 9 multiuser systems a place where users can store files for other users to access.
System/	Contains a subdirectory, *Library*, which holds support files for the system and system applications, among other things. See Table A-3.
System Folder/	The Mac OS 9 System Folder.
Temporary Items/	Contains temporary files used by Mac OS 9.
TheVolumeSettingsFolder/	Keeps track of details such as open windows and desktop printers.
tmp/	Holds temporary files. It is a symbolic link to */private/tmp*.
Trash/	Where Mac OS 9 stores deleted files until the Trash is emptied.
User Guides And Information/	An alias to */Library/Documentation/User Guides and Information*, and contains hardware-specific documentation and information about Panther.

File or directory	Description
Users/	Contains home directories for the users on the system. The *root* user's home directory is */var/root*.
usr/	Contains BSD Unix applications and support files.
var/	Contains frequently modified files, such as log files. It is a symbolic link to */private/var*.
VM Storage	Mac OS 9 virtual memory file.
Volumes/	Contains all mounted filesystems, including removable media and mounted disk images.

The /etc Directory

The */etc* directory contains configuration files for Unix applications and services, as well as scripts that control system startup. Table A-2 lists the contents of the */etc* directory.

Table A-2. The /etc directory

File or directory	Description
6to4.conf	Configuration file for encapsulating IPv6 within IPv4. See *ip6config(8)*.
afpovertcp.cfg	Causes Mac OS X to use TCP/IP as the default transport for Apple File Protocol (AFP). Use this file to configure the defaults for AFP over TCP/IP.
aliases	Mail aliases file. Symbolic link to */etc/postfix/aliases*.
aliases.db	Mail aliases db file created when you run *newaliases*.
amd.conf.template	Sample configuration file for the *automount* daemon.
amd.map.template	Sample map file for the *automount* daemon.
auth/	Contains an Open Directory authentication module for Samba.
appletalk.cfg	AppleTalk configuration file for routing or multihoming. See the *appletalk.cfg(5)* manpage.
authorization	Controls how applications, such as installers, can temporarily obtain *root* privileges.
authorization.cac	Description unavailable at time of printing. Please see the errata at *http://www.oreilly.com/catalog/mpantherunix/*.
bashrc	Global configuration file for *bash*, the Bourne-again shell.
charset/	Contains localization files.
crontab	*root's crontab*. See "Default cron Jobs" in Chapter 2.
csh.cshrc	Global *csh* configuration file, processed when the shell starts up. If you have a *.cshrc* or *.tcshrc* file in your home directory, *tcsh* will execute its contents as well.
csh.login	Global *csh* login file, processed when a login shell starts up. If you have a *.login* file in your home directory, *tcsh* will execute its contents as well.
csh.logout	Global *csh* logout file, processed when a user logs out of a login shell.

Table A-2. The /etc directory (continued)

File or directory	Description
cups/	Contains configuration files for Common Unix Printing System (CUPS).
daily	*cron* job that is run once a day (see *crontab*). This is a symlink to */etc/periodic/daily/500.daily*.
defaults/	Contains default configuration files for applications and utilities.
dumpdates	Dump date records created by *dump(5)*, which is run by */etc/daily*.
find.codes	Description not available at time of writing; see errata page at *http://www.oreilly.com/catalog/mpantherunix*.
fonts/	Configures fonts for X11.
fstab	Specifies filesystems that you want to mount at startup. See the comments in the file for examples.
fstab.hd	Unused.
ftpusers	List of users who are prohibited from using FTP.
gdb.conf	Global *gdb* configuration file.
gettytab	Terminal configuration database.
group	Group permissions file. See Chapter 3.
hostconfig	System configuration file that controls many of the startup items described in the "SystemStarter" section in Chapter 2.
hosts	Host database; a mapping of IP addresses to hostnames. You can use this as a supplement to other Directory Services, such as DNS. Mac OS X 10.1 and earlier consulted this file only in single-user mode, but Mac OS X 10.2 (Jaguar) uses this file at other times. For more information, see Chapter 3.
hosts.equiv	List of trusted remote hosts and host-user pairs. This is used by *rsh* and is inherently insecure. You should use *ssh* instead, which is a secure alternative. See *ssh-keygen(1)* to generate key pairs that can be used to set up a trust relationship with remote users.
hosts.lpd	List of hosts that are allowed to connect to the Unix *lpd* service.
httpd/	Contains Apache's configuration files.
idmap/	Description unavailable at time of printing. Please see the errata at *http://www.oreilly.com/catalog/mpantherunix/*.
inetd.conf	Internet super-server (*inetd*) configuration file.
kcpassword	Description unavailable at time of printing. Please see the errata at *http://www.oreilly.com/catalog/mpantherunix/*.
kern_loader.conf	Description unavailable at time of printing. Please see the errata at *http://www.oreilly.com/catalog/mpantherunix/*.
localtime	Symbolic link to your system's time zone, such as: */usr/share/zoneinfo/US/Eastern*.
lowcase.dat	Used by Samba to determine lowercase characters for various locales.
mail/	Contains configuration files for *sendmail*. Note that Open Directory handles the mail aliases (see Chapter 3).
mach_init.d/	Mach bootstrap daemons. See Chapter 2.

Table A-2. The /etc directory (continued)

File or directory	Description
mach_init_per_user.d/	Per-user Mach bootstrap daemons. See Chapter 2.
mail.rc	Global configuration file for /usr/bin/mail.
manpath.config	Configuration file for man.
master.passwd	Shadow passwd file, consulted only in single-user mode. During normal system operation, Open Directory manages user information (see Chapter 3).
moduli	System-wide prime numbers used for cryptographic applications such as ssh.
monthly	Monthly cron job (see crontab); a symlink to /etc/periodic/monthly/500. monthly.
motd	Message of the day; displayed each time you launch a new Terminal or log in remotely.
named.conf	Configuration file for named, the DNS daemon. For more details, see named(8).
networks	Network name database.
notify.conf	Configuration for the Notification Center.
ntp.conf	Configuration file for the Network Time Protocol daemon, which synchronizes system time by accessing a remote server.
openldap/	Contains configuration files for OpenLDAP, an implementation of the Lightweight Directory Access Protocol.
pam.d/	Contains configuration files for PAM.
passwd	Password file. For more information, see Chapter 3.
pdb/	Contains an Open Directory authentication module for Samba.
periodic/	Contains configuration files for the periodic utility, which runs cron jobs on a regular basis.
ppp/	Contains configuration files for Point-To-Point Protocol (PPP).
printcap	Printer configuration file for lpd. CUPS automatically generates this file. For more information, see cupsd(8).
profile	Global profile for the Bourne-again shell.
protocols	Network protocol database.
racoon/	Contains configuration files for racoon, the IKE key management daemon.
rc	Startup script for multiuser mode.
rc.boot	Startup script for single-user mode.
rc.cleanup	Cleanup script invoked by /etc/rc.
rc.common	Common settings for startup scripts.
rc.netboot	Startup script for booting from the network using NetBoot.
resolv.conf	DNS resolver configuration. Symlink to /var/run/resolv.conf.
resolver/	Contains files used to resolve hostnames.
rmt	Symbolic link to /usr/sbin/rmt.
rmtab	Remote NFS mount table.

Table A-2. The /etc directory (continued)

File or directory	Description
rpc	RPC number-to-name mappings. Mac OS X 10.1 and earlier consulted this file only in single-user mode, but Mac OS X 10.2 (Jaguar) uses this file at other times. For more information, see Chapter 3.
rtadvd.conf	Configuration file for the router advertisement daemon. For more details, see *rtadvd(8)*.
services	Internet service name database. Mac OS X 10.1 and earlier consulted this file only in single-user mode, but Mac OS X 10.2 (Jaguar) uses this file at other times. For more information, see Chapter 3.
shells	List of shells.
slpsa.conf	Configuration file for the service locator daemon (*slpd*).
smb.conf	Samba configuration file.
smb.conf.template	Template configuration file for Samba.
ssh_config	Global configuration file for OpenSSH client programs.
ssh_host_dsa_key	Private DSA host key for OpenSSH. This file, and the other *ssh_host_* * files, are created the first time you start Remote Login in the Sharing System Preferences.
ssh_host_dsa_key.pub	Public DSA host key for OpenSSH.
ssh_host_key	Private host key for OpenSSH when using SSH 1 compatibility.
ssh_host_key.pub	Public host key for OpenSSH when using SSH 1 compatibility.
ssh_host_rsa_key	Private RSA host key for OpenSSH.
ssh_host_rsa_key.pub	Public RSA host key for OpenSSH.
sshd_config	Configuration file for the OpenSSH *sshd* daemon.
sudoers	Configuration file for the *sudo* command. Make sure you use the *visudo* command only to edit this file.
syslog.conf	*syslogd* configuration file.
ttys	Terminal initialization file.
upcase.dat	Used by Samba to determine uppercase characters for various locales.
valid.dat	Used by Samba to determine valid characters for various locales.
vfs/	Description unavailable at time of printing. Please see the errata at *http://www.oreilly.com/catalog/mpantherunix/*.
weekly	Weekly *cron* job (see *crontab*). This is a symlink to */etc/periodic/weekly/500.weekly*.
X11/	X11 configuration directory. This file is present only if you have installed X11.
xinetd.conf	Configuration file for *xinetd*, the extended Internet superserver daemon.
xinetd.d/	Contains service-specific configuration files for *xinetd*.
xtab	Lists current NFS exports.

The /System/Library Directory

Table A-3 lists the directories stored under the */System/Library* directory. You should not modify the contents of these directories or add new files to them. Instead, use their counterparts in the */Library* folder. For example, to install a new font, drag it into */Library/Fonts*, not */System/Library/Fonts*.

Table A-3. The /System/Library directory

File or directory	Description
Caches/	Contains caches used by various parts of the operating system.
CFMSupport/	Holds shared libraries used by Carbon applications.
Classic/	Description unavailable at time of printing. Please see the errata at *http://www.oreilly.com/catalog/mpantherunix/*.
ColorPickers/	Includes localized resources for Mac OS X color pickers.
Colors/	Contains the names and values of colors used in the color picker control.
ColorSync/	Contains ColorSync profiles.
Components/	Contains application building blocks (components), such as AppleScript and color pickers. Components are not applications themselves and are generally shared between applications.
Contextual Menu Items/	Contains plug-ins for the Finder's contextual menu (Control-click or Right-click).
CoreServices/	Contains system applications, such as *SystemStarter*, *BootX*, the Finder, and the login window.
Displays/	Contains ColorSync information for external monitors.
DTDs/	Contains document type definitions for XML documents used by the system, such as property lists.
Extensions/	Holds Darwin kernel extensions.
Extensions.kextcache	Contains information about extensions in the cache; a compressed XML document.
Extensions.mkext	Contains the kernel extension cache. It is created at boot by */etc/rc*.
Filesystems/	Contains drivers and utilities for various filesystems (MS-DOS, AppleShare, UFS, etc.).
Filters/	Contains Quartz Filters that are used in the Print dialog's ColorSync section.
Find/	Includes support files for Sherlock's content indexing.
Fonts/	Contains core Mac OS X fonts.
Frameworks/	Holds a collection of reusable application frameworks, including shared libraries, headers, and documentation.
Image Capture/	Contains device support files for the Image Capture application.
Java/	Contains Java *class* and *jar* files.
Keyboard Layouts/	Contains bundles that support internationalized keyboard layouts.
Keychains/	Contains system-wide keychain files.
LoginPlugins/	Contains helper applications that are launched as you log in.
Modem Scripts/	Contains modem configuration scripts.

Table A-3. The /System/Library directory (continued)

File or directory	Description
MonitorPanels/	Includes panels used by System Preferences → Displays.
OpenSSL/	Holds OpenSSL configuration and support files.
Perl/	Holds Perl Libraries.
PHP/	Contains PHP Libraries.
PreferencePanes/	Contains all the preference panes for the Preferences application.
Printers/	Contains printer support files.
PrivateFrameworks/	Holds private frameworks meant to support Mac OS X. These frameworks are not meant for programmers' use.
QuickTime/	Holds QuickTime support files.
QuickTimeJava/	Includes support files for the QuickTime/Java bridge.
Rulebooks/	Contains information used for text handling, such as word-breaking rules for hyphenation.
Screen Savers/	Contains screensavers that you can select from System Preferences → Desktop & Screen Saver.
ScriptingAdditions/	Includes AppleScript plug-ins and libraries.
Services/	Contains services that are made available through the Services menu.
Sounds/	Contains sounds that are available in System Preferences → Sound.
Speech/	Includes speech recognition and generation support files.
StartupItems/	Contains startup scripts as described in Chapter 2.
SyncServices/	Contains iSync conduits.
SystemConfiguration/	Contains plug-ins used to monitor various system activities (for Apple use only).
SystemProfiler/	Contains support files for System Profiler.
SystemResources/	Contains precompiled header lists for the C compiler (see "Precompiled Header Files" in Chapter 9).
TextEncodings/	Contains localized text encodings.
User Template/	Holds localized skeleton files for user directories. See "Creating a User's Home Directory" in Chapter 3.

The /Library Directory

Table A-4 lists the contents of the */Library* directory. This directory contains counterparts to many directories found in */System/Library*. You can use the */Library* counterparts for system-wide customization. If you find a directory of the same name in your home *Library* directory (*~/Library*), you can use that for user-level customization. For example, you can install fonts for one particular user by moving them into *~/ Library/Fonts*.

Table A-4. The /Library directory

File or directory	Description
Address Book Plug-Ins	Contains plug-ins for the Address Book application.
Application Support/	Contains support files for locally installed applications.
Audio/	Contains audio plug-ins and sounds.
Caches/	Contains cached data used by various parts of the operating system.
CFMSupport/	Holds shared libraries used by Carbon applications.
ColorSync/	Contains user-installed ColorSync profiles and scripts.
Contextual Menu Items/	Contains plug-ins for the Finder's contextual menu (Control-Click or Right-Click).
Desktop Pictures/	Contains desktop pictures used by System Preferences → Desktop & Screen Saver.
Documentation/	Provides documentation for locally installed applications.
Filesystems/	Contains authentication support for the Apple Share network client.
Fonts/	Contains locally installed fonts.
Image Capture/	Contains locally installed scripts and plug-ins for the Image Capture application.
Internet Plug-Ins/	Contains locally installed browser plug-ins.
iTunes/	Holds iTunes plug-ins.
Java/	Contains locally installed Java classes (you can drop jar files into */Library/Java/Extensions*), as well as a suitable directory to use as your $JAVA_HOME (*/Library/Java/Home*).
Keyboard Layouts/	Contains keyboard mappings.
Keychains/	Contains keychain files.
Logs/	Holds logs for services such as Apple File Services, the Crash Reporter, and the Directory Service.
Modem Scripts/	Holds support files for various modem types.
Packages/	Description unavailable at time of printing. Please see the errata at *http://www.oreilly.com/catalog/mpantherunix/*.
Perl/	Contains locally installed Perl modules (MakeMaker's INSTALLSITELIB).
PreferencePanes/	Contains system preference panes for locally installed utilities such as TinkerTool.
Preferences/	Holds global preferences.
Printers/	Contains printer drivers and utilities.
Python/	Contains locally installed Python modules.
QuickTime/	Contains locally installed QuickTime components.
Receipts/	Leaves a receipt in the form of a *.pkg* directory after you install an application with the Mac OS X installer. The *.pkg* directory contains a bill of materials file (*.bom*), which you can read with the *lsbom* command.
Screen Savers/	Contains locally installed screensavers.
Scripts/	Contains a variety of AppleScripts installed with Mac OS X.
StartupItems/	Holds locally installed startup items. See "Adding Startup Items" in Chapter 2.
User Pictures/	Contains user pictures that are used in the login panel.
WebServer/	Contains the Apache CGI and document *root* directories.

The /var Directory

The */var* directory contains transient and volatile files, such as PID files (which tell you the process ID of a currently running daemon), log files, and many others. Table A-5 lists the contents of the */var* directory.

Table A-5. The /var directory

File or directory	Description
at/	Contains information about jobs scheduled with the *at* command.
automount	Contains information about servers and volumes that have been browsed on the network.
backups/	Contains backups of the NetInfo database.
cron/	Contains user *crontab* files.
db/	Includes a grab bag of configuration and data files, including the *locate* database, the NetInfo database, and network interface information.
empty/	Used as an unwritable `chroot(8)` environment.
log/	Contains a variety of log files, including *syslog*, mail, and web server logs.
mail/	Contains inboxes for local users' email.
msgs/	Holds system-wide messages that were delivered using *msgs –s*.
named/	Includes various files used for local DNS services.
netboot/	Contains various files used for NetBoot.
root/	Serves as the *root* user's home directory.
run/	Holds PID files for running processes. Also contains working files used by programs such as *sudo*.
rwho/	Contains information used by the *rwho* command.
slp.regfile	List of servers found with Service Location Protocol (SLP).
spool/	Serves as a spool directory for mail, printer queues, and other queued resources.
tmp/	Serves as a temporary file directory.
vm/	Contains your swap files.
yp/	Contains files used by NIS.

The /dev Directory

The */dev* directory contains files that represent devices attached to the system, including physical devices, such as serial ports, and pseudodevices, such as a random number generator. Table A-6 lists the contents of the */dev* directory.

Table A-6. The /dev directory

File or directory	Description
bpf[0-3]	Berkeley Packet Filter devices. See *bpf(4)*.
console	The system console. This is owned by whoever is currently logged in. If you write to it, the output will end up in */var/tmp/console.log*, which you can view with the Console application (*/Applications/Utilities*).
cu.*	Modem devices for compatibility with the Unix *cu* (call up) utility.
disk[0-n]	Disk.
disk[0-n]s[0-n]	Disk partition. For example, */dev/disk0s1* is the first partition of */dev/disk0*.
fd/	Devices that correspond to file descriptors. See the *fd* manpage for more details.
klog	Device used by *syslogd* to read kernel messages.
kmem	Image of kernel memory.
mem	Image of the system memory.
null	Bit bucket. You can redirect anything here, and it will disappear.
ptyp[0-f]	Master ends of the first sixteen pseudo-*ttys*.
pty[q-w][0-f]	Master ends of the remaining pseudo-*ttys*.
random	Source of pseudorandom data. See *random(4)*.
rdisk[0-n]	Raw disk device.
rdisk[0-n]s[0-n]	Raw disk partition.
stderr	Symbolic link to */dev/fd/2*.
stdin	Symbolic link to */dev/fd/0*.
stdout	Symbolic link to */dev/fd/1*.
tty	Standard output stream of the current Terminal or remote login.
tty.*	Various modem and serial devices.
ttyp[0-f]	Slave ends of the first sixteen pseudo-*ttys*.
tty[q-w][0-f]	Slave ends of the remaining pseudo-*ttys*.
urandom	Source of pseudorandom data, not guaranteed to be strong. See *random(4)*.
vn[0-3]	Pseudo disk devices.
zero	Infinite supply of null characters. Often used with *dd* to create a file made up of null characters.

Command-Line Tools: The Missing Manpages

Unfortunately, many of the command-line utilities in Mac OS X have no corresponding manpages, and documentation of any sort can be difficult to find. This appendix offers a quick reference to tools that may be helpful or interesting to Mac OS X system administrators and developers, but which have missing, incomplete, or inaccurate manpages.

Each of the following sections includes command syntax, a brief description, and the directory location of the command. (Note that some of these commands are available only if you've installed the Xcode Tools that comes with Mac OS X.) Table B-1 is a list of all the commands documented in this appendix.

Table B-1. Documented commands

AuthorizationTrampoline	hwprefs	open-x11
autodiskmount	ipconfig	pdisk
automount	kdumpd	pdump
CCLEngine	kuncd	postfix-watch
cd9660.util	languagesetup	register_mach_bootstrap_servers
certtool	makekey	screencapture
checkgid	mDNS	scselect
chkpasswd	mDNSResponder	scutil
configd	mount_devfs	SecurityServer
CpMac	mount_ftp	service
create_nidb	mount_smbfs	sips
DirectoryService	mount_synthfs	SplitForks
disktool	mount_volfs	systemkeychain
fixmount	msdos.util	udf.util
fixPrecomps	notifyd	ufs.util

Table B-1. Documented commands (continued)

FixupResourceForks	ntp-wait	unzip
gcc_select	ntptimeset	vndevice
hfs.util	od	vsdbutil
hostinfo	opendiff	zip

AuthorizationTrampoline

AuthorizationTrampoline *command filedesc argument...*

Description

An SUID *root* program that invokes actions with superuser privileges on behalf of applications calling the *AuthorizationExecuteWithPrivileges* routine (part of the Security framework's Authorization Services API). Successful use of this routine requires authorization against the system.privilege.admin right defined in */etc/authorization*, meaning that it's limited to *root* and to those in the *admin* group.

Options/Usage

argument
> A list of arguments to be passed to *command*.

command
> The path to the program to be executed with superuser privileges.

filedesc
> A file descriptor for a temporary file containing the authorization reference obtained by the application calling *AuthorizationExecuteWithPrivileges*. The reference is used by *AuthorizationTrampoline* to determine if the request should be allowed.

Location

/System/Library/CoreServices

autodiskmount

autodiskmount [-d] [-v] [-a] [-F [-V *vol_name*]]

Description

Automatically discovers and mounts disk volumes.

Options/Usage

−*a* Mounts removable disk volumes, as well as volumes on fixed disks.

−*d* Prints debugging information to standard output.

−F Prints the device name and filesystem type of the largest unmounted HFS+ or UFS volume on an internal fixed disk to standard output. If all volumes are the same size, prints information for the first one found. If *−a* is specified, prints information for all such volumes.

−v Should print a list of mounted volumes to standard error after it's finished working, but does not work in Panther.

−V Prints information only for the specified volume, if found.

Location

/sbin

---

automount

```
automount -help
```

```
automount -V
```

```
automount [-m map_directory map [-mnt mount_directory] [-1]]... [-a mount_
directory] [-d] [-D { mount | nsl | options | proc | select | all }]... [-f]
[-s] [-tcp] [-tl timeout] [-tm timeout]
```

Description

Provides transparent, automated access to NFS and AFP shares. When running, any filesystem access to *map_directory* is intercepted by *automount*. Typically, *automount* will then set up a symbolic link from *map_directory* or one of its subdirectories to a mount point under *mount_directory*, automatically creating directories and mounting remote volumes as needed. It will also unmount remote volumes that have been idle for too long. Directories or mounts set up by *automount* are removed when *automount* exits.

automount makes use of *maps* to determine how to mount volumes. When using a file as a map, the format is similar to that used by NFS automounters on other Unix platforms. Each entry in the file consists of a single line, either a comment beginning with a hash mark (#), or a mount directive of the form:

```
subdirectory server:/pathname
```

If this line were included in a file named */etc/mountmaps*, and *automount* were called like so:

```
# automount -m /mount_directory /etc/mountmaps
```

upon accessing */mount_directory*, *automount* would mount the NFS-exported *server:/pathname* on */private/mount_directory/subdirectory* and create a symlink to that mount point from */mount_directory/subdirectory*.

At one time it was also possible to use a map stored in a NetInfo database under */mountmaps/*, but that functionality has been deprecated in future versions of Mac OS X.

AFP URLs

The format of the AFP URLs in the *automount* examples is described in the manpage for *mount_afp*, but there are certain constraints you should be aware of:

- First, *server* must be a valid TCP/IP hostname or IP address, which may be different than the AFP name that shows up, for example, in a Connect to Server... dialog window.

- Second, *share_name* is the AFP name for the share point, which is not necessarily the same as the full pathname to the share point on the server.

- Finally, there are a few ways to handle authentication to the AFP server. If guest access to the share is allowed, then you may use a URL like those in the examples for *automount*:

    ```
    afp://;AUTH=NO%20USER%20AUTHENT@server/share_name
    ```

If user authentication is required, then you have two options. The first is to specify the necessary authentication information in the URL like so:

```
afp://username:password@server/share_name
```

However, this makes the authentication password available to anyone with access to the configuration stored in Open Directory. The other option is to leave out the authentication parameters:

```
afp://server/share_name
```

In this case, a user logged into the graphical console is presented with an authentication dialog to enable access to the share. Of course, if no one is logged into the GUI, this won't work, and the mount attempt will fail.

In addition to map files, there are several special maps available. Foremost among them are those used by default on Mac OS X systems, **-fstab**, **-static**, and **-nsl**. The following commands are run from the *NFS* startup item:

```
automount -m /Network -nsl
automount -m /automount/Servers -fstab -mnt /private/var/automount/Network/
Servers↵
  -m /automount/static -static -mnt /private/var/automount
```

Both **-fstab** and **-static** maps use similar configuration formats, stored in an Open Directory database under */mounts/*. The following configuration line triggers *automount* when using the **-fstab** map:

```
server:/subdirectory /mount_point url↵
  net,url==afp://;AUTH=NO%20USER%20AUTHENT@server/share_name 0 0
```

The AFP mount is used as an example for the remainder of this section, but an equivalent NFS configuration would look like this:

```
server:/subdirectory /mount_point nfs net 0 0
```

There are several options for getting this configuration into Open Directory; one is to use **niload fstab** *domain*, then enter the configuration line, followed by Ctrl-D. The configuration will be stored in Open Directory like this (as displayed by **nidump -r /mounts** *domain*):

```
{
  "name" = ( "mounts" );
  CHILDREN = (
    {
      "dir" = ( "/mount_point" );
      "dump_freq" = ( "0" );
      "name" = ( "server:/subdirectory" );
      "opts" = ( "net", "url==afp://;AUTH=NO%20USER%20AUTHENT@server/share_
name" );
      "passno" = ( "0" );
      "vfstype" = ( "url" );
    }
  )
}
```

The net option is the signal for *automount* to use this configuration line with the **-fstab** map. If the net option is not used, this configuration line is picked up by the **-static** map.

With this configuration, and *automount* called like so:

```
# automount -m /automount/Servers -fstabø
 -mnt /private/var/automount/Network/Servers
```

upon accessing */automount/Servers*, *automount* mounts *share_name* from *server* on */private/var/automount/Network/Servers/server/subdirectory*, and creates a symlink from */automount/Servers/server*. (Alternatively, the mount may be accessed via */Network/Servers/server*, thanks to a symlink created by the *NFS* startup item.) The configured mount point (the value of the *dir* property) is ignored by the **-fstab** map.

 Don't use a *map_directory* argument to *–m* that traverses a symlink, or any accesses to the mount will hang. For example, it's OK to do this:

```
# automount -m /private/tmp/map_dir -fstab
```

but not this:

```
# automount -m /tmp/map_dir -fstab
```

since */tmp* is a symlink to */private/tmp*.

While the **-static** map uses a configuration very much like this for **-fstab**, its mounting and linking behavior is significantly different. With a configuration like this (viewed as the output of **nidump fstab** *domain*):

```
server:/subdirectory /mount_point url ↵
    url==afp://;AUTH=NO%20USER%20AUTHENT@server/share_name 0 0
```

and *automount* called like so:

automount -m /automount/static -static -mnt /private/var/automount

upon accessing */mount_point*, *automount* mounts *share_name* from *server* on */private/var/automount/mount_point*, creates a symlink to this directory from */automount/static/mount_point*, and then makes another from */mount_point* to */automount/static/mount_point*. The configured server:/subdirectory (the value of the *name* property) is ignored by the **-static** map for AFP shares. (Incidentally, the term "static" is a misnomer. Mounts are made dynamically when they're accessed, just as with the **-fstab** map.)

In order to avoid networking overhead, *automount* attempts to create symlinks directly to folders that are shared from the same machine. In other words, , rather than mounting a share that exists locally on a file server, *automount* sets up the symlinks to provide for direct access.

However, as of this writing, *automount* exhibits what is apparently a bug—the symlinks created for local shares always point to the server's root directory (/). In most cases this means that shares accessed from the server are useless, as the path to those shares doesn't match what is seen on remote clients.

The **-nsl** map uses the Network Services Location service discovery API to automatically find available shares on the network (just as the Finder's Connect to Server... menu item does) and create mounts for them. With *automount* invoked like this:

automount -m /Network -nsl

discovered shares are mounted on subdirectories of */private/var/automount/Network/server*, with a symlink created from */Network/server*.

Before version 10.3, the **-nsl** map didn't really work, and generated I/O errors when access to a mount was attempted. The *automount* command making use of the **-nsl** map in the NFS startup item was added in Panther.

Another special map is the **-user** map, which doesn't actually cause any remote filesystems to be mounted on its own. It merely sets up symlinks to every user account's home directory from the *map_directory*, which may be useful if you want a single place to look in for everyone's home directory. But proceed cautiously if you have a very large number of user accounts.

The **-host** map is meant to automatically mount NFS exports from hosts listed in a NIS hosts map when accessing a subdirectory of the *map_directory* with the same name as the host. For example, accessing */net/hostname/export* should mount *hostname:/export* if */net* is the *map_directory*. This is similar to the -hosts map of other NFS automounters.

The **-null** map mounts... well, nothing. It will, however, intercept filesystem calls for the *map_directory*, thus effectively mounting an empty directory over whatever might have been there before. In the original *automount*, from which NeXT's and Apple's versions are descended, this was meant to nullify configuration entries included from a network-wide NIS map.

When running in daemon mode, *automount* stores its process ID in */var/run/ automount.pid*, and responds to SIGHUP by reloading its configuration.

Options/Usage

−1

> Creates directories on the path to a **-fstab** mount point one at a time, as they're traversed, rather than creating the entire path to a mount point when the mount is accessed. However, using this option leads to I/O errors when trying to access the mount.

−a

> Specifies the directory in which mounts are made. Symbolic links from the directory specified in the *−m* option are used to access these mounts. The default directory is */private/var/automount*.

−d

> Sends debugging output to standard error, and prevents daemonization.

−D

> Outputs debugging messages of the specified type. If the *−d* option is used, output is to standard error; otherwise it's via *syslog*. Multiple occurrences of this option may be used to specify multiple types.

−f

> Used internally by *automount* to indicate that the process has already forked during daemonization. (You can see in the output of *ps −ax* that the *automount* daemon runs with the *−f* flag, even though it isn't invoked that way from the *NFS* startup item.)

−help

> Prints a usage statement to standard output.

−m

> Uses the specified map to mount shares and create symlinks from the specified directory to the mount points. The map argument can be an absolute pathname to a file, a map in the */mountmaps/* directory of an Open Directory domain, or one of the special values **-fstab**, **-host**, **-nsl**, **-null**, **-static**, or **-user**. Multiple *−m* options enable the use of multiple maps. In the absence of a *−m* option, *automount* attempts to find maps in Open Directory.

−mnt

> Like *−a*, but specific to a single map.

−s

> Supposedly creates all mounts at startup, and never unmounts them. However, mounts are still attempted only upon access when using this option, at which point *automount* prints a bus error and dumps core.

−tcp

> Attempts to mount NFS volumes over TCP, instead of the default UDP.

−tl

> Specifies a time-to-live (TTL) value for mount names, in seconds. After the timeout expires, mounts are rechecked. A timeout of **0** sets an infinite TTL. The default TTL is **10000**.

−tm

> Specifies a timeout to retry failing mounts, in seconds. The timeout roughly doubles with each mount attempt, until giving up after a few tries. The default timeout is **20**.

−V

> Prints version number and host information to standard output.

Location

/usr/sbin

CCLEngine

CCLEngine -l *integer* −f *filename* −s { 0 | 1 } −e { 0 | 1 } −c { 0 | 1 } −p { 0 | 1 } −d { 0 | 1 } −m { 0 | 1 | 2 } [-v] [-E] −S *octal_integer* −I *string* −i *URL* −C *string* −T *phone_num* −U *username* −P *password*

Description

Parses a modem script and initiates a PPP dialout. When a PPP connection is attempted, *pppd* starts up, parses */Library/Preferences/SystemConfiguration/ preferences.plist*, and calls *CCLEngine* with the appropriate arguments.

Options/Usage

−c If set to **1**, enables Van Jacobson TCP/IP header compression. This option is the opposite of the *novj* option to *pppd*, and is obtained from the IPCPCompressionVJ parameter in */Library/Preferences/SystemConfiguration/ preferences.plist*.

−C If the modem script asks for input, this option provides the label for the alternate button (i.e., the one that's not labeled "OK") on the dialog that pops up. Normally this option is set to "Cancel".

–d If set to **1**, starts dialing the modem without waiting for a dial tone. This option corresponds to the *modemdialmode* option to *pppd*, and is obtained from the `DialMode` parameter in */Library/Preferences/SystemConfiguration/ preferences.plist.*

–e If set to **1**, enables compression and error correction in the modem. This option corresponds to the *modemcompress* and *modemreliable* options to *pppd*, and is obtained from the `ErrorCorrection` parameter in */Library/ Preferences/SystemConfiguration/preferences.plist.*

–E Prints output to standard error.

–f Provides the name of a modem script, normally in */System/Library/Modem Scripts/*. This option corresponds to the *modemscript* option to *pppd*, and is obtained from the `ConnectionScript` parameter in */Library/Preferences/ SystemConfiguration/preferences.plist.*

–i If the modem script asks for input, this option provides a URL for the pop-up dialog icon. This URL is usually *file://localhost/System/Library/Extensions/ PPPSerial.ppp/Contents/Resources/NetworkConnect.icns.*

–I If the modem script asks for input, this option provides the title for the dialog that pops up. Normally the title is set to "Internet Connect".

–l Specifies the service ID for the network configuration to use from */Library/Preferences/SystemConfiguration/preferences.plist*. This option corresponds to the *serviceid* option to *pppd*.

–m Determines whether the modem should try to connect (**0**), disconnect (**1**), or be set up to answer calls (**2**).

–p If set to **1**, the modem uses pulse dialing. This option corresponds to the *modempulse* and *modemtone* options to *pppd*, and is obtained from the `PulseDial` parameter in */Library/Preferences/SystemConfiguration/preferences. plist.*

–P Specifies the password for PPP authentication.

–s If set to **1**, enables sound output from the modem through the computer speakers. This option corresponds to the *modemsound* option to *pppd*, and is obtained from the Speaker parameter in */Library/Preferences/ SystemConfiguration/preferences.plist.*

–S Specifies the *syslog* priority level and facility to use for logging errors. The argument is an octal integer which serves as the first argument to a *syslog* system call, as described in the *syslog* manpage and in */usr/include/sys/syslog. h*. The low-order digit specifies priority level from **0** (*emerg*) to **7** (*debug*), while the higher-order digits specify facility. The default value is **150**, which logs to the *remoteauth* facility at *emerg* level.

–T Specifies the telephone number to dial. This option corresponds to the *remoteaddress* and *altremoteaddress* options in *pppd*, and is obtained from the `CommRemoteAddress` and `CommAlternateRemoteAddress` parameters in */Library/ Preferences/SystemConfiguration/preferences.plist.*

–U   Specifies the username to use for PPP authentication. This option corresponds to the *user* option to *pppd*, and is obtained from the AuthName
parameter in */Library/Preferences/SystemConfiguration/preferences.plist*.

–v   If set to **1**, enables verbose logging to */tmp/ppp.log*. This option is taken from
the VerboseLogging parameter in */Library/Preferences/SystemConfiguration/
preferences.plist*.

Location

/usr/libexec

---

cd9660.util

cd9660.util { -m | -M } *device mount_point*

cd9660.util { -p | -u } *device*

Description

Mounts ISO-9660 (CD-ROM) filesystems into the directory hierarchy.

Options/Usage

–m   Mounts the device.

–M   Attempts to force the mount.

–p   Probes the device, and prints the volume name to standard output.

–u   Unmounts the device. This function doesn't appear to work.

device
    The CD device filename, e.g., **disk1s2**.

mount_point
    The directory on which the CD filesystem is mounted.

Location

/System/Library/Filesystems/cd9660.fs

certtool

certtool { v | d | D } *filename* [h] [v] [d]

certtool y [h] [v] [k=*keychain* [c [p=*password*]]]

certtool c [h] [v] [a] [k=*keychain* [c [p=*password*]]]

certtool { r | I } *filename* [h] [v] [d] [a] [k=*keychain* [c [p=*password*]]]

certtool i *filename* [h] [v] [d] [a] [k=*keychain* [c [p=*password*]]]
[r=*filename* [f={ 1 | 8 | f }]]

Description

Manages X.509 SSL/TLS certificates. It uses the Common Data Security Architecture (CDSA) in much the same way that */System/Library/OpenSSL/misc/CA.pl* uses OpenSSL to ease the process of managing certificates.

As arguments, it takes a single-letter command, often followed by a filename, and possibly some options.

Options/Usage

a   When adding an item to a keychain, this option creates a key pair and includes a private key with a more restrictive ACL than usual. (The default behavior creates a private key with no additional access restrictions, while specifying this option adds a confirmation requirement to access the private key which only *certtool* is allowed to bypass.)

c   As a command, walks you through a series of interactive prompts to create a certificate and a public/private key pair to sign and possibly encrypt it. The resulting certificate (in DER format) is stored in your default keychain. (Note that the first prompt, for a key and certificate label, is asking for two space-separated items. Common choices are an organization name for the key, and a label designating the purpose of the certificate.)

   As an option, instructs *certtool* to create a new keychain by the name given in the *k* option.

d   As a command, displays the certificate contained in *filename*.

   As an option, indicates that the format of the CSR or CRL contained in *filename* is DER (a binary format), instead of the default PEM (an ASCII format, which is essentially a DER certificate with Base64 encoding).

D   Displays the certificate revocation list (CRL) contained in *filename*.

f   Specifies the format of the private key in the file specified with the *r* option. A single character specifies the format: **1** (for OpenSSL's PKCS1, the default), **8** (PKCS8), or **f** (FIPS186, or BSAFE).

h   Prints a usage statement to standard output, negating whichever command was given.

i   Imports the certificate contained in *filename* into the default keychain.

I   Imports the CRL contained in *filename* into the default keychain.

k Specifies the name of a keychain (in *~/Library/Keychains*) to use other than the default.

p Specifies the keychain password on the command line. To avoid password exposure, it's better to let *certtool* prompt for it.

r As a command, walks you through a series of interactive prompts to create a certificate-signing request (CSR) and a public/private key pair to sign and possibly encrypt it. The resulting CSR is stored in `filename`.

As an option, specifies the file containing a private key for the certificate being imported. This is useful if you've used OpenSSL to generate a certificate, instead of *certtool*.

v As a command, verifies the CSR contained in `filename`.

As an option, should enable verbose output, but it doesn't actually seem to make a difference.

y As a command, displays the certificates and CRLs in the specified keychain.

Location

/usr/bin

---

checkgid

checkgid `group_name`...

Description

Checks for the existence of the specified groups. If all groups exist, the return value is 0 and nothing is printed. If any groups do not exist, the return value is 255 and the following is printed to standard error for each nonexistent `group_name`:

    checkgid: group 'group_name' not found

checkgid should be run with superuser privileges.

This tool is part of the Apache distribution.

Options/Usage

`group_name`
Takes a list of group names as arguments. It should also be able to take numeric group IDs as `#groupID`, but *checkgid* always returns successful for arguments of that form.

Location

/usr/bin

chkpasswd

chkpasswd [-c] [-i *infosystem*] [-l *location*] [*username*]

Description

Useful for scripts, *chkpasswd* prompts for a password, which is then compared against the appropriate directory service for the user specified. If the password is correct, *chkpasswd* returns 0; otherwise, it returns 1 and the string Sorry is printed to standard error.

Options/Usage

–*c*   Compares user input with the password hash directly, rather than running it through the *crypt* algorithm first.

–*i*   Specifies the directory service to use, which may be **file**, **netinfo**, **nis**, or **opendirectory**.

–*l*   Depending on the directory service being used, it's a file (the default is */etc/master.passwd*), a NetInfo domain or server/tag combo, a NIS domain, or an Open Directory node (like */NetInfo/root*).

username
    Designates whose password will be checked. It defaults to that of the user running the command.

Location

/usr/libexec

---

configd

configd [-b] [-B *bundle_ID*] [-d] [-t *pathname*] [-v] [-V *bundle_ID*]

Description

The System Configuration Server, which monitors changes to network-related items such as link status, DHCP assignments, PPP connections, and IP configuration, and provides an API for applications to be notified of these changes. To monitor various items, it uses a set of plug-in configuration agents, including the Preferences Monitor, the Kernel Event Monitor, the PPP Controller Agent, the IP Configuration Agent, and the IP Monitor Agent. The agent plug-ins are located in */System/Library/SystemConfiguration/*. More information on the System Configuration framework can be found at *http://developer.apple.com/techpubs/macosx/Networking/SysConfigOverview926/*.

It's started as a bootstrap daemon, from */etc/mach_init.d/configd.plist* (processed by *register_mach_bootstrap_servers*). When running in daemon mode, *configd* stores its process ID in */var/run/configd.pid*.

Options/Usage

−*b* Disables loading of all agents.

−*B* Disables loading of the specified agent.

−*d* Runs the process in the foreground, preventing daemonization.

−*t* Loads the agent specified by *pathname*.

−*v* Enables verbose logging.

−*V* Enables verbose logging for the specified agent.

Location

/usr/sbin

CpMac

CpMac [-mac] [-p] [-r] *source_path* [*source_path...*] *dest_path*

Description

Copies files, keeping multiple forks and HFS attributes intact.

Options/Usage

−*mac*
  Arguments use legacy Mac OS pathname syntax (i.e., colons as path separators, paths as viewed from the Finder).

−*p* Preserves file attributes.

−*r* Recursively copies directory contents.

Location

/Developer/Tools

---

create_nidb

create_nidb [*tag* [*master_hostname* [*root_dir*]]]

Description

A Perl script that creates and populates an Open Directory database from the contents of flat files in */etc/*. This may be especially useful if you have configuration information you wish to carry over from another Unix system. Currently *create_nidb* makes use of the following files:

> */etc/master.passwd*
> */etc/group*
> */etc/hosts*
> */etc/networks*

create_nidb should be run with superuser privileges.

Options/Usage

master_hostname
> The name of the host serving the master copy of the Open Directory database. The default is **localhost** if the tag is **local**; otherwise, it's the hostname of the system on which *create_nidb* is run.

root_dir
> The directory in which *var/db/netinfo/tag.nidb* will be created. The default is **/**.

tag
> The tag of the Open Directory database. The default is **local**.

Location

/usr/libexec

DirectoryService

```
DirectoryService [-h | -v]

DirectoryService [-appledebug | -appleframework | -applenodaemon |
-appleoptions | -appleperformance | -appleversion]
```

Description

The server process for the Directory Service framework. It's started as a bootstrap daemon, from */etc/mach_init.d/DirectoryService.plist* (processed by *register_mach_bootstrap_servers*).

The manpage for *DirectoryService* on Panther is very good, but this entry details the additional *–apple* options.

Options/Usage

–appledebug
> Runs the service in debug mode, disabling daemonization, and logging to */Library/Logs/DirectoryService/DirectoryService.debug.log*.

–appleoptions
> Prints a usage statement for the second form of command invocation to standard output.

–appleperformance
> Runs the service in the foreground and logs extensively.

–appleversion
> Prints software build version to standard output.

–h

Prints a usage statement for the first form of command invocation to standard output.

–v

Prints software release version to standard output.

Location

/usr/sbin

---

disktool

```
disktool [-l | -r | -x | -y]
disktool [-d | -e | -g | -m | -p | -u | -A | -D | -S] device
disktool -s device integer_flag
disktool -n device vol_name
disktool -a device vol_name vol_flags
disktool -c userID
```

Description

Controls disks, including mounting, unmounting, ejecting, enabling permissions, and volume naming. Most options require a device name argument (e.g., **disk0**), and some require additional parameters.

Options/Usage

–a Adds disk to Disk Arbitration tables, to notify applications of a mounted volume. This is useful if you have forced a mount, thus bypassing standard notification.

–A Activates permissions on the volume, adding an entry to */var/db/volinfo. database* if one does not already exist.

–c Specifies user ID of account to use when mounting disks.

–d Removes disk from Disk Arbitration tables, to notify applications of a dismount. This is useful if you have forced a dismount, thus bypassing standard notification.

–D Deactivates permissions on the volume.

–e Ejects disk.

–g Prints HFS encoding on a volume to standard output.

–l Lists disk volumes to standard output.

–m Mounts disk.

–n Gives the device a new volume name. For HFS, HFS+, and UFS partitions only.

–p Unmounts partition. Device name is that of a partition (e.g., **disk0s5**).

-r Refreshes Disk Arbitration tables.

-s Sets HFS encoding on a volume. Takes encoding as additional integer argument.

-S Prints status of volume in */var/db/volinfo.database* to standard output.

-u Unmounts disk.

-x Disallows dismounts and ejects.

-y Allows dismounts and ejects.

Location

/usr/sbin

fixmount

```
fixmount [-q] [-a | -d | -e] [-v [-h hostname_or_IP] | -r | -A] [-f]
nfs_server...
```

Description

Communicates with the NFS mount daemon, *mountd*, to remove invalid records of client mounts from the NFS server. *fixmount* is run from the client, and when called without flags, prints the client's IP address to standard output if the server has a record of NFS mounts from the client.

mountd maintains records of which clients have mounted exports from the server, and writes the records to a file so that this information is retained through process or system restarts. (On most Unix platforms, this file is */etc/rmtab*; on Mac OS X, it's */var/db/mountdtab*.) Over time, this file accumulates a lot of outdated information, primarily due to clients rebooting or otherwise dropping their mounts without properly informing the server, or changing their hostnames.

The primary purpose of *fixmount* is to clear bogus entries from the file kept by *mountd*. On most Unix systems, it does this by comparing the current set of mounts on the client (as listed in */etc/mtab*) to the server's list of mounts from the client, and asking the server's *mountd* to remove any entries that don't match up.

However, a Mac OS X system keeps a current list of mounts in the kernel, and doesn't use */etc/mtab*. Therefore, when *fixmount* checks this file and finds it empty (or nonexistent), it perceives all of the server's entries as bogus—even those that do match up to current mounts on the client. This makes *fixmount*, at least as currently implemented, of very limited utility on Mac OS X.

Options/Usage

-a Lists mounts from the client in the form *IP_addr:pathname*. This option is similar to *showmount -a*, but limited to providing information about the client on which *fixmount* is run.

-A Removes all of the entries for the client from the server's */var/db/mountdtab*.

-*d*   Lists exports that are mounted on the client, instead of the client's IP address. This option is similar to *showmount –d*, but limited to providing information about the client on which *fixmount* is run.

-*e*   Prints the server's list of NFS exports to standard output. This option is the same as *showmount –e*.

-*f*   Forces all entries for the client to be interpreted as bogus. This option makes –*f* –*r* equivalent to –*A*. On a Mac OS X client, it's as if this flag is always set.

-*h*   Communicates with the server's *mountd* as if the client's hostname or IP address were that given by the argument to this option. This option is useful when the client has changed its hostname or IP address, but the server retains invalid entries with the old information.

-*q*   Minimizes output from error messages.

-*r*   Removes bogus entries for the client from the server's */var/db/mountdtab*.

-*v*   Runs the verification procedure to determine the list of bogus entries for the client (which is printed to standard output), but doesn't actually remove anything from the server's */var/db/mountdtab*.

Location

/usr/sbin

---

fixPrecomps

```
fixPrecomps -help

fixPrecomps [-checkOnly] [-force] [-relroot directory] [-all |
-precompsList filename] [-precomps filename...] [-find_all_precomps] [-gcc2
| -gcc3all] [-skipIfMissing] [-output directory] [-precompFlags flag...]
```

Description

Compiles header files to improve performance for programs including them. When invoked without arguments, *fixPrecomps* reads any files in */System/Library/ SystemResources/PrecompLists/* in alphanumeric order by filename. Normally this includes *phase1.precompList* and *phase2.precompList*. These files are expected to consist of lists of precompiled header filenames to generate. *fixPrecomps* then runs *cc -precomp* on the ordinary header files where the precompiled headers are either out-of-date (i.e., have modification times less recent than the ordinary headers) or nonexistent.

The headers listed in the *precompList* files have filename extensions of either *.p* or *.pp*. *fixPrecomps* finds ordinary headers with the same base filenames but extensions of *.h*. The *.p* headers are compiled with GCC Version 2 for use with C and Objective-C programs, while the *.pp* headers are compiled with GCC Version 2 for C++ and Objective-C++ programs. By default, *fixPrecomps* compiles headers with GCC Version 3, in which case C/Objective-C precompiled header filenames end in –*gcc3.p*, and C++/Objective-C++ precompiled header filenames end in –*gcc3.pp*.

Options/Usage

–all

> Uses all files contained in */System/Library/SystemResources/PrecompLists/*. This is the default.

–checkOnly

> For each header file listed in the *precompList* files, prints a status message to standard output indicating whether the precompiled header exists and is up-to-date with the ordinary header.

–find_all_precomps

> Requires specification of *–all*, *–precompList* or *–precomps*, but otherwise doesn't appear to do anything.

–force

> Produces precompiled headers even if they're up-to-date. Using this flag causes the *–checkOnly* flag to be ignored.

–gcc2

> Applies the command to GCC Version 2 C/Objective-C (*.p*) and C++/Objective-C++ (*.pp*) precompiled headers.

–gcc3all

> Applies the command to GCC Version 3 C++/Objective-C++ (*-gcc3.pp*) precompiled headers, as well as to those for C/Objective-C (*-gcc3.p*).

–help

> Prints a usage statement to standard error.

–output

> Checks for and creates precompiled headers in locations relative to the specified directory. Intermediate directories must already exist, or compilation will fail.

–precompFlags

> Specifies additional *cc* command-line flags to use when compiling headers.

–precompList

> Uses only the *precompList* files specified.

–precomps

> Specifies a list of precompiled headers to check or create.

–relroot

> Looks for *System/Library/SystemResources/PrecompLists/* relative to the specified directory. The default is */*.

–skipIfMissing

> Compiles precompiled headers if they're out-of-date, but not if they don't exist. Using this flag causes the *–checkOnly* flag to be ignored.

Location

/usr/bin

FixupResourceForks

FixupResourceForks [-nodelete] [-nosetinfo] [-q[uiet]] *pathname*...

Description

Recombines the resource fork and HFS metadata split out into a separate file (named *._filename*) with the file's data fork (in a file named *filename*), resulting in a single multi-forked file (named *filename*) with HFS attributes. As such, this option works only on HFS and HFS+ volumes. It reverses the effect of running *SplitForks*.

FixupResourceForks does a recursive descent into the directory specified by *pathname*, working on every file within it.

Options/Usage

–nodelete
> Prevents deletion of *._filename* after recombination with *filename*.

–nosetinfo
> Disables setting of HFS attributes on the recombined files.

–quiet
> Suppresses printing the name of each recombined file to standard output.

Location

/System/Library/CoreServices

---

gcc_select

gcc_select [-v | --version] [-h | --help] [-l | --list]

gcc_select [-v | --version] [-n] [-force] [-root] [-dstroot *pathname*] { 2 | 3 | 3.*x* }

Description

A shell script that sets the default version of GCC (either 2.95.2 (**2**), 3.1 (**3**), or some other version (specified as **3.***x*)) by creating various symlinks for compiler tools, libraries, and headers. With no arguments (or with just **–v**), the current default version is printed to standard output.

Options/Usage

–dstroot
> Specifies the root-level directory where changes are made. The default is */usr*.

–force
> Recreates symlinks for the specified version, even if it is already the current default version.

–h | *--help*
>   Prints a usage statement to standard output.

–l | *--list*
>   Lists available GCC versions.

–n
>   Prints the list of commands that would be executed to standard output, but does not actually execute them.

–root
>   Disables the initial check for *root* access before executing commands.

–v | *--version*
>   Prints the version of *gcc_select* to standard output.

Location

/usr/sbin

---

hfs.util

```
hfs.util { -m | -M } device mount_point { fixed | removable }
{ readonly | writable } { suid | nosuid } { dev | nodev }

hfs.util -p device { fixed | removable } { readonly | writable }

hfs.util { -a | -k | -s | -u } device

hfs.util { -J | -U | -I } mount_point
```

Description

Mounts HFS and HFS+ filesystems into the directory hierarchy.

Options/Usage

–a Enables (adopts) permissions on the volume, creating an entry for it in */var/db/volinfo.database* if one does not already exist. Unlike *disktool –A* or *vsdbutil –a*, this option functions only on an unmounted volume.

–I Prints information about the journal file to standard output.

–J Enables journaling on the volume.

–k Reads the disk's UUID key and prints it to standard output. Functions only on an unmounted volume.

–m Mounts the device.

–M Attempts to force the mount.

–p Probes the device, and prints the volume name to standard output.

–s Generates a new disk UUID key and sets it on the volume. Functions only on an unmounted volume.

–u Unmounts the device. This function doesn't appear to work.

–U Disables journaling on the volume.

device

The disk device filename, e.g., **disk0s5**.

mount_point

The directory on which the filesystem is mounted.

Location

/System/Library/Filesystems/hfs.fs

---

hostinfo

hostinfo

Description

Prints basic information about the system to standard output, including Darwin version number, number and types of processors, amount of physical memory, current number of Mach tasks and threads running in the kernel, and CPU load.

Example

```
% hostinfo
Mach kernel version:
        Darwin Kernel Version 7.0.0:
Wed Sep 17 20:12:58 PDT 2003; root:xnu/xnu-510.obj~1/RELEASE_PPC


Kernel configured for a single processor only.
1 processor is physically available.
Processor type: ppc750 (PowerPC 750)
Processor active: 0
Primary memory available: 320.00 megabytes.
Default processor set: 51 tasks, 114 threads, 1 processors
Load average: 0.18, Mach factor: 0.89
```

Location

/usr/bin

---

hwprefs

hwprefs [-h]

hwprefs [-v] *parameter*[=*value*] [*parameter*[=*value*]]...

Description

Prints some information about the system to standard output. This option is installed as part of the Computer Hardware Understanding Development (CHUD) set of developer tools.

Options/Usage

−*h*   Prints a usage statement to standard error.

−*v*   Prints information verbosely.

parameter
> One of the following: **cpus** reports the number of CPUs (either 1 or 2), **cpunap** reports whether the CPU may slow down to conserve energy (either 0 or 1), **hwprefetch** reports the number of prefetch engines used by a G5 CPU (either 4 or 8), and **ostype** reports the code name for the system's OS: Cheetah (Mac OS X 10.0), Puma (10.1), Jaguar (10.2), Smeagol (10.2.7), or Panther (10.3).

Location

/usr/bin

---

ipconfig

```
ipconfig getifaddr interface

ipconfig getoption { interface | "" } { option_name | option_code }

ipconfig getpacket interface

ipconfig ifcount

ipconfig set interface { BOOTP | DHCP }

ipconfig set interface { INFORM | MANUAL } IP_addr netmask

ipconfig waitall
```

Description

Interacts with the IP Configuration Agent of *configd* to manage network configuration changes.

Options/Usage

getifaddr
> Prints the specified network interface's IP address to standard output.

getoption
> Prints the value of the specified DHCP option to standard output. If *interface* is specified, the option is interface-specific. If empty quotes are used instead, the option is global. Option names and numeric codes are DHCP-standard (such as **host_name**, **domain_name**, **netinfo_server_address**, etc.).

getpacket
> Prints DHCP transaction packets to standard output.

ifcount
> Prints the number of network interfaces to standard output.

set

Sets the method by which the specified network interface is assigned an IP address. Using *BOOTP* or *DHCP* causes the system to attempt to contact a server of the appropriate type to obtain IP configuration information. Using *INFORM* sets the IP address locally, but initiates a DHCP request to obtain additional IP configuration information (DNS servers, default gateway, etc.). Using *MANUAL* indicates that all IP configuration information is set locally.

waitall

Sets the configurations of all network interfaces according to the specifications in */etc/iftab*.

Location

/usr/sbin

kdumpd

kdumpd [-l] [-s *directory* [-u *username*] [-c | -C]] [-n] [*directory*]

Description

Provides a service meant to accept transfers of kernel core dumps from remote Mac OS X clients. Based on *tftpd*, *kdumpd* offers a simplistic file drop service. Setting it up involves:

- Adding a *kdump* entry to */etc/services*, recommended on UDP port 1069.
- Creating a *kdump* service file in */etc/xinetd.d/*, modeled after that for *tftp*.
- Executing *sudo service kdump start*.

Once that's done, you can invoke *tftp* on a client system, enter *connect server_name 1069*, and use *put filename* to transfer a file. The file will be saved on the server in the directory specified in the arguments to *kdumpd*. There are restrictions: the filename cannot include / or .., so the target file will be deposited into the target directory only and must not already exist.

This service is apparently not used by any current facility, but may exist for future use by Apple.

Options/Usage

−c Same as −C. Using this option should reject the connection if the path including the client IP address doesn't exist, but a bug prevents it from doing this.

−C Adds the client's IP address to the end of the *chroot* directory path. If this path doesn't already exist, it falls back to the one specified for −s.

−l Enables logging via *syslog* using the ftp facility. However, logging is enabled by default, so this option doesn't actually do anything.

–n Suppresses a negative acknowledgment if the client requests a relative path-name that doesn't exist.

–s Performs a *chroot* to the specified directory.

–u Changes user ID to the specified username. Defaults to *nobody*.

Location

/usr/libexec

---

kuncd

```
kuncd [-d]
```

Description

The Kernel-User Notification Center server, which handles communication to users from kernel processes. *kuncd* is started as a bootstrap daemon from */etc/mach_init.d/kuncd.plist* (processed by *register_mach_bootstrap_servers*). For more information, check out *http://developer.apple.com/documentation/DeviceDrivers/Conceptual/WritingDeviceDriver/KernelUserNotification/*.

Options/Usage

–d Enables debugging output.

Location

/usr/libexec

---

languagesetup

```
languagesetup -h

languagesetup -langspec language

languagesetup [-English | -Localized]
```

Description

Changes the default language used by the system. If invoked with no arguments, or with the *–English* or *–Localized* flags, *languagesetup* enters an interactive session in which the new language may be chosen from a menu.

Options/Usage

–English
> Presents interactive prompts in English.

–h
> Prints a usage statement to standard output.

–langspec
> Specifies the new system language on the command line, instead of interactively.

–Localized
> Presents interactive prompts in the system's default language.

Location

/usr/sbin

---

makekey

makekey

Description

Produces *crypt* password hashes. This command could be used to automatically populate a password database from known passwords, or to make hashes of prospective passwords that could be subjected to cracking attempts before being put into use.

Options/Usage

makekey takes no command-line arguments. It accepts a character string on standard input, consisting of an eight-character password combined with a two-character *salt*, which is used to permute the DES password encryption algorithm. (Use *man crypt* for more information.) It prints a thirteen-character string to standard output, with the first two characters being the salt, and the other eleven characters being the password hash. The entire string is suitable for use as the password field in a standard Unix */etc/passwd*-format file, or as the value of the passwd property in an Open Directory entry for a user employing Basic authentication.

Example

```
% echo password12 | /usr/libexec/makekey
12CsGd8FRcMSM
```

Location

/usr/libexec

mDNS

mDNS [-E | -F | -A | -U | -N | -T | -M]

mDNS -B *type domain*

mDNS -L *service_name _app_protocol._transport_protocol domain*

mDNS -R *service_name _app_protocol._transport_protocol domain port*
[*string*]...

Description

A basic client for Rendezvous multicast DNS (mDNS), primarily used for testing local mDNS service. When invoked with no arguments, it prints a usage statement to standard error. In most instances, the command doesn't return on its own, so you'll need to use Ctrl-C to break out.

When registering or looking up a name like *website._http._tcp.local.*, *website* is the *service_name*, *http* is the *app_protocol*, *tcp* is the *transport_protocol*, and *local* is the *domain*. For example, to register such a service:

```
% mDNS -R website _http._tcp local 80 "my web site"
```

Options/Usage

-A   Tests mDNS by repeatedly adding, updating, and then deleting an HINFO resource record for *Test._testupdate._tcp.local.*.

-B   Browses for services (although this doesn't seem to work).

-E   Discovers and lists domains recommended for registration of services.

-F   Discovers and lists domains recommended for browsing of services.

-L   Looks up a service, displaying its host address, port number, and TXT records if found.

-M   Tests mDNS by registering a service (*Test._testdualtxt._tcp.local.*) with multiple TXT resource records.

-N   Tests mDNS by registering a service (*Test._testupdate._tcp.local.*) with a large NULL resource record.

-R   Registers a service.

-T   Tests mDNS by registering a service (*Test._testlargetxt._tcp.local.*) with a large TXT resource record.

-U   Tests mDNS by repeatedly updating a TXT resource record for *Test._testupdate._tcp.local.*.

Location

/usr/bin

mDNSResponder

mDNSResponder [-d]

Description

The server for Rendezvous multicast DNS (mDNS). *mDNSResponder* is started by the *mDNSResponder* startup item, creates a PID file in */var/run/*, and responds to TERM and INT signals by quitting cleanly.

Options/Usage

-d Runs in debug mode, preventing daemonization, although it doesn't appear to be particularly useful in this state.

Location

/usr/sbin

---

mount_devfs

mount_devfs [-o *mount_options*] devfs *mount_point*

Description

Mounts the *devfs* filesystem in */dev*, where block and character device special files exist.

Options/Usage

-o

    Takes *-o* options as listed in the *mount* manpage. Not normally used for *mount_devfs*.

mount_point

    The directory on which the filesystem will be mounted, normally */dev*.

Location

/sbin

---

mount_ftp

mount_ftp [-o *mount_options*] [ftp://][*username:password@*]*ftp_server:port_num*[*/pathname*] *mount_point*

Description

Mounts FTP archives as filesystem volumes.

Options/Usage

−o

    Takes *−o* options as listed in the *mount* manpage.

username

    The login name to use with an FTP server that requires authentication.

password

    The password to use with an FTP server that requires authentication. Note that specifying this option on the command line exposes the password in a process listing.

ftp_server

    The hostname or IP address of an FTP server.

port_num

    The port number on which the server offers FTP service.

pathname

    The path to the directory you wish to access on the FTP server, relative to the site's default FTP root directory (e.g., */Library/FTPServer/FTPRoot* on Mac OS X Server). Defaults to */*.

mount_point

    The directory on which the filesystem will be mounted. It must be an absolute pathname.

Location

/sbin

---

mount_smbfs

mount_smbfs { -h | -v }

mount_smbfs [-u *username_or_ID*] [-g *groupname_or_ID*] [-f *mode*] [-d *mode*] [-I *hostname_or_IP*] [-n *long*] [-N] [-U *username*] [-W *workgroup_name*] [-O *c_user*[:*c_group*]/*s_user*[:*s_group*]] [-M *c_mode*[/*s_mode*]] [-R *num_retries*] [-T *timeout*] [-o *mount_options*] [-x *max_mounts*] //[*workgroup*;][*username*[:*password*]@]*smb_server*[/*share_name*] *mount_point*

Description

Mounts Server Message Block (SMB) shares as filesystem volumes. It takes a share UNC and a mount point as arguments.

mount_smbfs can make use of the same configuration files used by *smbutil*: either *.nsmbrc* in the user's home directory, or the global */usr/local/etc/nsmb.conf*, which overrides per-user files. The following example *.nsmbrc* demonstrates some of the parameters available:

```
[default]
username=leonvs
# NetBIOS name server
```

```
nbns=192.168.1.3

[VAMANA]
# server IP address
addr=192.168.1.6
workgroup=TEST

[VAMANA:LEONVS]
password= $$178465324253e0c07
```

The file consists of sections, each with a heading in brackets. Besides the [default] section, headings have a server name to which the parameters in the section apply, and can also include a username and a share name.

Sections of the configuration file may not be read properly unless the hostnames and usernames in the section headings are rendered in uppercase characters.

All sections and parameter definitions in *.nsmbrc* are optional; everything can be specified right on the *mount_smbfs* command line. This option may come in handy for providing passwords for automated connections, when prompting for a password (which is the most secure method of providing it) is impractical. The value of the password parameter can be a cleartext password, but it's derived from the output of *smbutil crypt password* in this example. While this is better than cleartext, don't trust the encryption too much, as it's fairly weak. Make sure you restrict permissions on *.nsmbrc* to prevent anyone from reading your passwords.

Options/Usage

−d Specifies directory permissions on the mounted volume, which default to the same as file permissions, plus an execute bit whenever a read bit is set. The argument is an octal mode, as described in the *chmod* manpage.

−f Specifies file permissions on the mounted volume, which default to the same as those set on the mount point. The argument is an octal mode, as described in the *chmod* manpage.

−g Specifies group ownership for files and directories on the mounted volume, which defaults to the same as that set on the mount point.

−h Prints a brief usage statement to standard error.

−I Avoids NetBIOS name resolution, connecting directly to the hostname or IP address specified as an argument.

−M Assigns access rights to the SMB connection.

−n With an argument of **long**, disables support for long filenames, restricting them to the "8.3" naming standard.

−N Suppresses the prompt for a password. Unless a password is specified in a configuration file, authentication will fail for non-guest users.

−o Takes −o options, as listed in the *mount* manpage.

−O Assigns owner attributes to the SMB connection.

-R   Specifies the number of times to retry a mount attempt. The default is **4**.

-T   Specifies the connection request timeout (in seconds). The default is **15**.

-u   Specifies ownership for files and directories on the mounted volume, which defaults to the same as that set on the mount point.

-U   Specifies a username for authentication. This may also be part of the UNC.

-v   Prints software version to standard error.

-W   Specifies an SMB workgroup or NT domain for authentication. This may also be part of the UNC.

-x   Automatically mounts all shares from the SMB server. The argument specifies a maximum number of shares that *mount_smbfs* is willing to mount from a server, to forestall resource starvation when the server has a very large number of shares. If the server has more shares than *max_mounts*, the mount attempt is cancelled.

workgroup
> The name of the SMB workgroup or NT domain to use for authentication to the SMB server.

username
> The name to use for authentication to the SMB server.

password
> The password to use for authentication. Note that specifying this option on the command line exposes the password in a process listing.

smb_server
> The NetBIOS name of an SMB server.

share_name
> The name of the SMB share you wish to access.

mount_point
> The directory on which the filesystem will be mounted.

Location

/sbin

---

mount_synthfs

mount_synthfs [-o *mount_options*] synthfs *mount_point*

Description

Mounts a *synthfs* filesystem, which is a simple mapping of memory into the filesystem hierarchy (i.e., the contents of a *synthfs* filesystem are contained in memory). While creation of files in the filesystem is prevented (in fact, you may cause the system to hang after attempting to create files), directory hierarchies are allowed. This option could be used to set up transient mount points for other volumes on, for example, read-only media with a shortage of spare directories to serve as mount points (such as an installation CD).

Options/Usage

−o

> Takes *−o* options as listed in the *mount* manpage.

mount_point

> The directory on which the filesystem will be mounted.

Location

/sbin

---

mount_volfs

```
mount_volfs [-o mount_options] mount_point
```

Description

Mounts the *volfs* filesystem in */.vol*. The *volfs* filesystem enables the Carbon File Manager API to map a file ID to a file, without knowing the BSD path to it. Thus, HFS aliases, which use file IDs, remain consistent, even if the targets of the aliases move around within the volume.

The */.vol* directory contains subdirectories named with numeric IDs, each associated with a volume on the system. While the directories appear empty if listed, with a file or directory ID one can access any object on those volumes. A file ID is a unique number associated with each file on a volume (analogous to an inode number on a UFS-formatted filesystem), and can be viewed with the *−i* option of *ls*.

If you know a file's ID, you can access it as */.vol/vol_ID/file_ID*. If you know the ID of the directory the file is in, you can also access it as */.vol/vol_ID/dir_ID/ filename*. The root directory of a volume always has a directory ID of 2, so you can map volume IDs to volumes with:

```
% cd /.vol/vol_ID/2; pwd
```

Options/Usage

−o

> Takes *−o* options as listed in the *mount* manpage. Not normally used for *mount_volfs*.

mount_point

> The directory on which the filesystem will be mounted, normally */.vol*.

Location

/sbin

msdos.util

```
msdos.util -m device mount_point { fixed | removable }
{ readonly | writable } { suid | nosuid } { dev | nodev }

msdos.util -p device { fixed | removable } { readonly | writable }

msdos.util -u device

msdos.util -n device name
```

Description

Mounts FAT (MS-DOS) filesystems into the directory hierarchy.

Options/Usage

–m Mounts the device.

–n Resets the volume name of the device. This function doesn't appear to work.

–p Probes the device, and prints the volume name to standard output.

–u Unmounts the device. This function doesn't appear to work.

device
> The disk device filename, e.g., **disk0s5**.

mount_point
> The directory on which the filesystem is mounted.

Location

/System/Library/Filesystems/msdos.fs

---

notifyd

```
notifyd [-no_restart] [-no_startup] [-shm_pages integer]
```

Description

The notification server for the API described in the *notify(3)* manpage. (Use *man 3 notify* to display this page.) Using the API, processes may post notifications associated with arbitrary names, and other processes can register to be informed of such notification events. (A name should follow the convention used for Java classes: the reversed DNS domain name associated with the responsible organization, followed by one or more segments; for example, com.apple.system.timezone.) *notifyd* sets up the shared memory used for the *notify_register_check* call, and directly answers *notify_check* requests for other notification methods (signal, Mach port, and file descriptor).

notifyd also reads a configuration file, */etc/notify.conf*. Each line begins with one of two keywords: reserve or monitor. The reserve keyword lays out access restrictions for portions of the namespace. The arguments are a name, a user and a group that "owns" the name, and a set of read /write permissions for the user, the group, and others, similar to those applied to files. For example, the following line:

```
reserve com.apple.system. 0 0 rwr-r-
```

states that any names starting with *com.apple.system.* are owned by UID 0 (*root*) and GID 0 (*wheel*), and that anyone can receive notifications for these names, but only *root* (the owner) can post notifications.

The monitor keyword takes a name and a filename as arguments. When the specified file is changed, a notification is posted for the name. For example, the following line from the stock */etc/notify.conf* can be used by processes wishing to keep track of time zone changes:

```
monitor com.apple.system.timezone /etc/localtime
```

Another use would be to monitor changes to a daemon's configuration file. When the file is changed, the daemon or another process could receive notification and cause the daemon to automatically reread the configuration.

notifyd is started as a bootstrap daemon, from */etc/mach_init.d/notifyd.plist* (processed by *register_mach_bootstrap_servers*). It responds to HUP or TERM signals by restarting (unless the *–no_restart* flag was used), thus rereading */etc/ notify.conf*. Before *notifyd* exits, it sends notifications for all registered names; after it restarts, processes registered for notifications must register again, as their tokens become invalid.

Options/Usage

–no_restart

Disables automatic restart. Normally, if *notifyd* is killed, it's restarted within a few seconds.

–no_startup

Apparently prevents *notifyd* from issuing notifications, while using all available CPU time. The purpose of this option is unknown.

–shm_pages

Specifies the number of pages (i.e., units of 4096 bytes) to reserve for shared memory (although it appears to use about twice that). Defaults to **1**.

Location

/usr/sbin

---

ntp-wait

```
ntp-wait [-v] [-f] [-n num_tries] [-s time]
```

Description

A Perl script that reports whether the local *ntpd* has synchronized yet. Returns 0 if synchronized; 1 if not.

Options/Usage

–f   Causes *ntp-wait* to return 1 if an indeterminate result is received from *ntpd*; otherwise, *ntp-wait* returns 0.

–n Specifies the number of times to try for a successful result before quitting. Defaults to **1000**.

–s   Specifies the number of seconds between tries. Defaults to **6**.

–v Enables verbose output to standard output.

Location

/usr/bin

---

ntptimeset

```
ntptimeset [-l] [-d]... [-v] [-s] [-c filename] [-u] [-S integer]
[-V integer] [-t timeout] [-H] [-a key_id] [-e delay]
```

Description

Synchronizes the system clock in a manner similar to *ntpdate*, but in a way that attempts to compensate for current, possibly degraded, network conditions.

Options/Usage

–a Enables secure authentication with the key specified by the given identifier.

–c Specifies the location of the configuration file. Defaults to */etc/ntp.conf*.

–d Enables debugging output.

–e Specifies the delay, in seconds, caused by authentication. Normally this value is negligible.

–H Simulates poor network conditions by dropping a proportion of network packets.

–l   Enables logging to *syslog*.

–s   Sets the system clock. Otherwise, *ntptimeset* merely reports the clock's offset.

–S Specifies a minimum number of servers that must respond. Defaults to **3**.

–t   Specifies time, in seconds, spent waiting for a server response. Defaults to **1**.

–u Uses an unprivileged client port.

–v Enables verbose output.

–V Specifies a minimum number of servers that must respond with a valid time. Defaults to **1**.

Location

/usr/sbin

od

od [-c] [-a] [-b] [-B] [-o] [-O] [-d] [-D] [-i] [-I] [-l] [-L] [-f] [-e]
[-F] [-h] [-x] [-H] [-X] [-v] [*filename*]

Description

Prints the contents of a file to standard output in a variety of formats. (If no file-name is specified, it acts on the contents of standard input.) The name is an acronym for *octal dump*, from its default behavior of displaying files as series of octal numbers.

od has been deprecated in favor of *hexdump*; in fact, the two binaries are hard-linked to the same data. However, traditional *od* syntax applies when invoked by that name. See the *hexdump* manpage for more.

Options/Usage

−*a* Displays content in 1-byte chunks of ASCII characters, hexadecimal numbers, and short strings representing control characters.

−*b* Displays content in 1-byte chunks of octal numbers.

−*B* Displays content in 2-byte chunks of octal numbers. This option is the default.

−*c* Displays content in 1-byte chunks of ASCII characters, octal numbers, and escape sequences representing control characters. This is probably the most commonly used option.

−*d* Displays content in 2-byte chunks of unsigned decimal integers.

−*D* Displays content in 4-byte chunks of unsigned decimal integers.

−*e* Displays content in 8-byte chunks of decimal floating-point numbers.

−*f* Displays content in 4-byte chunks of decimal floating-point numbers.

−*F* Same as −*e*.

−*h* Displays content in 2-byte chunks of hexadecimal numbers.

−*H* Displays content in 4-byte chunks of hexadecimal numbers.

−*i* Displays content in 2-byte chunks of signed decimal integers.

−*I* Displays content in 4-byte chunks of signed decimal integers.

−*l* Same as −*I*.

−*L* Same as −*I*.

−*o* Same as −*B*.

−*O* Displays content in 4-byte chunks of octal numbers.

−*v* Disables the suppression of duplicate lines, which are normally represented by a single asterisk.

−*x* Same as −*h*.

−*X* Same as −*H*.

Location

/usr/bin

opendiff

opendiff *file1* *file2* [-ancestor *ancestor_file*] [-merge *merge_file*]

Description

Opens the two designated files in the FileMerge application.

Options/Usage

–ancestor
>   Compares the two files against a common ancestor file.

–merge
>   Merges the two files into a new file.

Location

/usr/bin

---

open-x11

open-x11 *app_name*...

Description

Starts specified X Window System applications using the X11 application.

Options/Usage

app_name
>   The name of an executable X11 application. Those delivered with Mac OS X are in */usr/X11R6/bin/*. If located in a standard directory, the application pathname is not required.

Location

/usr/bin

pdisk

pdisk

pdisk *device* { -diskSize | -isDiskPartitioned | -dump | -blockSize | -initialize }

pdisk *device* { -partitionEntry | -partitionName | -partitionType | -partitionBase | -partitionSize | -deletePartition } *part_num*

pdisk *device* { -setWritable | -setAutoMount } *part_num* { 0 | 1 }pdisk *device*

-makeBootable *part_num boot_addr boot_bytes load_addr goto_addr*

pdisk *device* -createPartition *part_name part_type part_base part_size*

pdisk *device* -splitPartition *part_num part1_size part2_name part2_type*

pdisk *device* -getPartitionOfType *part_type instance_num*

pdisk *device* -getPartitionWithName *part_name instance_num*

Description

Provides control over Apple partition maps on disk devices in Macintosh systems.

Options/Usage

–blockSize
> Prints the block size of the specified device, in bytes, to standard output.

–createPartition
> Adds a partition to the partition map with the specified name, type (such as **Apple_HFS** or **Apple_UFS**), base (i.e., starting block number), and size (in blocks).

–deletePartition
> Deletes the specified partition from the partition map.

–diskSize
> Prints the size of the specified device, in megabytes, to standard output.

–dump
> Prints the partition map on the specified device to standard output.

–getPartitionOfType
> Prints the number of a partition with the specified type to standard output. An *instance_num* of **0** refers to the lowest-numbered partition of the specified type, **1** refers to the second partition of that type, etc.

–getPartitionWithName
> Prints the number of a partition with the specified name to standard output. An *instance_num* of **0** refers to the lowest-numbered partition with the specified name, **1** refers to the second partition of that name, etc.

–initialize
> Creates a partition map on the device.

–isDiskPartitioned

Returns 0 if the device has an Apple partition map on it, 1 if not.

–makeBootable

Sets the startup bit on a partition. This is unused by Mac OS X.

–partitionBase

Prints the starting block number of the specified partition to standard output.

–partitionEntry

Prints a line to standard output containing the name, type, base, and size of the specified partition.

–partitionName

Prints the name of the specified partition to standard output.

–partitionSize

Prints the size of the specified partition, in blocks, to standard output.

–partitionType

Prints the type of the specified partition to standard output.

–setAutoMount

Sets (**1**) or clears (**0**) the automount bit on a partition. This option is unused by Mac OS X.

–setWritable

Sets (**1**) or clears (**0**) the writable bit on a partition.

–splitPartition

Splits an existing partition in two. The arguments include the size (in blocks) of the first partition formed from the split, and the name and type of the second partition.

device

The disk device filename, e.g., **/dev/disk0**.

Commands

pdisk enters interactive mode when invoked without arguments. Interactive commands that take arguments will prompt for any that are missing.

?   Displays a summary list of commands.

a   Toggles the abbreviate flag. When in abbreviate mode, partition type names are shortened. For example, `Apple_HFS` is displayed as `HFS`.

d   Toggles the debug flag. When in debug mode, some extra commands are enabled, including commands to display block contents and partition map data structures.

e device

Edits the partition map on a device.

E device

Should open a partition map for editing after prompting for a redefinition of the logical block size from the default 512 bytes, but doesn't appear to work at present.

| *h* | Displays a summary list of commands. |

l device
Displays the partition map on a device.

L	Displays the partition maps on all devices.
p	Toggles the physical flag. When in physical mode, block positions and sizes are reported according to the physical limits of the partitions, which may not be the same as their logical limits.
q	Quits interactive mode.
r	Toggles the read-only flag. When in read-only mode, changes to the partition map are disallowed.
v	Prints the version number and release date of *pdisk*. (The output is currently far out of date, listing a release in 1997, when it was still used for MkLinux.)

x device block_num
Displays the contents of the block given by *block_num*. While it always appears to produce a bus error when called at this level, the same functionality is available from an expert level while editing a map, where it does work.

Location

/usr/sbin

---

pdump

```
pdump [-v] [-s] [-h] [-p] [-d] [-d0] [-d1] [-d2] [-d3] [-d4] [-d5] [-d6]
[-st] [-i] [-e] [-x] [-if] [-t] [-o] [-k] [-m] [-class class] [-protocol
protocol] [-arch arch] [-f]
```

Description

Prints information about precompiled header files to standard output. See the entry for *fixPrecomps* for more on precompiled headers.

Options/Usage

–arch
Appears to do nothing.

–class
Lists the method declarations for the specified class.

–d Lists all declarations.

–d0 Lists type definition declarations.

–d1 Lists class declarations.

–d2 Lists category declarations.

–d3 Lists protocol declarations.

–d4 Lists enumerated constant declarations.

–d5 Lists function declarations.

–d6 Lists variable declarations.

–e Lists entry macros.

–f Appears to do nothing.

–h Lists included headers.

–i Lists all identifiers.

–if Lists conditional macros defined outside the precompiled header.

–k Lists "must keeps".

–m Lists method names and their classes.

–o Lists preprocessed tokens.

–p Lists paths to included headers.

–protocol
    Lists the method declarations for the specified protocol.

–s Lists bytes taken up by each of several kinds of elements in the precompiled header.

–st Lists all strings.

–t Lists all tags.

–v Enables verbose output.

–x Lists exit macros.

Location

/usr/bin

postfix-watch

```
postfix-watch
```

Description

Starts Postfix processes necessary to send email on demand. For a system that isn't providing mail service, Mac OS X runs those processes only when mail is queued for sending in */var/spool/postfix/maildrop*.

postfix-watch is started by the *Postfix* startup item.

Location

/usr/sbin

register_mach_bootstrap_servers

register_mach_bootstrap_servers *config_source*

Description

Registers a Mach port with the bootstrap task of *mach_init* on behalf of a specified daemon. (A Mach *task* is analogous to a process that runs within the kernel of Mac OS X; a *port* is used to communicate between tasks.) When another task sends a request to the bootstrap task for access to a port, *mach_init* starts up the associated daemon if necessary.

This program serves as a replacement for certain startup items on Panther. Instead of launching services from */System/Library/StartupItems/* (processed by *SystemStarter*), files in */etc/mach_init.d/* are processed by *register_mach_bootstrap_servers*, which is called from */etc/rc*. (Per-user services are started by the login window application, which uses *register_mach_bootstrap_servers* to process */etc/mach_init_per_user.d/*.) One advantage of this program over startup items is that a daemon can be run only when needed, if another process needs to communicate with it, thus reducing resource consumption.

Options/Usage

config_source
> Either an XML property list (*.plist*) file, or a directory containing such files. Each file is usually named after the associated daemon, and contains some of the following keys:

Command
> The path to the server executable. This is a required key.

isKUNCServer
> Specifies whether the daemon is *kuncd*, the Kernel-User Notification Center server, used by the kernel to communicate with users. Defaults to false.

OnDemand
> Specifies whether the daemon should only be started when it first receives a request for its bootstrap port. If set to false, the daemon is started immediately. Defaults to true.

ServiceName
> An identifier for the service. The name should follow the convention used for Java classes: the reversed DNS domain name associated with the responsible organization, followed by one or more segments specifically identifying the service (e.g., com.apple.DirectoryService). This is a required key.

Username
> The user under which the daemon is started.

Location

/usr/libexec

screencapture

screencapture [-i [-s | -w | -W] | -m] [-x] { -c | *pathname* ...}

Description

Saves the contents of the screen to a PDF file or to the Clipboard. Unless using the *–i* option to start an interactive screen capture, the contents of the entire display are captured.

Options/Usage

–c Saves screenshot to the Clipboard for later pasting.

–i Initiates interactive screen capture. The mouse is used to select a region of the screen to capture. Pressing the spacebar toggles between this mouse selection mode and a window selection mode, in which clicking on a window captures the portion of the screen taken up by that window. Pressing the Control key saves the screenshot to the Clipboard. Pressing the Escape key cancels the interactive screen capture.

–m Captures only the main display, if multiple displays are in use.

–s Disables window selection mode in an interactive screen capture; only mouse selection is allowed.

–w Disables mouse selection mode in an interactive screen capture; only window selection is allowed.

–W Starts an interactive screen capture in window selection mode instead of mouse selection mode.

–x Disables sound effects.

pathname
    The name of a file in which to save the screenshot. You should terminate the filename with a *.pdf* extension.

Location

/usr/sbin

---

scselect

scselect [[-n] *location*]

Description

Changes active network Location. With no arguments, a usage statement and a list of defined Locations (or "sets") are printed to standard output, along with an indication of which Location is currently active. Locations can be referred to by name or by integer ID.

Options/Usage

−n   Changes the active network Location, but does not apply the change.

Location

/usr/sbin

---

scutil

```
scutil [-v] [-p]
scutil [-v] [-d] -r { hostname | IP_addr [IP_addr] }
scutil [-v] -w key [-t timeout]
scutil [-v] --get { ComputerName | LocalHostName }
scutil [-v] --set { ComputerName | LocalHostName } [hostname]
```

Description

Provides control of the System Configuration framework's dynamic store. *scutil* is used to open an interactive session with *configd*, in which various commands are available to view and modify System Configuration keys.

As a quick example of interactive use, try this:

- Invoke *scutil*. You will be placed at the *scutil* prompt.
- Enter **open** to open the session with *configd*.
- Enter **list**. You will see a set of keys, some of which are provided by the System Configuration framework (such as the keys in the File: domain), some of which are obtained from */Library/Preferences/ SystemConfiguration/preferences.plist* (the Setup: keys), and some of which are published by the configuration agents (the State: keys).
- Enter **show State:/Network/Global/DNS** to display the DNS dictionary. You should see a list of DNS servers and search domains configured on your system.
- Enter **close**, then **quit**.

Options/Usage

−d   Enables debugging output to standard error.

--get
     Prints the system's computer name or Rendezvous hostname to standard output.

−p   Enables a private API with additional commands, including *lock*, *unlock*, *touch*, *snapshot*, *n.file*, *n.signal*, *n.wait*, and *n.callback*.

–r   Determines how the specified node (given as a hostname or an IP address) would be reached, printing the result to standard output. Possibilities include **Reachable**, **Directly Reachable Address** (the address is on the local network), and **Local Address** (the address resolves to the host on which the command is run). For systems with more than one network interface, two arguments may be given, where the first is the system's local address, and the second is the remote address. Note that this option does not determine whether a machine at the specified address is currently active, only whether that address is reachable.

--set
    Sets the system's computer name or Rendezvous hostname. If the new hostname isn't specified on the command line, it's taken from standard input.

–t   Specifies the timeout to wait for the presence of a data store key, in seconds. Defaults to **15**.

–v   Enables verbose output to standard error.

–w   Exits when the specified key exists in the data store, or until the timeout has expired.

Commands

scutil enters interactive mode when invoked with no arguments.

add key [temporary]
    Adds a key to the data store with the value of the current dictionary. The **temporary** keyword causes it to be flushed when the session to *configd* is closed.

close
    Closes a session with *configd*.

d.add key [* | ? | #] value...
    Adds an entry to the current dictionary. The optional type specifier can be used to designate the values as arrays (*****), booleans (**?**), or numbers (**#**).

d.init
    Creates an empty dictionary.

d.remove key
    Removes the specified key from the current dictionary.

d.show
    Displays the contents of the current dictionary.

exit
    Exits the *scutil* session.

f.read file
    Reads prepared commands from a file.

get key
    Causes the value of the specified key to become the current dictionary.

help
    Prints a list of available commands.

list [regex]

Lists keys in the System Configuration data store. A regular expression may be specified to restrict which keys are listed.

lock

Prevents changes to the data store by other processes.

n.add key [pattern]

Requests notification of changes made to the specified key, or to keys matching a regular expression (when the **pattern** argument is used).

n.callback [verbose]

Sends notifications via a callback function defined in the *scutil* code. This isn't particularly useful without modifying the source code.

n.cancel

Cancels *n.watch* settings.

n.changes

Lists changed keys that have been marked with notification requests, and resets the state of notification.

n.file [identifier]

Sends notifications to a file descriptor. After issuing this command, the prompt returns only after a notification is received.

n.list [pattern]

Lists keys upon which notification requests have been set. With the **pattern** argument, lists notification requests for keys matching regular expressions.

n.remove key [pattern]

Removes notification requests for the specified key or regular expression (when the **pattern** argument is used).

n.signal signal [process_ID]

Sends notifications by signaling a process. If a process ID isn't specified, the signal is sent to the *scutil* process. The signal is specified either as a name or a number (as described in the *kill* manpage).

n.wait

Sends notifications via Mach messaging.

n.watch [verbose]

Causes changes to keys marked with notification requests to issue immediate notices, obviating the need to use *n.changes* to notice that the change has occurred.

notify key

Sends a notification for the specified key.

open

Opens a session with *configd*.

q

Exits the *scutil* session.

quit

Exits the *scutil* session.

remove key
> Removes the specified key from the data store.

set key
> Sets the specified key to the value of the current dictionary.

show key [pattern]
> Same as *get key*, followed by *d.show*.

snapshot
> Saves current store and session data to XML property lists in */var/tmp/*.

touch key
> "Touches" the specified key, spurring notifications as if it had changed, but leaving it unaltered.

unlock
> After issuing a *lock* command, allows other processes to make changes to the data store.

Location

/usr/sbin

SecurityServer

SecurityServer [-a *config_file*] [-d] [-E *entropy_file*] [-f]
[-N *bootstrap_name*] [-t *max_threads*] [-T *thread_timeout*] [-X]

Description

Provides services to the Security framework, including authorization and secure key management.

Options/Usage

−a Specifies an Authorization Services configuration file. Defaults to */etc/authorization*.

−d Runs process in debug mode, and disables daemonization. Output is sent to standard error and to *syslog*.

−E Specifies a file to use as a source of entropy for cryptographic operations. Defaults to */var/db/SystemEntropyCache*.

−f Forces immediate initialization of the Common Security Services Manager (CSSM), the central access point for services provided by the Common Data Security Architecture (CDSA). Normally the CSSM will be initialized when it is first needed.

−N Specifies a service name used to register a Mach bootstrap port. Defaults to **SecurityServer**; any other setting will prevent authorization from working.

−t Limits the number of Mach threads started by the *SecurityServer* process. Defaults to **100**.

-*T*   Specifies a timeout for Mach threads started by the *SecurityServer* process, in seconds. Defaults to **120**.

-*X*   Directs *SecurityServer* to re-execute itself when in daemon mode, needed to work around Mach-related bugs in libraries.

Location

/System/Library/CoreServices

---

service

```
service --list
service { --test-if-available | --test-if-configured-on } service
service service { start | stop }
```

Description

A shell script used to list, start, and stop network services. *service* is primarily an interface to services managed by *xinetd*, but it also includes support for Postfix (with a service name of **smtp**) and for receipt of faxes (**fax-receive**) on Panther.

Options/Usage

--list
> Prints a list of services available for management to standard output.

--test-if-available
> Returns 0 if the specified service is available on the system; 1 if not.

--test-if-configured-on
> Returns 0 if the specified service is currently configured to run; 1 if not.

Location

/sbin

sips

sips [-h | --help | -H | --helpProperties]

sips [--debug] { -g | --getProperty } *property image_or_profile_filename...*

sips [--debug] { -x | --extractProfile } *profile_filename image_filename...*

sips [--debug] { -X | --extractTag } *tag tag_filename profile_filename...*

sips [--debug] { -v | --verify } *profile_filename...*

sips [--debug] { -s | --setProperty } *property value* [--out *filename*]
image_or_profile_filename...

sips [--debug] { -d | --deleteProperty } *property* [--out *filename*]
image_or_profile_filename...

sips [--debug] { -r | --rotate } *degrees* [--out *filename*] *image_filename...*

sips [--debug] { -f | --flip } { horizontal | vertical } [--out *filename*]
image_filename...

sips [--debug] { -c | --cropToHeightWidth | -p | --padToHeightWidth |
-z | resampleHeightWidth } *height_pixels width_pixels* [--out *filename*]
image_filename...

sips [--debug] { -Z | --resampleHeightWidthMax | --resampleHeight |
--resampleWidth } *pixels* [--out *filename*] *image_filename...*

sips [--debug] { -i | --addIcon } [--out *filename*] *image_filename...*

sips [--debug] { -e | --embedProfile | -E | --embedProfileIfNone | -m |
--matchTo } *profile_filename* [--out *filename*] *image_filename...*

sips [--debug] { -M | --matchToWithIntent } *profile_filename* { absolute |
relative | perceptual | satuation } [--out *filename*] *image_filename...*

sips [--debug] --deleteTag *tag* [--out *filename*] *profile_filename...*

sips [--debug] --copyTag *src_tag dst_tag* [--out *filename*]
profile_filename...

sips [--debug] --loadTag *tag tag_filename* [--out *filename*]
profile_filename...

sips [--debug] --repair [--out *filename*] *profile_filename...*

Description

The Scriptable Image Processing System (SIPS) tool can be used to manipulate
images and ColorSync profiles from the command line.

ColorSync profiles are International Color Consortium (ICC) files that characterize the color properties of different devices, so that accurate color matching can be performed between them. There are ColorSync profiles located under /System/Library/ColorSync/Profiles/, /Library/ColorSync/Profiles/, /Library/Printers/, and /Library/Image Capture/Devices/, among other places. For more on ColorSync, see *http://www.apple.com/macosx/features/colorsync/*.

Options/Usage

−c | --cropToHeightWidth
    Crops an image to the specified size (in pixels). The image is cropped equally from both top and bottom, and from both sides.

--copyTag
    Copies the value of a tag in a ColorSync profile to another tag in the same profile.

−d | --deleteProperty
    Deletes the specified property. A list of possible properties may be obtained with *sips −H*.

--debug
    Enables debugging output.

--deleteTag
    Deletes the specified tag from a ColorSync profile.

−e | --embedProfile
    Embeds the specified ColorSync profile into the image.

−E | --embedProfileIfNone
    Embeds the specified ColorSync profile into the image only if another profile is not already embedded.

−f | --flip
    Flips an image in the specified direction.

−g | --getProperty
    Prints the value of the specified property to standard output. A list of possible properties may be obtained with *sips −H*.

−h | --help
    Prints a usage message to standard output.

−H | --helpProperties
    Prints a list of image and profile properties to standard output.

−i | --addIcon
    Adds an icon for an image file to its resource fork, which is used in Finder previews.

--loadTag
    Copies the value of a tag from a file to a ColorSync profile. (This is the opposite of *--extractTag*.)

–m | --matchTo

Matches an image to the specified ColorSync profile.

–M | --matchToWithIntent

Matches an image to the specified ColorSync profile with the given rendering intent. (Note the misspelled **satuation**; this is a typo in the *sips* code.)

--out

Specifies the filename of the modified image file. By default, sips modifies the file in place; this option lets you save the modified file under a different name, leaving the original unchanged.

–p | --padToHeightWidth

Pads an image with blank space to the specified size (in pixels). The image is padded equally on both top and bottom, and on both sides.

–r | --rotate

Rotates an image the specified number of degrees clockwise.

--repair

Attempts to repair a malformed **desc** tag in a ColorSync profile. This option is the same as the Repair operation under Profile First Aid in the ColorSync Utility application.

--resampleHeight

Stretches or compresses an image to the specified height (in pixels).

--resampleWidth

Stretches or compresses an image to the specified width (in pixels).

–s | --setProperty

Sets a property to the specified value. A list of possible properties may be obtained with *sips –H*.

–v | --verify

Verifies the syntax of a ColorSync profile. This option is the same as the Verify operation under Profile First Aid in the ColorSync Utility application.

–x | --extractProfile

Copies an embedded ColorSync profile from an image to a file with the specified name.

–X | --extractTag

Copies the value of a tag (such as **desc**) from a ColorSync profile to a file with the specified name.

–z | --resampleHeightWidth

Stretches or compresses an image to the specified size (in pixels).

–Z | --resampleHeightWidthMax

Stretches or compresses an image while maintaining the aspect ratio. The largest dimension (height or width) is set to the specified size (in pixels).

Examples

Show the properties of a ColorSync profile (similar to what's displayed under the Profiles tab of the ColorSync Utility application):

```
% sips -g all /Library/ColorSync/Profiles/WebSafeColors.icc
/Library/ColorSync/Profiles/WebSafeColors.icc
  size: 10644
  cmm: appl
  version: 2.2.0
  class: nmcl
  space: RGB
  pcs: Lab
  creation: 2003:07:01 00:00:00
  platform: APPL
  quality: normal
  deviceManufacturer: 0
  deviceModel: 0
  deviceAttributes0: 0
  deviceAttributes1: 0
  renderingIntent: perceptual
  creator: appl
  md5: 14487F1ED8F8947B15F6682BFCF21E00
  description: Web Safe Colors
  copyright: Copyright 2001 - 2003 Copyright Apple Computer Inc., all rights
reserved.
```

Convert a TIFF to a JPEG from the command line (also works for PNG, GIF, PICT, BMP, and other image formats):

```
% sips -s format jpeg --out sample.jpeg sample.tiff
```

Location

/usr/bin

SplitForks

SplitForks { -u | [-v] *pathname* }

Description

Copies the resource fork and HFS attributes from a file named *filename* into a separate file named *.filename*, equivalent to an AppleDouble Header file. The original file retains the resource fork and HFS metadata as well.

If *pathname* refers to a file, that file's resource fork and metadata are split out. If *pathname* is a directory, *SplitForks* does a recursive descent into the directory, working on every file within it.

FixupResourceForks undoes the actions of *SplitForks*.

Options/Usage

−*u* Prints a usage statement to standard output.

−*v* Enables verbose output.

Location

/Developer/Tools

systemkeychain

```
systemkeychain [-v] [-f] -C [password]
systemkeychain [-v] -t
systemkeychain [-v] [-c] [-k dest_keychain] -s keychain
```

Description

Creates and manages the system keychain, */Library/Keychains/System.keychain*. (*systemkeychain* also creates */var/db/SystemKey*, which presumably contains a randomly generated keychain password in encrypted form.) This keychain is used by system processes that run as *root*, such as daemons and boot processes, and is created automatically by the *SecurityServer* startup item.

Options/Usage

−*c* Creates the destination keychain if it doesn't already exist.

−*C* Creates a new system keychain, unless one already exists. The keychain password can be specified with an optional argument.

−*f* Forces the overwrite of an existing system keychain when creating a new one.

−*k* Instead of adding a key to the system keychain, adds it to the specified destination keychain.

−*s* Adds a key to the system keychain that can be used to unlock the specified keychain.

−*t* Unlocks the system keychain.

−*v* Enables verbose output.

Location

/usr/sbin

udf.util

```
udf.util -m device mount_point
udf.util { -p | -u } device
```

Description

Mounts UDF (DVD) filesystems into the directory hierarchy.

Options/Usage

−m Mounts the device.

−p Probes the device, and prints the volume name to standard output.

−u Unmounts the device.

device
> The DVD device filename, e.g., **disk1**.

mount_point
> The directory on which the DVD filesystem is mounted.

Location

/System/Library/Filesystems/udf.fs

---

ufs.util

```
ufs.util { -k | -p | -s } device
ufs.util -n device name
```

Description

Manipulates UFS filesystems.

Options/Usage

−k Reads the disk's UUID key and prints it to standard output.

−n Resets the volume name of the device. It takes effect after the next remount.

−p Probes the device, and prints the volume name to standard output.

−s Generates a new disk UUID key and sets it on the volume.

device
> The disk device filename, e.g., **disk0s5**.

mount_point
> The directory on which the filesystem is mounted.

Location

/System/Library/Filesystems/ufs.fs

unzip

unzip [-v]

unzip –Z [-v] [-M] [-s | -m | -l | -1] [-T] *archive_filename* [*pathname...*]
[-x *pathname...*]

unzip –Z [-v] [-M] [-2] [-h] [-t] [-z] *archive_filename* [*pathname...*]
[-x *pathname...*]

unzip [-q[q] | -v] [-M] [-l | -t | -z | -p | -c [-a[a]]] [-b] [-C]
archive_filename [*pathname...*] [-x *pathname...*]

unzip [-q[q] | -v] [-M] [-f | -u] [-a[a] | -b] [-C] [-L] [-j] [-V] [-X]
[-n | -o] [-d *directory*] *archive_filename* [*pathname...*] [-x *pathname...*]

Description

Lists or extracts files from a ZIP archive (such as one created by the *zip* command). If the name of the archive file ends in *.zip*, that extension need not be specified in *archive_filename*. If *pathname* arguments are given, only archive items matching those arguments are processed; otherwise, *unzip* lists or extracts all items in the archive. When called with no arguments, it prints a usage statement to standard output.

Options/Usage

–*a*   Converts text files in the archive to native format. For instance, this option translates DOS linefeeds to Unix linefeeds on Mac OS X. When doubled (-*aa*), it attempts to convert all files, whether text or binary.

–*b*   Treats all files as binary, so that no text conversions are attempted.

–*c*   Extracts file data to standard output.

–*C*   Uses case-insensitive matching of *pathname* arguments to archive items.

–*d*   Extracts files into the given directory. Otherwise, files are extracted into the current working directory.

–*f*   Extracts files only if they already exist, and if the modification timestamps in the archive are more recent than those on disk.

–*j*   Discards the paths of archived files, so that all files are extracted into the same directory.

–*l*   Lists archive contents, along with sizes, modification timestamps, and comments. More information is printed if –*v* is also used.

–*L*   Converts filenames to lowercase if they were archived from a single-case filesystem (such as FAT). When doubled (-*LL*), all filenames are converted to lowercase.

–*M*   Displays output a page at a time.

–*n*   Never overwrites existing files when extracting. By default, *unzip* prompts the user if an existing file would be overwritten.

–*o*   Overwrites existing files when extracting, without prompting.

-p   As –c, except that text conversions are not allowed.

-q   Minimizes output. When doubled (-qq), produces even less output.

-t   Performs a CRC check on archive items to determine if they have changed since being archived.

-u   As –f, but also extracts files that don't already exist on the disk.

-v   Enables verbose output. If it's the only argument, prints version information, compile settings, and environment variable settings to standard output.

-V   For items archived on a VMS system, this argument retains file version numbers in filenames.

-x   Excludes the files specified by the additional *pathname* arguments, which usually include wildcards to match filenames of a certain pattern.

-X   Restores owner and group information for extracted files. Successful use of this flag will most likely require superuser privileges.

-z   Prints comments stored in the archive file to standard output.

-Z   Provides more control over information displayed to standard output about archive contents. When invoked as the only argument, prints usage information for the following options to standard output.

-h   Prints archive name, size, and number of archived items.

-l   As –s, but compressed size is also displayed.

-m   As –s, but compression ratio is also displayed.

-M   Displays output a page at a time.

-s   Prints information about each item in the archive: permissions, version of *zip* used to create the archive, uncompressed size, file type, compression method, modification timestamp, and name. This is the default behavior if no other options are specified.

-t   Prints number of archived items, cumulative compressed and uncompressed sizes, and compression ratio.

-T   Prints timestamps in a sortable format, rather than the default human-readable format.

-v   Enables verbose output.

-x   Excludes the files specified by the additional *pathname* arguments, which usually include wildcards to match filenames of a certain pattern.

-z   Prints comments stored in the archive file.

-1   Prints only filenames of archived items.

-2   As –1, but –h, -t, and –z flags may be used to print additional information.

Location

/usr/bin

vndevice

Syntax

```
vndevice { attach | shadow } device pathname
vndevice detach device
```

Description

Attaches or detaches a virtual device node to or from a disk image file. (Note that the functionality of *vndevice* is incorporated within *hdiutil*.) Modifications to data on the attached disk image will instead be written to the virtual node, or *shadow image*, and subsequent access to that data will be from the shadow. This allows effective read/write access to data on a disk image that should not or cannot be modified.

Options/Usage

attach
> Attaches a device node to a disk image designated by *pathname*.

detach
> Detaches a device node from a disk image.

shadow
> Associates an attached device node to a shadow disk image designated by *pathname*.

device
> The device node filename; e.g., **/dev/vn0**.

Examples

Create a disk image, attach a virtual device node to it, and mount it:

```
% hdiutil create test.dmg -volname test -size 5m -fs HFS+ -layout NONE
% sudo vndevice attach /dev/vn0 test.dmg
% mkdir mount_point
% sudo mount -t hfs /dev/vn0 mount_point
```

Wait a minute, and then:

```
% touch mount_point/test_file
% ls -l test.dmg
```

Note that the modification time on the disk image is current, reflecting the change you made by creating a test file.

Now set up shadowing. Unmount the volume first, then create the shadow disk image, attach the virtual node to it, and mount it again:

```
% sudo umount /dev/vn0
% hdiutil create shadow.dmg -volname shadow -size 5m -fs HFS+ -layout NONE
% sudo vndevice shadow /dev/vn0 shadow.dmg
% sudo mount -t hfs /dev/vn0 mount_point
```

Wait a minute, and then:

```
% rm mount_point/test_file
% ls -l test.dmg; ls -l shadow.dmg
```

The modification time on the test image wasn't updated, but the shadow image reflects the change you just made, indicating that writes are being passed through to the shadow.

Finish up by unmounting the volume and detaching the virtual node:

```
% sudo umount /dev/vn0
% sudo vndevice detach /dev/vn0
```

Location

/usr/libexec

vsdbutil

vsdbutil { -a | -c | -d } *pathname*

vsdbutil -i

Description

Enables or disables the use of permissions on a disk volume. This is equivalent to using the "Ignore Privileges" checkbox in the Finder's Info window for a mounted volume. The status of permissions usage on mounted volumes is stored in the permissions database, */var/db/volinfo.database*.

Options/Usage

−a   Activates permissions on the volume designated by *pathname*.

−c   Prints the status of permissions usage on the volume designated by *pathname* to standard output.

−d   Deactivates permissions on the volume designated by *pathname*.

−i   Initializes the permissions database to include all mounted HFS and HFS+ volumes.

Location

/usr/sbin

zip

zip [-h | -v]

zip [-q | -v] [-T] [-0 | -1 | -9] [-F[F]] [-o] [-f | -u] [-g] [-b *directory*]
[-J] *archive_filename*

zip [-q | -v] [-T] [-0 | -1 | -9] [-r [-D]] [-m] [-t *MMDDYY*] [-o] [-c] [-z]
[-X] [-j] [-k] [-l[l]] [-y] [-n *suffix*[:*suffix*]...] [-f | -u] [-d] [-g]
[-b *directory*] [-A] *archive_filename* { *pathname*... | -@ } [{ -i | -x }
pathname...]

Description

The files given by the *pathname* arguments are collected into a single archive file
with some metadata (as with *tar*), where they are compressed using the PKZIP
algorithm. The archive file is named with a *.zip* extension unless another extension is specified. If pathname is given as -, then data to be archived and
compressed is read from standard input; if *archive_filename* is -, the ZIP archive
data is written to standard output instead of to a file. If *archive_filename* already
exists, then the specified files are added to or updated in the existing archive.
When called with no arguments, it prints a usage statement to standard output.

Unlike the creation of ZIP archives from the Finder, *zip* does not preserve resource
or attribute forks.

Options/Usage

–*A* Adjusts the file offsets stored in the ZIP archive to prepare it for use as a self-
extracting executable archive.

–*b* When updating an existing archive, this option specifies the directory in
which the new archive is temporarily stored before being copied over the old.
Normally the temporary file is created in the current directory.

–*c* Prompts for one-line comments associated with each file in the archive.

–*d* Removes files from an existing archive, instead of adding or updating them.

–*D* Disables the creation of directory entries in the archive.

–*f* Updates files in an existing archive if the modification timestamps of the
source files are more recent than those in the archive. Does not add new files
to an existing archive.

–*F* Attempts to repair an archive file that has been corrupted or truncated. When
doubled (-*FF*), it performs a more thorough analysis of the archive.

–*g* When updating an existing archive, attempts to append to the existing file,
rather than creating a new file to replace the old.

–*h* Prints a usage statement to standard output.

–*i* Includes only the files specified by the additional *pathname* arguments, which
usually include wildcards to match filenames of a certain pattern.

–*j* Discards the paths of archived files, retaining only the filenames.

−*J*   Strips data prepended to an archive, such as code to make the archive a self-extracting executable.

−*k*   Attempts to archive files using DOS-compatible names and attributes.

−*l*   Translates Unix-style newlines in files to DOS newlines. When doubled (-*ll*), converts DOS newlines to Unix newlines.

−*m*   Deletes the source files after they've been archived.

−*n*   Disables compression for files with names ending in the specified strings.

−*o*   Sets the modification timestamp of the ZIP archive to that of the most recently modified item in the archive.

−*q*   Minimizes output.

−*r*   Performs a recursive traversal of directories specified in the *pathname* arguments, and archives their contents.

−*t*   Only archives files with modification timestamps more recent than the given date.

−*T*   Tests the integrity of the ZIP archive created by the command. If the test fails, then a preexisting archive file will not be overwritten, and source files will not be deleted (if using −*m*).

−*u*   Updates files in an existing archive if the modification timestamps of the source files are more recent than those in the archive. Unlike −*f*, new files are also added.

−*v*   Enables verbose output. If it's the only argument, prints version information, compile settings, and environment variable settings to standard output.

−*x*   Excludes the files specified by the additional *pathname* arguments, which usually include wildcards to match filenames of a certain pattern.

−*X*   Disables storage of file metadata in the archive, such as owner, group, and modification date.

−*y*   Archives symbolic links as symlinks, rather than archiving the targets of symlinks.

−*z*   Prompts for comments to be stored in the archive file.

−*0*   Disables compression.

−*1*   Compresses more quickly, at the cost of space efficiency.

−*9*   Compresses better, at the cost of time.

−*@*   Takes the list of source files from standard input.

Location

/usr/bin

Mac OS X's Unix Development Tools

The version of Unix that you'll encounter in Mac OS X's Terminal is similar to other versions you have seen, but dissimilar in some fundamental and often surprising ways. Although most tools are in their usual place, some are not on the system, while others are not where you would typically expect to find them on other Unix systems.

The lists shown in this Appendix contain a sampling of the Unix commands developers will find on Mac OS X. It is, by no means, a complete list of the Unix utilities found on your system. Because there are so many commands, they are organized into several categories. If you are an experienced Unix user, many of these commands will be familiar to you, but we've referenced them here so you can quickly determine whether a command you need is available. Unless otherwise specified, all of the tools in the following lists can be found in */usr/bin* or */usr/libexec*. Some tools are available with the standard distribution of Mac OS X, but others are available only after installing the Xcode Tools. (See Chapter 8 for more information about the Xcode Tools). Appendix B contains a listing of Unix commands that don't have manpages on Mac OS X Panther.

Standard Unix Development Tools

The following commands are development tools that are commonly found on Unix and Linux systems.

bison
> *yacc*-compatible parser generator.

bsdmake
> BSD make program. Use this if you have any BSD makefiles.

cvs

High-level revision control system that sits on top of RCS.

distcc

Frontend that distributes gcc builds across a network.

flex, flex++

A tool that generates lexical analyzers. See *lex & yacc* (O'Reilly).

cc, gcc

Apple's customized version of *gcc*, the GNU C compiler.

gdb

Source-level debugger.

gnumake, make

Automate the steps necessary to compile a source code package. GNU and BSD make are included. See *Managing Projects with make* (O'Reilly).

lex

Generates lexical analyzers. See *lex & yacc* (O'Reilly).

rcs

Manages file revisions.

unzip

Extracts files from a zip archive.

zip

Creates a zip archive.

Apple's Command-Line Developer Tools

The following list of utilities can be found in */Developer/Tools* after you have installed the Xcode Tools package. Xcode depends on some of these tools; some of them have their roots in Macintosh Programmer's Workshop (MPW), which is Apple's old development environment.

agvtool

Acts as a versioning tool for Xcode projects.

BuildStrings

Creates resource string definitions.

CpMac

Serves as an alternative to *cp*; preserves resource forks when copying.

cvs-unwrap

Extracts a tar file created by *cvs-wrap*.

cvs-wrap
Combines a directory into a single *tar* file.

cvswrappers
Checks an entire directory into CVS as a binary file.

DeRez
Displays the contents of a resource fork.

GetFileInfo
Displays extended information about a file, including creator code and file type.

MergePef
Merges code fragments from one file into another.

MvMac
Serves as an alternative to *mv*; preserves resource forks when copying.

pbhelpindexer
Creates an index of Apple's API documentation for Xcode.

pbprojectdump
Used by Xcode's FileMerge feature to produce more readable diffs between file versions.

pbxcp
Supports Xcodes's build system; an internal tool.

pbxhmapdump
Debugs header maps; also internal to Xcode.

ResMerger
Merges resource manager resource files. Xcode's build system compiles . *r* files into *.rsrc* files using *Rez*, and if needed, Xcode merges multiple files using *ResMerger*.

Rez
Compiles resource files.

RezWack
Embeds resource and data forks in a file.

sdp
Converts a scripting definition file into another format.

SetFile
Sets HFS+ file attributes.

SplitForks

Splits the resource fork, moving it from a dual-forked file into a file named *._ pathname*.

uninstall-devtools.pl

Uninstalls Xcode and the rest of the developer tools.

UnRezWack

Removes resource and data forks from a file.

WSMakeStubs

Generates web service stubs from a WSDL file.

Also available in the */Developer/Tools* directory is a Perl script (*uninstall-devtools.pl*), which can be used to uninstall the Xcode Tools.

Macintosh Tools

You can use the following tools to work with Macintosh files and disks, Macintosh applications, and the Macintosh clipboard.

bless

Makes a system folder bootable.

diskutil

Manipulates disks and volumes.

ditto

Copies directories, and optionally includes resource forks for copied files.

hdiutil

Manipulates disk images.

installer

Installs packages; command-line tool.

lsbom

Lists the contents of a Bill of Materials (BOM) file, such as those deposited under */Library/Receipts*.

open

Opens a file or directory. See "The open Command" in Chapter 1.

pbcopy

Copies standard input to the clipboard.

pbpaste

Sends the contents of the clipboard to standard output.

pstopdf

Convert EPS and PS files to PDF format.

screencapture
>Takes a screenshot of a window or the screen.

sips
>Scriptable image processing system for altering image files. (See Appendix B for more information.)

Java Development Tools

You can use the following tools to develop, debug, and run Java applications.

appletviewer
>Java applet viewer.

jar
>Java archive tool.

java
>Java Virtual Machine.

javac
>Java compiler.

javadoc
>Java documentation generator.

javah
>Generates C and header files for JNI programming.

javap
>Disassembles class files and inspects member signatures.

jdb
>Java Debugger.

jikes
>Fast open source Java compiler (installed as part of the Developer Tools package).

Text Editing and Processing

You can use the following tools to edit, convert, and otherwise manipulate text.

awk
>Pattern-matching language for textual database files.

cut
>Tool that selects columns for display.

emacs
> GNU Emacs.

ex
> Line editor underlying *vi*.

fmt
> Produces roughly uniform line length.

groff
> Document formatting system that can render *troff* typesetting macros to PostScript, HTML, and other formats.

join
> Merges different columns into a database.

paste
> Merges columns or switches their order.

pico
> Simple text editor designed for use with the Pine mailer. Note that the version of *pine* that ships with Mac OS X is much older than the current release.

sed
> Stream editor.

texi2html
> Converts Texinfo to HTML.

tr
> Command that substitutes or deletes characters.

vim
> Visual text editor.

Scripting and Shell Programming

The following commands include shells and programs useful in shell scripts.

bash
> Bourne Again shell (default).

csh
> C shell.

echo
> Repeats command-line arguments on standard output.

expr
> Performs arithmetic and comparisons.

line
> Reads a line of input.

lockfile
> Makes sure that a file is accessed by only one script at a time.

perl
> Practical Extraction and Report Language, Version 5.8.1 RC3.

php
> PHP scripting language Version 4.3.2, used for web development.

printf
> Formats and prints command-line arguments.

python
> Python scripting language, Version 2.3.

ruby
> Ruby scripting language, Version 1.6.8.

sh
> Standard Unix shell.

sleep
> Causes a pause during processing.

tclsh
> Tool Command Language (Tcl) shell, Version 8.4.

tcsh
> Tenex C shell.

test
> Command that tests a condition.

xargs
> Command that reads arguments from standard input and passes them to a command.

zsh
> Enhanced Unix shell.

Working with Files and Directories

You can use the following tools to compare, copy, and examine files.

cat
> Concatenates and displays files.

cd
> Changes directory.

chflags

Changes file flags.

chmod

Changes access modes on files.

cmp

Compares two files, byte-by-byte.

comm

Compares two sorted files.

cp

Copies files.

diff

Compares two files, line-by-line.

diff3

Compares three files.

file

Determines a file's type.

head

Shows the first few lines of a file.

less

Serves as an enhanced alternative to *more*.

ln

Creates symbolic or hard links.

 Symbolic and hard links are not the same as Carbon aliases that you create in the Finder (File → Make Alias). Unix programs cannot follow Carbon aliases, but all Mac OS X applications (Carbon, Cocoa, Classic, and Unix) can follow symbolic or hard links.

ls

Lists files or directories.

mkdir

Makes a new directory.

more

Displays files one screen at a time.

mv

Moves or renames files or directories.

patch

Merges a set of changes into a file.

pwd
> Prints the working directory.

rcp
> Insecurely copies a file to or from a remote machine. Use *scp* instead.

rm
> Removes files.

rmdir
> Removes directories.

scp
> Secures alternative to *rcp*.

sdiff
> Compares two files, side-by-side and line-by-line.

split
> Splits files evenly.

tail
> Shows the last few lines of a file.

vis
> Displays nonprinting characters in a readable form.

unvis
> Restores the output of *vis* to its original form.

wc
> Counts lines, words, and characters.

zcmp
> Compares two compressed files, byte-by-byte.

zdiff
> Compare two compressed files, line-by-line.

File Compression and Storage

The following tools will compress, decompress, and archive files.

bzip2
> Compresses files.

bzip2recover
> Recovers data from corrupted bzip2-compressed files.

bzcat
> Displays contents of compressed files.

bunzip2
> Uncompresses a files that was compressed with *bzip2*.

compress
> Compresses files to free up space (use *gzip* instead).

cpio
> Copies archives in or out.

gnutar
> GNU version of *tar*; available only if you have installed the Developer Tools package.

gunzip
> Uncompresses a file that was compressed with *gzip*.

gzcat
> Displays contents of compressed files.

gzip
> Compresses a file with Lempel-Ziv encoding.

tar
> Tape archive tool. GNU *tar* has more features and fewer limitations.

uncompress
> Expands compressed (.Z) files.

zcat
> Displays contents of compressed files.

Searching and Sorting

You can use the following tools to search and sort files.

egrep
> Extended version of *grep*.

fgrep
> Searches files for literal words.

find
> Searches the system for filenames.

grep
> Searches files for text patterns.

locate
> Faster version of *find*; however, it depends on a database that is periodically updated by the weekly *cron* job in */etc/weekly*. If the database is out of date, *find* is more accurate.

sort
> Sorts a file (use *-n* for numeric sorting, *-u* to eliminate duplicates).

strings
> Searches binary files for text patterns.

uniq
Reports or filters duplicate lines in a file.

zgrep
Searches compressed files for text patterns.

Miscellaneous Tools

The following tools will help you perform such tasks as searching the online documentation, switching user IDs, and controlling how programs run.

apropos
Locates commands by keyword.

clear
Clears the screen.

dc
Serves as a reverse-polish arbitrary precision calculator.

man
Gets information on a command.

nice
Changes a job's priority.

nohup
Keeps a job running even if you log out.

passwd
Changes your password.

script
Produces a transcript of your login session.

su
Allows you to become the superuser. Since the *root* account is disabled by default, you should use *sudo* instead.

sudo
Executes a command as another user. This tool is usually used to temporarily gain superuser privileges.

Index

Symbols

^[(ASCII ESC character), 11
* (asterisk)
   passwords set to, 48
      quoting or escaping, 49
\ (backslash)
   escaping spaces or special characters
      in file or directory names, 12
   line continuation escape symbol,
      removal in preprocessing, 135
$, bash shell prompt, xv
" (quotation marks)
   file or directory names with spaces,
      escaping, 12
      path to Classic application, 13
#, root user prompt for bash shell, xv

Numbers

128-bit integers, arithmetic operations
   on, 158
32-bit systems, 129
3D modeling, 89–91
64-bit systems, 129

A

acct daemon, starting, 28
acid command-line tool, 154
Active Directory plug-in (Directory
   Access), 41

ADC (Apple Developer Connection)
   documentation for Xcode, 116
   Xcode Tools, xiii
AddModule and LoadModule directives
   (httpd.conf), 206
administrative privileges, granting, 49
Advanced Package Tool (APT), 169
AFP (AppleTalk Filing Protocol), 205
   AFP URLs, 263
   automated access to AFP
      shares, 262–267
agvtool, 321
AirPort Base Station, sending traffic to
   Mac acting as server, 201
alloc.h header file, 140
AltiVec Velocity Engine (Motorola), 118
Amber command-lline tool, 154
anacron, setting up, 213
animation, 3D graphics package, 89
anonymous server, configuring ProFTPd
   as, 215
ANSI
   C predefined macros, 135
   escape sequences, 11
   trigraph preprocessing, 136
Apache server, 205, 206–212
   hostconfig entry for, 24
   optional modules, 206–212
      hfs_apple_module, 211
      perl_module (mod_perl), 207
      php4_module (mod_php4), 211
      rendezvous_apple_module, 211

We'd like to hear your suggestions for improving our indexes. Send email to *index@oreilly.com*.

Directory Access Authentication
tab, 42
Linux-PAM, using, 38–40
NetInfo database and, 36
PostgreSQL and, 223
Windows users logging onto
Mac, 205
X11, configuring for, 71
authentication server, starting, 28
AuthorizationTrampoline
command, 261
autoconf utility, 118
detecting sytems that require
malloc.h file, 139
determining supported compiler
features, 121
autodiskmount command, 261
automount command, 262–267
automount daemon, NFS, 23
awk tool, 324

B

backups of NetInfo database, 52
bash shell, 3, 325
# prompt for root user, xv
$ user prompt, xv
DISPLAY variable, enabling X11
forwarding, 73
escape sequences used with, 11
basic arithmetic operations (vBasicOps
library), 158
basic linear algebra subprograms
(BLAS), 158
BBEdit, forcing file to be opened
with, 19
beeps (system alert), for X11, 71
Berkeley-compatible command-line
interface, 59
biendian byte order, PowerPC, 130
big- or little-endian order for bytes, 130
bill of materials (.bom) file
describing package contents, 178
listing contents of, 323
binaries
installation, mixing with source, 176
installing via dselect, 174
binary formats
ELF, 142
Mach-O, 142
BIND DNS server, 24

binding, prebinding Mach
executables, 151
/bin/sh, 3
bison command, 320
BLAS (basic linear algebra
subprograms), 158
Blender 3D graphics package, 89–91
installing on Mac OS X, 89
OpenGL, use of, 90
bless tool, 323
Bluetooth device, sending file to, 15
Bombich Software, SMD application, 81
bookmarks
iTerm support for, 17
KDE Konsole terminal emulator, 17
BootCacheControl, launching, 25
booting Mac OS X, 20–29
BootX loader, 21
/etc/rc script, 25
/etc/rc.boot script, 22–24
fsck command, failure of, 24
initialization, 22
Login Window, 29
Open Firmware variables that control
behavior of, 242–244
register_mach_bootstrap_
servers, 301
in single-user mode, 21
SystemStarter, 28
in verbose mode, 20
bootstrap script, running for Fink
installation, 171
bootstrap services (Mach)
launching, 26
listing of, 27
BootX loader, 20, 21
Bourne shell, 3
(see also bash shell; shells)
BSD operating system, 20
flat files (see flat files)
initialization of supporting data
structures, 22
osx2x application, 75
bsdmake command, 320
build type, 119
building software
gnuplot application, 133
Unix-based, on Mac OS X, 134–158
header files, 134–140
X-11 based applications, 131

D

G

^G (ASCII BEL character), terminating
    escape sequences, 11
G4 processors, Motorola AltiVec
    Velocity Engine, 118
G5 processors
    Apple notes on code optimization
        for, 129
    support by GCC, 115
g77 (GNU FORTRAN 77
    compiler), 117
game creation and playback, 89
gcc compiler
    distcc command, 321
    --dump-pch switch, 138
    --load-pch switch, 138
GCC (GNU Compiler Collection), 115
    AltiVec Velocity Engine,
        Motorola, 118
    command for, 321
    differences between Mac OS X and
        Unix versions, 117
        g77 (FORTRAN 77
           compiler), 117
    documentation for, 116
    Mac OS X GCC compiler
        flags, 127–128
    programming languages supported
        by, 121
gcc_select command, 117, 279
gdb (GNU debugger), 152, 321
GeekTool, 245
GetFileInfo tool, 322
gethostent( ), 36
getpw* functions, passwords and, 37
getty, 29
gftp (SSH GUI), 96
GIMP (GNU Image Manipulation
    Program), 72, 88
    CinePaint version for film
        professionals, 89
    installing via Fink, 131
    using as iPhoto's default image
        editor, 88
Gimp-Print, 61
    HP Inkjet Project (HPIJS), 62
    web site for Mac OS X, 61
Glade, on Fink web site, 69

glib
    on Fink web site, 69
    GUI for SSH, 96
    installation via Fink, 131
GLterm, 4, 16
    interesting features of, 15
gluemac utility, 160
GNOME desktop environment, xiii, 66
    installation via Fink, 131
    installing from Fink, 69
    Mac OS X desktop displayed and
        controlled on Solaris
        machine, 81
    Solaris machine connected to Mac
        OS X via VNC, 78
    tabbed terminal sessions, 16
GNU
    autoconf (see autoconf utility)
    C preprocessor (see cpp)
    Compiler Collection (see GCC)
    debugger tool (gdb), 152
    General Public License, 59, 81
    gnutar tool, 177, 185, 329
    Image Manipulation Program (see
        GIMP)
    libiconv utility, 140
    Library General Public License, 59
GNU-Darwin, xiv
    web site, 68
    (see also Darwin kernel)
gnumake tool, 321
gnuplot data plotting program, 133
gnutar tool, 177, 185, 329
google.com, searching with, 15
gprof tool, 153
graphical environments for Mac OS
    X, 63
graphical user interfaces (see GUIs)
graphics formats, AquaTerm
    output, 133
grep tool, 329
groff tool, 325
groups, 45–47
    adding user to admin group, 49
    adding users to group with dscl
        merge command, 46
    checkgid command, 271
    creating with dscl utility, 46
    creating with niload, 46, 48

deleting with dscl's delete
command, 47
listing all GIDs with nireport, 45
listing with nidump utility, 47
/groups directory, 45
GTK+
on Fink web site, 69
GUI for SSH (gftp), 96
installation via Fink, 131
GUIs
Cocktail, for system administrative
tasks, 245
FinkCommander, for Fink, 173
for SSH, 96–99
Fugu, for OpenSSH, 96
gunzip tool, 329
gzcat tool, 329
gzip tool, 177, 185, 329

H

.h file extension (header files), 134
hardware acceleration support, X11, 64
HAVE_MALLOC_H macro, 139
hdiutil, 85, 323
creating a disk image, 191
creating Internet-enabled disk
image, 192
head command, 327
header files, 134–140
alloc.h, 140
dlfcn.h, 140
framework, including in Objective-C
code, 135
functions of, 134
generating for JNI
programming, 324
header.h file, 138
including in C Source file, 135
including in vecLib framework
code, 158
lcrypt.h, 140
malloc.h, 139
poll.h, 139
POSIX.4 compliance
mechanism, 134
precompiled, 136–139, 277
listing of, 137
PFE mechanism, 138
printing information about, 299

types of, in Mac OS X, 134
values.h, 140
wchar.h and iconv.h, 140
heap, 152
here document, using in group
creation, 46
Hewlett-Packard InkJet Project
(HPIJS), 62
HFS+ filesystem
case-insensitivity of, 118
file attributes, setting, 322
HFS filesystem, FixupResourceForks
command and, 279
hfs_apple_module, 211
hfs.util, 280
hiding an application, 92
hints (Mac OS X Hints), xiv
home directory
creating, 49
sharing with connected
machine, 205
host type, 119–121
canonical form, 120
guessing and validating with config.*
files, 120
macros to detect Mac OS X, 120
hostconfig file, 22
AppleTalk Filing Profile (AFP)
service, 205
default entries from, 22–24
enabling Postfix to receive email, 204
environment variables in, 31
postfix-watch daemon, entry
for, 203
VNCSERVER variable, 83
WEBSERVER entry, 206
hostinfo command, 281
hostnames
configuration of, 29
configuring to use Postfix on
standalone server, 203
managing with Directory
Services, 50
hosts, creating with niload, 50
hosts file, 50
HPIJS (Hewlett-Packard InkJet
Project), 62
httpd.conf file (Apache), 206
AddModule and LoadModule
directives, 206

Mail application, 14
    burning Mail folder disk image on a
        CD, 85
    disk image of Mail folder,
        making, 84
    Equation Services, using to typeset
        LaTeX within, 106
Mail Exchange (MX) record, 204
mail, startup of Postfix mail server, 23,
    29
mailing lists (Apple-hosted, for
    Darwin), xiii
main.c application, 139
main.cf file (Postfix)
    configuring inet_interfaces to listen
        on port 25, 204
    configuring Postfix for use on
        standalone server, 203
    relayhost entry, 204
Make New Sticky Note service, 15
make tool, 116, 118, 321
    building X-11 based
        applications, 132
    missing header files and, 139
makefiles
    bsdmake command, 320
    creating and testing shared library
        (example), 144
    generating for X11 applications, 132
makekey command, 285
MallocDebug tool, 152
malloc.h header file, 139
malloc_history tool, 152
man command, 330
Mandrake Linux, connecting to Mac
    printer, 60
manpages
    flat file formats and, 51
    hosts and, 50
master.cf file (Postfix), 204
math libraries
    libm, 141, 158
    vMathLib, 158
mathematical publications (see LaTeX)
MD5 passwords for PostgreSQL, 223
mDNS (Rendezvous multicast DNS
    client), 286
mDNSResponder, 287

memory
    contiguous memory accesses for
        G5, 130
    endian order for bytes, 130
        biendian order for PowerPC, 130
    information about (top utility), 227
    Panther tools for analyzing usage
        of, 152
    virtual memory allocation by the
        kernel, 27
    virtual memory statistics (vm_
        stat), 231
menu bar key equivalents, X11, 70
MergePef tool, 322
metacharacters (shell), escape sequences
    for, 11
metapackages, 177, 178
MH_BUNDLE file type, 142
MH_DYLIB file type, 142
microkernel operating system (see Mach
    kernel)
Microsoft
    Remote Desktop Client (RDC), 83
    (see also Windows)
middle mouse button, simulation with
    Option-click, 66
miscellaneous tools, 330
mkdir command, 327
mod_dav (dav_mod), 206
modeling, 3D, 89
mod_hfs_apple, 211
mod_perl module, 207
mod_php4, 211
mod_rendezvous_apple, 211
mod_ssl, 207–211
    configuring for Mac OS X, online
        information about, 211
modules
    Apache server, 206–212
    kernel, utilities for, 233
    loadable (see bundles)
    Perl, for database support, 225
Monster tool, 153
monthly cron jobs, 33
more command, 327
Motif window manager (mwm), 72, 131
Motorola AltiVec Velocity Engine, 118
mountd, removing invalid records of
    client mounts, 276
mount_devfs, 287

Windows
    consulting Active Directory domain
        on server editions, 41
    file sharing server (Samba), 24
    file sharing with Mac OS X, 205
    LyX WYSIWYM document
        processor, 105
    users connecting to Mac OS X
        printer, 58
    VNC clients and servers for, 83
windows
    Terminal (see Terminal application)
    xterm (see X Window System; xterm)
WindowServer, 27
WSMakeStubs tool, 323
WYSIWYM (What you see is what you
    mean), 105

X

X Window System, 4
    Apple X11 distribution (see X11)
    AquaTerm application and, 133
    connecting from Mac OS X to, 73
X11, 63–83
    applications and libraries, 131–133
        building, 131
        installing via Fink, 131
    applications and libraries, installing
        via Fink, 72
    connecting to other X Window
        Systems, 73
        Applications menu, using, 74
        OSX2X, using, 75
    customizing, 68–72
        Applications menu, 71
        dot-files, desktops, and window
           managers, 68
        input devices, interaction
           with, 70
        output, 70
        security features, 71
    features of, 64
    forwarding, 73
    graphics, using from R console, 110
    installing, 64
    interactions with Aqua, 72
    open-x11 command, 296
    running, 65
        rootless and full-screen
           modes, 66
        xterm vs. Terminal windows, 65

video viewing applications, 86
VNC (Virtual Network
    Computer), 76–83
    connecting to Mac OS X VNC
        server, 79–83
    launching, 77–79
X11 .bdf fonts, 16
X11SDK, 64
X.509 SSL/TLS certificates, 270
xargs command, 326
Xcode Tools, xiii, 321
    CHUD tools, 153
    documentation for, 115, 116
    IDE for Mac OS X, 116
    IDE provided by, 115
    precompiled header files, building
        and using, 136
    uninstalling, 322
    X11 SDK, 64, 131
Xfce desktop environment, 66
xfig/transfig drawing tool, 72, 131
XFree86 Project, 63
xinetd
    FTP server, 213
    OpenSSH server, 212
    Printer Sharing, 215
    starting, 28
.xinitrc script, for X11
        customization, 68
xmkmf script, 132
XML property lists (see property lists)
xmodmap utility, 66
XProg.tgz, 131
xterm
    customizing window in X11, 69
    R commands entered in, 110
    replacements for, 65
    Terminal vs., 3

Y

yacc-compatible parser generator, 320

Z

zcat tool, 329
zcmp command, 328
zdiff command, 328
zgrep tool, 329
ZIP archives, 314
zip command, 318, 321
zsh shell, 3, 326

About the Authors

Brian Jepson is an O'Reilly editor, programmer, and coauthor of *Learning Unix for Mac OS X Panther*. He's also a volunteer system administrator and all-around geek for AS220, a nonprofit arts center in Providence, Rhode Island. AS220 gives Rhode Island artists uncensored and unjuried forums for their work. These forums include galleries, performance space, and publications. Brian sees to it that technology, especially free software, supports that mission.

Ernest E. Rothman is an Associate Professor of Mathematics at Salve Regina University (SRU) in Newport, Rhode Island, where he is also Chair of the Mathematical Sciences Department. Ernie holds a Ph.D. in Applied Mathematics from Brown University and held positions at the Cornell Theory Center in Ithaca, New York, before coming to SRU. His academic interests are in scientific computing, computational science, and applied mathematics education. A longtime Unix aficionado, Ernie has enjoyed tinkering with Mac OS X since the day it was first released. Ernie has recently become interested in digital photography, especially when it comes to taking pictures of his Newfoundland dogs. You can see many of his photos and keep abreast of his latest activities at *http://homepage.mac.com/samchops*.

Colophon

Our look is the result of reader comments, our own experimentation, and feedback from distribution channels. Distinctive covers complement our distinctive approach to technical topics, breathing personality and life into potentially dry subjects.

The animal on the cover of *Mac OS X Panther for Unix Geeks* is a foxhound. The foxhound's coat is short, hard, and glossy and can be black, tan, white, or a combination of these colors. Foxhounds are generally free of many of the heritable defects that afflict other large dog breeds. They usually stand 21 to 27 inches tall at the shoulder, and their average weight is 55 to 75 pounds.

The English foxhound traces its ancestry back to the 1600s. Foxhounds were bred specifically to hunt foxes, so they require great stamina, strength, and speed. They are known for their superior scenting powers and strong, melodious voices. American foxhounds, developed from stock brought over from England in the 1650s, are hardier and finer-boned than their English counterparts. They were bred to adapt to more rugged terrain, where they hunted foxes, coyotes, and deer.

Foxhounds are friendly, intelligent, courageous pack hounds with a cheerful, determined disposition. They tend to be easygoing and affectionate, and although they can be strong-willed, they are not aggressive. Foxhounds were bred mainly as hunting dogs, rather than as family pets. They are a very active breed, requiring lots of exercise, and they tend to be happiest with owners who live in rural areas or on large farms. Foxhounds enjoy the company of other dogs and can become bored if kept alone.

Philip Dangler was the production editor and copyeditor for *Mac OS X Panther for Unix Geeks*. Marlowe Shaeffer was the proofreader. Reg Aubry and Claire Cloutier provided quality control. Ellen Troutman Zaig wrote the index.

Emma Colby designed the cover of this book, based on a series design by Edie Freedman. The cover image is a 19th-century engraving from the *Royal Natural History*. Emma Colby produced the cover layout with QuarkXPress 4.1, using Adobe's ITC Garamond font.

David Futato designed the interior layout. This book was converted to FrameMaker 5.5.6 by Julie Hawks with a format conversion tool created by Erik Ray, Jason McIntosh, Neil Walls, and Mike Sierra that uses Perl and XML technologies. The text font is Linotype Birka; the heading font is Adobe Myriad Condensed; and the code font is LucasFont's TheSans Mono Condensed. The illustrations that appear in the book were produced by Robert Romano and Jessamyn Read using Macromedia FreeHand 9 and Adobe Photoshop 6. The tip and warning icons were drawn by Christopher Bing. This colophon was written by Rachel Wheeler.